# SFML Blueprints

Sharpen your game development skills and improve your C++ and SFML knowledge with five exciting projects

**Maxime Barbier**

[PACKT] open source *
PUBLISHING    community experience distilled

BIRMINGHAM - MUMBAI

# SFML Blueprints

First published: May 2015

Production reference: 1220515

Published by Packt Publishing Ltd.
Livery Place
35 Livery Street
Birmingham B3 2PB, UK.

ISBN 978-1-78439-847-7

www.packtpub.com

# Credits

**Author**
Maxime Barbier

**Reviewers**
Nolwenn Bauvais
Jason Bunn
Tom Ivanyo
Vittorio Romeo
Richa Sachdeva
Michael Shaw

**Commissioning Editor**
Edward Bowkett

**Acquisition Editor**
Shaon Basu

**Content Development Editor**
Akashdeep Kundu

**Technical Editors**
Tanmayee Patil
Shiny Poojary
Mohita Vyas

**Copy Editors**
Trishya Hajare
Aditya Nair
Shambhavi Pai
Merilyn Pereira
Aarti Saldanha

**Project Coordinator**
Milton Dsouza

**Proofreaders**
Safis Editing
Jonathan Todd

**Indexer**
Tejal Soni

**Graphics**
Abhinash Sahu

**Production Coordinator**
Aparna Bhagat

**Cover Work**
Aparna Bhagat

# About the Author

**Maxime Barbier** has recently finished his studies and is now a software engineer in Strasbourg, France. He loves programming crazy things and has been experimenting and sharing them with the open source community on GitHub since 2010. Also, he really likes game programming.

As his favorite technology is C++, he has become an expert in it because of his work. He has also developed several libraries with this language, and some of them are used in this book. Game programming is his hobby, and he really likes the challenges involved in such a project. He also loves sharing his knowledge with other people, which was the main reason he wrote this book and also the reason for his activity in the open source community.

Since 9 years, he has been working on different projects such as Anka Dreles, which is a pen and paper role-playing game, and is putting in effort to convert it into a computer game.

He also loves sailing and was a sailing teacher for several years while studying. His dream is to be able to combine sailing and computer sciences by traveling around the world.

Before starting with this book, Maxime had already reviewed some books, such as *SFML Game Development* and *Getting Started with OUYA*, both by Packt Publishing.

I would like to thank my girlfriend for her patience and efforts on this book, and in particular, for all the asserts made especially for this book. I would also like to thank my family and friends for supporting me during this process. Finally, I would like to thank the team at Packt Publishing for giving me the opportunity to work on this project.

# About the Reviewers

**Nolwenn Bauvais** is a French student of English literature, civilization, and translation. She took the opportunity to work with Maxime Barbier as a grammar reviewer for this book. She loves reading, and her final goal is to become an English-to-French translator in literature. She is also an independent photographer during her free time; Nature and human activities are her favorite subjects.

> I would like to thank Maxime Barbier for giving me the opportunity to work in my field of study.

**Jason Bunn** is a game developer from Tennessee and is currently pursuing a masters degree in applied computer science. He has worked in the game industry professionally for 3 years and will most likely return upon graduation.

Jason was a developer at On The Level Game Studios, where he helped create a couple of titles using the Unity3D engine. He has since begun tinkering with 2D games using SFML and SDL.

> Special thanks to my wife, Ashleigh, and our wonderful kids for being patient with me as I continue my life-long learning endeavors!

**Tom Ivanyo** is a game developer and computer science major. He started programming in 2007 with only the knowledge of Visual Basic. Since then, he has experimented with many languages, from assembly to C#, and has become familiar with many useful APIs and libraries.

For game development, he started off using SDL, but then played around with XNA. Less than a year later, he moved on to Unity. He stayed with Unity for almost 2 years before making the change to SFML. Currently, he is working with Doug Madden on his 2D physics-based game engine, S2D.

**Vittorio Romeo** is a computer science student at the University of Messina and a C++ enthusiast. Since childhood, he has been interested in computers, gaming, and programming. He learned to develop games and applications as an autodidact at a very young age, starting with VB/C# and the .NET environment, moving on to C++ and native cross-platform programming. He works on his open source general-purpose C++14 libraries in his spare time and develops free open source games using SFML2. The evolution of C++ is something that greatly interests him. He has also spoken about game development with the latest standard features at CppCon 2014.

**Richa Sachdeva** is an avid programmer. She believes in designing games that are high on educational content as well as entertainment and is contributing two cents towards creating and exploring different dimensions in the field of game programming. She is a physics graduate, who—somewhere along the course—found her true calling in computers and ever since has been amazed by this strange pixelated world. While not thinking about games or which movie to watch, she finds solace in writing.

**Michael Shaw**, growing up in the small city of Gympie, discovered an interest in the development of games. During his time at Gympie State High School, he attended a Certificate IV course in Interactive Digital Media run by a passionate teacher, Ken Brady. This led him toward Canberra for a bachelor's degree in. He completed this course through the Academy of Interactive Entertainment and the Canberra Institute of Technology. Throughout this course he learned a variety of 2D and 3D game programming and design skills in both C++ and C#. The software ranged from basic 2D frameworks to using Unity3D to develop major projects. He also learned essential programming to build engines. During his second year, he produced a project of his own design with a team of three other programmers and two artists.

I would like to thank my fiancée, Natasha, for supporting me through the reviewing of this book.

# www.PacktPub.com

## Support files, eBooks, discount offers, and more

For support files and downloads related to your book, please visit www.PacktPub.com.

Did you know that Packt offers eBook versions of every book published, with PDF and ePub files available? You can upgrade to the eBook version at www.PacktPub.com and as a print book customer, you are entitled to a discount on the eBook copy. Get in touch with us at service@packtpub.com for more details.

At www.PacktPub.com, you can also read a collection of free technical articles, sign up for a range of free newsletters and receive exclusive discounts and offers on Packt books and eBooks.

https://www2.packtpub.com/books/subscription/packtlib

Do you need instant solutions to your IT questions? PacktLib is Packt's online digital book library. Here, you can search, access, and read Packt's entire library of books.

## Why subscribe?

- Fully searchable across every book published by Packt
- Copy and paste, print, and bookmark content
- On demand and accessible via a web browser

## Free access for Packt account holders

If you have an account with Packt at www.PacktPub.com, you can use this to access PacktLib today and view 9 entirely free books. Simply use your login credentials for immediate access.

# Table of Contents

**Preface**                                                                        **vii**

**Chapter 1: Preparing the Environment**                                            **1**

  **C++11**                                                               **1**

  **SFML**                                                                **3**

  **Installation of a C++11 compiler**                                    **4**

    For Linux users                                             4

    For Mac users                                               4

    For Windows users                                           4

    For all users                                               4

  **Installing CMake**                                                    **5**

    For Linux users                                             5

    For other operating systems                                 5

  **Installing SFML 2.2**                                                 **5**

    Building SFML yourself                                       5

      Installing dependencies                         6

      Linux                                           6

      Other operating systems                         6

      Compilation of SFML                             6

    Code::Blocks and SFML                                       11

    A minimal example                                           14

  **Summary**                                                             **16**

**Chapter 2: General Game Architecture, User Inputs,**
**and Resource Management**                                                         **17**

  **General structure of a game**                                         **17**

    The game class                                              18

    Game loops                                                  21

      The frame rate                                  22

Move our player 27
The player class 27
**Managing user inputs** **31**
Polling events 32
Real-time events 33
Handling user inputs 35
Using the Action class 35
Action target 39
Event map 44
Back to action target 45
**Keeping track of resources** **50**
Resources in SFML 50
The texture class 51
The image class 52
The font class 52
The shader class 53
The sound buffer class 53
The music class 53
Use case 54
RAII idiom 55
Building a resources manager 55
Changing the player's skin 58
**Summary** **60**
**Chapter 3: Making an Entire 2D Game** **61**
**Turning our application to an Asteroid clone** **61**
The Player class 62
The levels 62
The enemies 62
The meteors 62
The flying saucers 63
**Modifying our application** **63**
The World class 65
The hierarchical entity system 70
The entity component system 70
**Designing our game** **71**
Prepare the collisions 72
The Entity class 73
The Player class 75
The Enemy class 78
The Saucer class 79
The Meteor class 83
The Shoot class 85

**Building a Tetris clone**    **88**
The Stats class    89
The Piece class    91
The Board class    96
The Game class    103
**Summary**    **107**
**Chapter 4: Playing with Physics**    **109**
**A physics engine – késako?**    **109**
3D physics engines    110
2D physics engines    110
**Physics engine comparing game engine**    **110**
**Using Box2D**    **111**
Preparing Box2D    111
Build    112
Installation    112
**Pairing Box2D and SFML**    **112**
Box2D, how does it work?    113
**Adding physics to a game**    **119**
The Piece class    121
The World class    125
The Game class    132
The Stats class    136
**Summary**    **137**
**Chapter 5: Playing with User Interfaces**    **139**
**What is a GUI?**    **139**
Creating a GUI from scratch    140
Class hierarchy    140
The Widget class    142
The Label class    144
The Button class    146
The TextButton class    148
The Container class    151
The Frame class    153
The Layout class    156
The VLayout class    157
**Adding a menu to the game**    **160**
Building the main menu    161
Building the pause menu    164
Building the configuration menu    166
**Using SFGUI**    **167**
Installing SFGUI    168
Using the features of SFGUI    168

| | |
|---|---|
| Building the starting level | 169 |
| **Summary** | **173** |
| **Chapter 6: Boost Your Code Using Multithreading** | **175** |
| **What is multithreading?** | **175** |
| The fork() function | 175 |
| The exec() family functions | 176 |
| **Thread functionality** | **177** |
| Why do we need to use the thread functionality? | 178 |
| Using threads | 179 |
| **Adding multithreading to our games** | **181** |
| **Summary** | **186** |
| **Chapter 7: Building a Real-time Tower Defense Game from Scratch – Part 1** | **187** |
| **The goal of the game** | **188** |
| **Building animations** | **189** |
| The Animation class | 190 |
| The AnimatedSprite class | 192 |
| A usage example | 197 |
| **Building a generic Tile Map** | **199** |
| The Geometry class as an isometric hexagon | 201 |
| VLayer and Layer classes | 203 |
| VMap and Map classes | 207 |
| Dynamic board loading | 208 |
| The MapViewer class | 213 |
| A usage example | 213 |
| **Building an entity system** | **215** |
| Use of the entity system | 216 |
| Advantages of the entity system approach | 218 |
| **Building the game logic** | **218** |
| Building our components | 219 |
| Creating the different systems | 220 |
| The level class | 223 |
| The game class | 223 |
| The Team GUI class | 224 |
| **Summary** | **225** |

## Chapter 8: Build a Real-time Tower Defense Game from Scratch – Part 2, Networking — 227

**Network architectures** — 227
  Peer-to-peer architecture — 228
  Client-server architecture — 228
    Client — 230
    Server — 230
**Network communication using sockets** — 231
  UDP — 231
  TCP — 232
  Selector — 232
  The Connection class — 233
    The goal of the Connection class — 233
**Creating a communication protocol** — 239
  Using the sf::Packet class — 239
  RPC-like protocol — 241
  The NetworkEvent class — 243
**Modifying our game** — 247
  Server — 247
    Building the Server entry point — 248
    Reacting to players' actions during a match — 253
    Synchronization between clients and the server — 256
  The Client class — 257
    Connection with the server — 258
    The Level class — 262
**Adding data persistence to the game** — 265
  What is ORM? — 266
  Using cpp-ORM — 266
  Turning our object persistent — 269
    Saving an object in a database — 269
    Loading an object from the database — 269
**Summary** — 270

## Index — 271

# Preface

Throughout this book, I'll try to share my knowledge on how to make video games and share them with you. Five different projects will be covered, which include many techniques and ways to resolve quite commons problems involved in game development.

The technologies used are the C++ programming language (2011 standard) and the SFML library (version 2.2).

Many aspects of game programming are developed over the different chapters and give you all the keys in hand to build every kind of game you want in 2D, with the only limit of your imagination.

## What this book covers

*Chapter 1, Preparing the Environment,* helps you install everything needed for this book, and build a small application using SFML to test whether everything is fine.

*Chapter 2, General Game Architecture, User Inputs, and Resource Management,* explains general game architectures, managing user inputs and finally, how to keep track of external resources.

*Chapter 3, Making an Entire 2D Game,* helps you build Asteroid and Tetris clones, learning entity models and board management.

*Chapter 4, Playing with Physics,* provides a description of physical engines. It also covers the usage of Box2D paired with SFML, and turns our Tetris into a new game, Gravitris.

*Chapter 5, Playing with User Interfaces,* helps you create and use a game user interface. It introductes you to SFGUI and adding them to our Gravitris game.

*Chapter 6, Boost Your Code Using Multithreading*, introduces multithreading and adapts our game to use it.

*Chapter 7, Building a Real-time Tower Defense Game from Scratch – Part 1*, helps you create animations, a generic tile map system (isometric hexagonal tiles), and an entity system. Finally, you will create all the game logic.

*Chapter 8, Build a Real-time Tower Defense Game from Scratch – Part 2, Networking*, introduces network architectures and networking. It helps you create a custom communication protocol, and modify our game to allow multiplayer matches over the network. Then, we finally add a save/load option to our game using Sqlite3 through an ORM.

# What you need for this book

To be able to build the projects covered throughout this book, you are assumed to have knowledge of the C++ language with its basic features, and also parts of the standard template library, such as strings, streams, and containers. It's important to keep in mind that game development is not an easy task, so if you don't have the prerequisites, it can get frustrating. So, don't hesitate to read some books or tutorials on C++ before starting with this one.

# Who this book is for

This book is for developers who know the basics of the SFML library and its capabilities for 2D game development. Minimal experience with C++ is required.

# Conventions

In this book, you will find a number of styles of text that distinguish between different kinds of information. Here are some examples of these styles, and an explanation of their meaning.

Code words in text, folder names, filenames, file extensions, pathnames, dummy URLs, user input, and Twitter handles are shown as follows: "We also add the point calculation to this class with the addLines() function."

A block of code is set as follows:

```
AnimatedSprite::AnimatedSprite(Animation* animation,Status
status,const sf::Time& deltaTime,bool loop,int repeat) :
onFinished(defaultFunc),_delta(deltaTime),_loop(loop),
_repeat(repeat),_status(status)
```

```
{
setAnimation(animation);
}
```

When we wish to draw your attention to a particular part of a code block, the relevant lines or items are set in bold:

```
int main(intargc, char* argv[])
```

Any command-line input or output is written as follows:

```
sudo make install
```

**New terms** and **important words** are shown in bold. Words that you see on the screen, in menus or dialog boxes for example, appear in the text like this: "We will also use this class to display the **Game Over** message if it's needed".

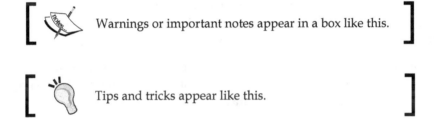

Warnings or important notes appear in a box like this.

Tips and tricks appear like this.

# Reader feedback

Feedback from our readers is always welcome. Let us know what you think about this book—what you liked or may have disliked. Reader feedback is important for us to develop titles that you really get the most out of.

To send us general feedback, simply send an e-mail to feedback@packtpub.com, and mention the book title via the subject of your message.

If there is a topic that you have expertise in and you are interested in either writing or contributing to a book, see our author guide on www.packtpub.com/authors.

# Customer support

Now that you are the proud owner of a Packt book, we have a number of things to help you to get the most from your purchase.

# Downloading the example code

You can download the example code files from your account at http://www.packtpub.com for all the Packt Publishing books you have purchased. If you purchased this book elsewhere, you can visit http://www.packtpub.com/support and register to have the files e-mailed directly to you.

# Errata

Although we have taken every care to ensure the accuracy of our content, mistakes do happen. If you find a mistake in one of our books—maybe a mistake in the text or the code—we would be grateful if you could report this to us. By doing so, you can save other readers from frustration and help us improve subsequent versions of this book. If you find any errata, please report them by visiting http://www.packtpub.com/submit-errata, selecting your book, clicking on the **Errata Submission Form** link, and entering the details of your errata. Once your errata are verified, your submission will be accepted and the errata will be uploaded to our website or added to any list of existing errata under the Errata section of that title.

To view the previously submitted errata, go to https://www.packtpub.com/books/content/support and enter the name of the book in the search field. The required information will appear under the **Errata** section.

# Piracy

Piracy of copyright material on the Internet is an ongoing problem across all media. At Packt, we take the protection of our copyright and licenses very seriously. If you come across any illegal copies of our works, in any form, on the Internet, please provide us with the location address or website name immediately so that we can pursue a remedy.

Please contact us at copyright@packtpub.com with a link to the suspected pirated material.

We appreciate your help in protecting our authors, and our ability to bring you valuable content.

# Questions

You can contact us at questions@packtpub.com if you are having a problem with any aspect of the book, and we will do our best to address it.

# 1

# Preparing the Environment

Through this book, I will try to teach you some elements to build video games using the SFML library. Each chapter will cover a different topic, and will require knowledge from the previous one.

In this first chapter, we will cover basics points needed for the future such as:

- Installing a compiler for C++11
- Installing CMake
- Installing SFML 2.2
- Building a minimal SFML project

Before getting started, let's talk about each technology and why we will use them.

## C++11

The C++ programming language is a very powerful tool and has really great performance, but it is also really complex, even after years of practice. It allows us to program at both a low and high level. It's useful to make some optimizations on our program such as having the ability to directly manipulate memory. Building software utilizing C++ libraries allows us to work at a higher level and when performance is crucial, at a low level. Moreover, the C/C++ compilers are very efficient at optimizing code. The result is that, right now, C++ is the most powerful language in terms of speed, and thanks to the zero cost abstraction, you are not paying for what you don't use, or for the abstraction you are provided.

I'll try to use this language in a modern way, using the object-oriented approach. Sometimes, I'll bypass this approach to use the C way for optimizations. So do not be shocked to see some "old school code". Moreover, all the main compilers now support the standard language released in 2011, so we can use it everywhere without any trouble. This version adds some really useful features in the language that will be used in this book, such as the following:

- Keywords are one such important feature. The following are a few of them:

  - ° `auto`: This automatically detects the type of the new variable. It is really useful for the instantiation of iterators. The auto keyword already existed in the past, but has been deprecated for a long time, and its meaning has now changed.

  - ° `nullptr`: This is a new keyword introducing a strong type for the old NULL value. You can always use NULL, but it's preferable to use `nullptr`, which is any pointer type with 0 as the value.

  - ° `override` and `final`: These two keywords already exist in some languages such as Java. These are simple indications not only for the compiler but also for the programmer, but don't specify what they indicate. Don't hesitate to use them. You can take a look to the documentation of them here `http://en.cppreference.com/w/cpp/language/override` and `http://en.cppreference.com/w/cpp/language/final`.

- The range-based `for` loops is a new kind of loop in the language `foreach`. Moreover, you can use the new `auto` keyword to reduce your code drastically. The following syntax is very simple:

  ```
  for(auto& var : table){...}.
  ```

  In this example, `table` is a container (vector and list) and `var` is a reference to the stored variable. Using & allows us to modify the variable contained inside the table and avoids copies.

- C++11 introduces the smart pointers. There are multiple pointers corresponding to their different possible utilizations. Take a look at the official documentation, this which is really interesting. The main idea is to manage the memory and delete the object created at runtime when no more reference on it exists, so that you do not have to delete it yourself or ensure that no double free corruptions are made. A smart pointer created on the stack has the advantages of being both fast and automatically deleted when the method / code block ends. But it is important to know that a strong use of this pointer, more especially `shared_ptr`, will reduce the execution speed of your program, so use them carefully.

- The lambda expression or anonymous function is a new type introduced with a particular syntax. You can now create functions, for example, as a parameter of another function. This is really useful for callback. In the past, functor was used to achieve this kind of comportment. An example of functor and lambda is as follows:

```
class Func(){ void operator()(){/* code here */}};
auto f = [](){/* code here*/};
```

- If you already know the use of the variadics function with the ellipse operator (. . .), this notion should trouble you, as the usage of it is different. The variadics template is just the amelioration of template with any number of parameters using the ellipse operator. A good example for this is the tuple class. A tuple contains any number of values of any type known at compile time. Without the variadics template, it was not really possible to build this class, but now it is really easy. By the way, the tuple class was introduced in C++11. There are several other features, such as threads, pair, and so on.

# SFML

**SFML** stands for **Simple and Fast Multimedia Library**. This is a framework written in C++ and is based on OpenGL for its graphical rendering part. This name describes its aim pretty well, that is, to have a user-friendly interface (API), to deliver high performance, and to be as portable as possible. The SFML library is divided into five modules, which are compiled in a separated file:

- **System**: This is the main module, and is required by all others. It provides clocks, threads, and two or three dimensions with all their logics (mathematics operations).

- **Window**: This module allows the application to interact with the user by managing windows and the inputs from the mouse, keyboard, and joystick.

- **Graphics**: This module allows the user to use all the graphical basic elements such as textures, shapes, texts, colors, shaders, and more.

- **Audio**: This module allows the user to use some sound. Thanks to this, we will be able to play some themes, music, and sounds.

- **Network**: This module manages not only socket and type safe transfers but also HTTP and FTP protocols. It's also very useful to communicate between different programs.

Each module used by our programs will need to be linked to them at compile time. We don't need to link them all if it's not necessary. This book will cover each module, but not all the SFML classes. I recommend you take a look at the SFML documentation at http://www.sfml-dev.org/documentation.php, as it's very interesting and complete. Every module and class is well described in different sections.

Now that the main technologies have been presented, let's install all that we need to use them.

# Installation of a C++11 compiler

As mentioned previously, we will use C++11, so we need a compiler for it.
For each operating system, there are several options; choose the one you prefer.

## For Linux users

If you are a Linux user, you probably already have GCC/G++ installed. In this case, check whether your version is 4.8 or later. Otherwise, you can install GCC/G++ (version 4.8+) or Clang (version 3.4+) using your favorite packet manager. Under Debian based distribution (such as Ubuntu and Mint), use the command line:

```
sudo apt-get install gcc g++ clang -y
```

## For Mac users

If you are a Mac user, you can use Clang (3.4+). This is the default compiler under Mac OS X.

## For Windows users

Finally, if you are a Windows user, you can use Visual Studio (2013), Mingw-gcc (4.8+), or Clang (3.4+) by downloading them. I suggest you not use Visual Studio, because it's not 100 percent standard compliant, even for the C99, and instead use another IDE such as Code::Blocks (see the following paragraph).

## For all users

I assume that in both cases, you have been able to install a compiler and configure your system to use it (by adding it to the system path). If you have not been able to do this, another solution is to install an IDE like Code::Blocks, which has the advantage of being installed with a default compiler, is compatible with C++11, and doesn't require any system configuration.

I will choose the IDE option with Code::Blocks for the rest of the book, because it does not depend on a specific operating system and everyone will be able to navigate. You can download it at `http://www.codeblocks.org/downloads/26`. The installation is really easy; you just have to follow the wizard.

# Installing CMake

CMake is a really useful tool that manages the build process in any operating system and in a compiler-independent manner. This configuration is really simple. We will need it to build the SFML (if you choose this installation solution) and to build all the future projects of this book. Using CMake gives us a cross-platform solution. We will need version 2.8 or later of CMake. Currently, the last stable version is 3.0.2.

# For Linux users

If you use a Linux system, you can install CMake and its GUI using your packet manager. For example, under Debian, use this command line:

```
sudo apt-get install cmake cmake-gui -y
```

# For other operating systems

You can download the CMake binary for your system at `http://www.cmake.org/download/`. Follow the wizard, and that's it. CMake is now installed and ready to be used.

# Installing SFML 2.2

There are two ways to get the SFML library. The easier way is to download the prebuilt version, which can be found at `http://sfml-dev.org/download/sfml/2.2/`, but ensure that the version you download is compatible with your compiler.

The second option is to compile the library yourself. This option is preferable to the previous one to avoid any trouble.

# Building SFML yourself

Compiling SFML is not as difficult as we might think, and is within the reach of everyone. First of all, we will need to install some dependencies.

# Installing dependencies

SFML depends on a few libraries. Before starting to compile it, make sure that you have all the dependencies installed along with their development files. Here is the list of dependencies:

- `pthread`
- `opengl`
- `xlib`
- `xrandr`
- `freetype`
- `glew`
- `jpeg`
- `sndfile`
- `openal`

# Linux

On Linux, we will need to install the development versions of each of these libraries. The exact names of the packages depend on each distribution, but here is the command line for Debian:

```
sudo apt-get install libglu1-mesa-dev freeglut3-dev mesa-common-dev
libxrandr-dev libfreetype6-dev libglew-dev libjpeg-dev libsndfile1-dev
libopenal-dev -y
```

# Other operating systems

On Windows and Mac OS X, all the needed dependencies are provided directly with SFML, so you don't have to download or install anything. Compilation will work out of the box.

# Compilation of SFML

As mentioned previously, the SFML compilation is really simple. We just need to use CMake, by following these steps:

1. Download the source code at `http://sfml-dev.org/download/sfml/2.2/` and extract it.

2. Open CMake and specify the source code directory and the build directory. By convention, the build directory is called `build` and is at the root level of the source directory.

3. Press the **Configure** button, and select **Code::Blocks** with the right option for your system.

   Under Linux, choose **Unix Makefiles**. It should look like this:

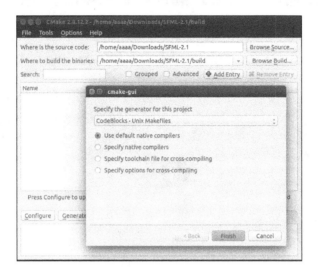

   Under Windows, choose **MinGW Makefiles**. It should look like this:

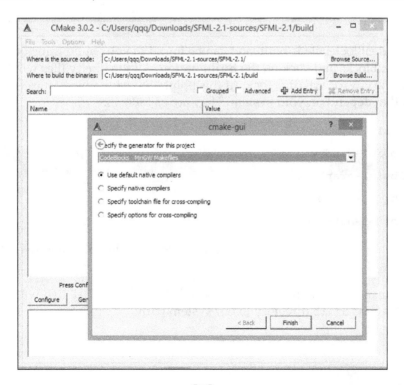

4. And finally, press the **Generate** button. You'll have an output like this:

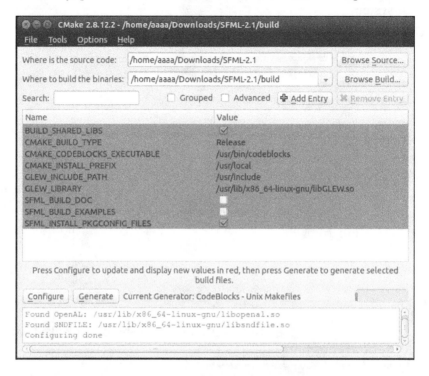

Now the Code::Blocks file is built, and can be found in your build directory. Open it with Code::Blocks and click on the **Build** button. All the binary files will be built and put in the build/lib directory. At this point, you have several files with an extension that depend on your system. They are as follows:

- libsfml-system
- libsfml-window
- libsfml-graphics
- libsfml-audio
- libsfml-network

Each file corresponds to a different SFML module that will be needed to run our future games.

Now it's time to configure our system to be able to find them. All that we need to do is add the build/lib directory to our system path.

## Linux

To compile in Linux, first open a terminal and run the following command:

```
cd /your/path/to/SFML-2.2/build
```

The following command will install the binary files under `/usr/local/lib/` and the headers files in `/usr/local/include/SFML/`:

```
sudo make install
```

By default, `/usr/local/` is in your system path, so no more manipulations are required.

## Windows

On Windows, you will need to add to your system path, the `/build/lib/` directory, as follows:

1.  Go to the **Advanced** tab in **System Properties**, and click on the **Environment Variables** button:

2. Then, select **Path** in the **System variables** table and click on the **Edit...** button:

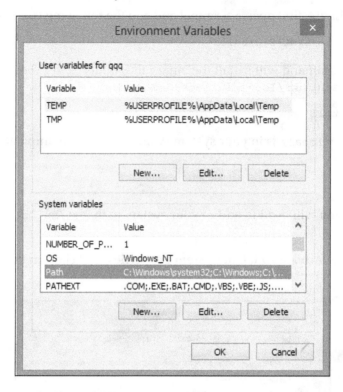

3. Now edit the **Variable value** input text, add `;C:\your\path\to\SFML-2.2\build\lib`, and then validate it by clicking on **OK** in all the open windows:

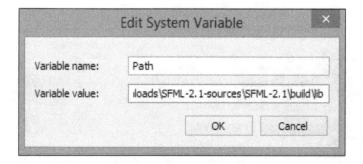

At this point, your system is configured to find the SFML `dll` modules.

# Code::Blocks and SFML

Now that your system is configured to find the SFML binary files, it's time for us to configure Code::Blocks and finally test whether everything is fine with your fresh installation. To do so, follow these steps:

1.  Run Code::Blocks, go to **File | New | Project**, and then choose **Console Application**.

2.  Click on **GO**.

3.  Choose **C++** as the programming language, and follow the instructions until the project is created. A default `main.cpp` file is now created with a typical `Hello world` program. Try to build and run it to check whether your compiler is correctly detected.

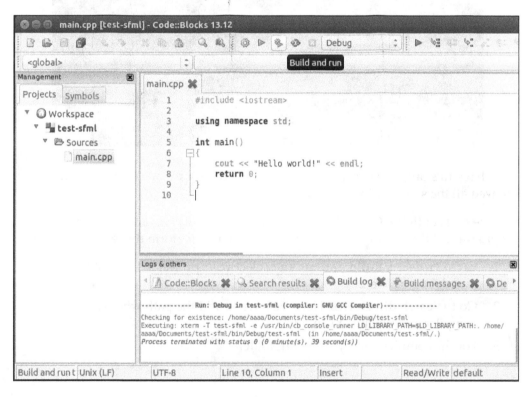

If everything works correctly, you will have a new window created that has a `Hello world!` message, as follows:

```
⊗ ⊖ ⊡   test-sfml
Hello world!

Process returned 0 (0x0)   execution time : 0.001 s
Press ENTER to continue.
```

If you have this output, everything is fine. In any other case, make sure you have followed all the steps for the installations.

Now we will configure Code::Blocks to find the SFML library, and ask it to link with our program at the end of the compilation. To do this, perform the following steps:

1. Go to **Project | Build options** and select your project at the root level (not debug or release).
2. Go to **Search directories**. Here we have to add the path where the compiler and the linker can find the SFML.
3. For the compiler, add your SFML folder.

4.  For the linker, add the `build/lib` folder, as follows:

Now we need to ask the linker which libraries our project needs. All our future SFML projects will need the System, Window, and Graphics modules, so we will add them:

1.  Go to the **Linker settings** tab.
2.  Add `-lsfml-system`, `-lsfml-window` and `-lsfml-graphics` in the **Other linker options** column.

3.  Now click on **OK**.

Good news, all the configurations are now finished. We will eventually need to add a library to the linker in the future (audio, network), but that's it.

# A minimal example

It's now time for us to test the SFML with a very basic example. This application will show us the window as in the following screenshot:

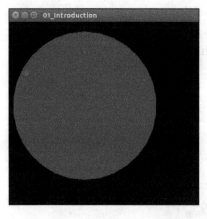

The following code snippet brings about this window:

```
int main(int argc, char* argv[])
{
    sf::RenderWindow window(sf::VideoMode(400,
400),"01_Introduction");
    window.setFramerateLimit(60);

    //create a circle
    sf::CircleShape circle(150);
    circle.setFillColor(sf::Color::Blue);
    circle.setPosition(10, 20);

    //game loop
    while (window.isOpen())
    {
        //manage the events
         sf::Event event;
         while(window.pollEvent(event))
         {
             if ((event.type == sf::Event::Closed)
                 or (event.type == sf::Event::KeyPressed and
event.key.code == sf::Keyboard::Escape))
                 window.close(); //close the window
         }
         window.clear(); //clear the windows to black
         window.draw(circle); //draw the circle
         window.display(); //display the result on screen
    }
    return 0;
}
```

All that this application does is to create a window with a width and height of 400 pixels and its title is 01_Introduction. Then a blue circle with a radius of 150 pixels is created, and is drawn while the window is open. Finally, the user events are checked on each loop. Here we verify if the close event has been asked (close the button or click *Alt* + *F4*), or if the user has pressed the *Esc* button on his keyboard. In both case, we close the window, that will result to the program exit.

# Summary

In this chapter we covered which technologies we will use and why to use them. We also learned the installation of the C++11 compiler on different environments, we learned about installing CMake and how this will help us build the SFML projects in this book. Then we installed SFML 2.2, and followed on to build a very basic SFML application.

In the next chapter we will gain knowledge on how to structure a game, manage user inputs, and keep trace of our resources.

# 2

# General Game Architecture, User Inputs, and Resource Management

Now that the boring part is over, let's start working with SFML. In this chapter, we are not yet going to build a complete game, but instead we'll learn some basic skills that are required to build a game. These are as follows:

- Understanding a basic game architecture
- Managing user inputs
- Keeping a track of external resources

All of these points are really important for any kind of game. But what do these points exactly mean? This is what I will explain to you in this chapter.

## General structure of a game

Before starting to build randomly and without any specific planning, we need to have some information: what kind of game you want to build (RPG, FPS, or action-adventure), what elements will be used, and so on. The aim of this chapter is to understand the general game structure, which can be used in any kind of game. Through this part, we will study:

- The game class
- The frame rate
- The player class
- Event management

# The game class

In the previous chapter, we have seen the minimal code required for a game, which contains:

- Window creation
- Creation of graphic display
- Handle user inputs
- Deal with the user inputs
- Display game objects on the screen

Instead of having one function do all the work, we will make use of object-oriented practices and define various states in different functions. Moreover, we will encapsulate the methods in a new class named `Game`, and we will minimize the `main` function. This `Game` class will be the starting point for all our future games:

```cpp
class Game
{
    public:
        Game(const Game&) = delete;
        Game& operator=(const Game&) = delete;
        Game();
        void run();

    private:
        void processEvents();
        void update();
        void render();

        sf::RenderWindow _window;
        sf::CircleShape  _player;
};


int main(int argc,char* argv[])
{
    Game game;
    game.run();

    return 0;
}
```

`= delete` is a C++11 feature that allows us to explicitly delete a special member function such as constructor, move constructor, copy constructor, copy-assignment operator, move copy-assignment operator, and destructor. It tells to the compiler to not build the default function. In this particular case, it makes the class noncopyable. Another solution would be to extend the class from `sf::NonCopyable`.

`= default` is also possible to explicitly tell the compiler to build the default version of this member function. It could, for example, be used to define a custom constructor and a default constructor.

Now we have the basic `Game` class structured, in which the functions are separated based on their features. Moreover, there is no loop anymore in the main function because we will be present in the `Game::run()` function. Now, we simply have to call the `Game::run()` function.

We can now move all the codes from the main function into the functions — `processEvents()`, `update()`, or `render()` — depending on what we are trying to achieve:

- `processEvents()`: This will manage all events from the user
- `update()`: This will update the entire game
- `render()`: This will manage all the rendering of the game

All the future features will also be put into one of these private functions.

Now, let's have a look at the implementation:

1. The constructor initializes the window and the player:

```
Game::Game()  :  _window(sf::VideoMode(800,  600),"02_Game_Archi"),
_player(150)
{
        _player.setFillColor(sf::Color::Blue);
        _player.setPosition(10, 20);
}
```

2. The `Game::run()` method hides the main game loop:

```
void Game::run()
{
    while (_window.isOpen())
    {
```

```
        processEvents();
        update();
        render();
    }
}
```

3. The `Game::processEvents()` method handles user inputs. It simply polls all the events received from the window since the last frame, such as a button in the window title bar or a keyboard key being pressed. In the following code, we check for the user pressing the window's close button and the keyboard's Esc key. In response, we close the window:

```
void Game::processEvents() {
  sf::Event event;
  while(_window.pollEvent(event)) {
    if ((event.type == sf::Event::Closed)
    or ((event.type == sf::Event::KeyPressed) and (event.key.code
== sf::Keyboard::Escape))) {
      _window.close();
    }
  }
}
```

4. The `update()` method updates our game logic. For the moment, we don't have any logic, but in the near future we will see how to modify the logic of our game:

```
void Game::update(){}
```

5. The `Game::render()` method renders the game to the screen. First, we clear the window with a color, usually `sf::Color::Black`, which is the default, then we render our object for the frame, and finally, we display it on the screen:

```
void Game::render() {
  _window.clear();
  _window.draw(_player);
  _window.display();
}
```

**Downloading the color images of this book**

We also provide you with a PDF file that has color images of the screenshots/diagrams used in this book. The color images will help you better understand the changes in the output. You can download this file from `https://www.packtpub.com/sites/default/files/downloads/B03963_84770S_Graphics.pdf`.

There is no change on the final render of the scene, compared to the minimal example of the previous chapter, except the title and the size. Even if there is more code, the application is easier to maintain with the new architecture because the functions have been reduced to the minimal, and it's easier for you to find what you want:

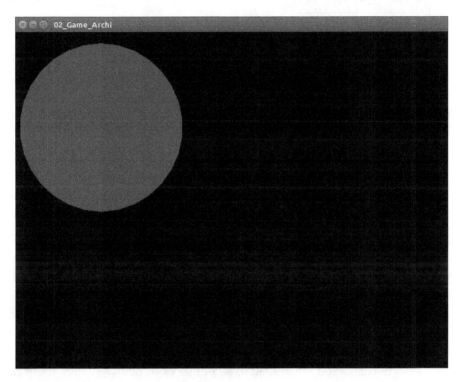

# Game loops

Now that the Game class has been introduced, let's talk about the loop inside the Game::run() function. This loop is called the game loop or main loop. It runs continuously during game play and performs several actions at each turn of the loop. Each iteration of this loop is called a frame. The term **frames per second (FPS)** is a measure that determines the number of iterations made by the game in 1 second. I will come back to this point later.

What you do inside this loop is quite simple. Firstly, we process the events. Then we update the games states. Finally, we render the game to the screen.

As you might have noticed, this sounds a lot like the `run` method of the `Game` class. To explain more visually, this loop is a flowchart representing the logic:

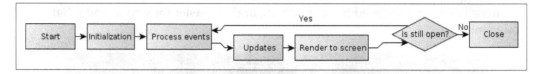

For the moment, the loop is reduced to the minimum. For example, we don't detail the `Game::processEvents()` method in depth here. For the moment, the game loop has been kept simple, so you can learn the basics first. Later, we will be getting back to each of the methods in the `Game::run()` method, such as the `Game::processEvents()` method, and adding more complexity.

## The frame rate

We are now coming back to the frames. As I have already said, a frame is a complete iteration of the game loop. The final result is the new game states that can be displayed on the screen.

Humans are unable to see unlimited number of images per second. There is some interpolation between each image that we perceive with our brain. The result is that we don't need to display a great amount of images each second. But the more images displayed, the greater will the quality of the final result be. For example, at the cinema, only 24 images are displayed per second.

In video games, most of the time, we try to make a loop as quick as we can. The number of images displayed reaches 30 to 60 per second. Below 30 FPS, there can be a lag effect which can be due to the game, and we need to handle it to avoid problems.

One of the most common problems caused by the lag effect is the displacement of the entities. Most of the time, each entity has its own speed and direction. The speed is often measured in pixels per second. Now imagine your game, for any reason, has some lag and the FPS dropped to a small number like 5, then the graphical effect is that all your entities will teleport themselves. But this is not the main issue. The big issue is with the collisions. Take an example of an entity that was walking in the direction of a wall when the lag happens, the entity will literally cross over the wall. Here is a figure that represents the problem:

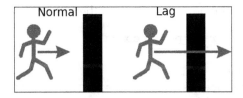

To fix this problem, there are three different approaches. The first is called variable time steps, second is fixed time steps, and third that mix them together.

## Fixed time steps

The fixed time steps approach, as its name suggests, is an approach where each call to the `Game::update()` function is made with the same time interval. The units used, for example, for the movement are relative to the frame. Because each frame is separate from the others of the same time, we don't need more complexity. The only thing we need to pay attention to is to choose the basic values to be sure that there are no problems.

Here is the new flowchart of the `game` loop:

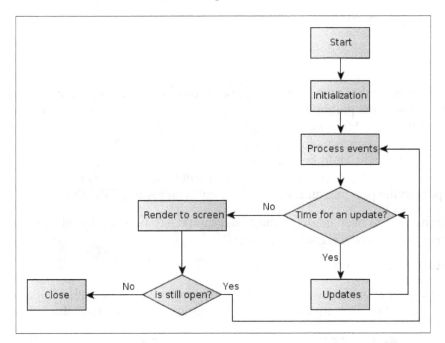

Now we will implement the new Game class in the following code snippet:

```cpp
void Game::run(int frame_per_seconds)
{
    sf::Clock clock;
    sf::Time timeSinceLastUpdate = sf::Time::Zero;
    sf::Time TimePerFrame = sf::seconds(1.f/frame_per_seconds);

    while (_window.isOpen())
    {
        processEvents();
        bool repaint = false;

        timeSinceLastUpdate += clock.restart();
        while (timeSinceLastUpdate > TimePerFrame)
        {
            timeSinceLastUpdate -= TimePerFrame;
            repaint = true;
            update(TimePerFrame);
        }
        if(repaint)
            render();
    }
}
```

This code ensures that each call to the Game::update() function will always take the same time as the parameter value. There no big difference with the previous version of the code. Here we just keep track of the time since the last call of the Game::update() function, and then we only call it again, when the time exceeds the frame rate. The code could be improved by sleeping with sf::sleep the remainder of the free time in the loop. It's a bit more difficult (because needs to measure the time spent in the previous update+render), but won't waste CPU time.

A little change has been made on the Game::update() function by adding a parameter to it. Its new signature is now:

```cpp
void update(sf::Time deltaTime);
```

This parameter allows us to know the time elapsed since the last call of Game::update(). Currently, there is no great interest in it, but later there will be.

Because the state of the game is changed only when Game::update() is called, the call to Game::render() is made when at least an update is made.

# Variable time steps

The variable time steps approach is different from fixed time steps, as the name suggests. The main idea here is to execute the game loop as quickly as we can, without any delay. This allows the game to be more reactive. The units here have to be like units per time (mostly, time refers to one second here). Because we cannot predict how many times the loop will run, we will make it a parameter in the Game::update() function, and multiply it with the base unit.

Our actual implementation of the game loop corresponds to the variable time steps approach; we just need to add a system to keep a track of the elapsed time since the last loop:

```
void Game::run()
{
    sf::Clock clock;

    while (_window.isOpen())
    {
        processEvents();
        update(clock.restart());
        render();
    }
}
```

The only thing new here is sf::Clock and the parameter to the Game::update() method. But there is still a problem with this approach: when the game is too slow (the time between two steps is important).

# Minimum time steps

There is another solution, wherein the last two approaches are merged. The idea is to run the game as quickly as possible by ensuring the time parameter passed in the Game::update() method is not too high. The consequence is that we ensure to have a minimal frame rate, but no maximal. To sum up, we want two things:

- To allow the game to run as quickly as possible
- If, for any reason, the time between the two loops becomes higher than, let's say, 30 FPS, we split this time as much as needed to ensure that the delta time pass to the Game::update() function is not higher than 30 FPS.

Here is the flowchart representing this solution:

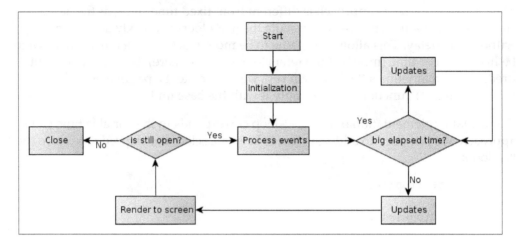

Now we will implement the new `run` function in the following code snippet:

```
void Game::run(int minimum_frame_per_seconds)) {
    sf::Clock clock;
    sf::Time timeSinceLastUpdate;
    sf::Time TimePerFrame = sf::seconds(1.f/minimum_frame_per_
seconds);

    while (_window.isOpen()) {
        processEvents();
        timeSinceLastUpdate = clock.restart();

        while (timeSinceLastUpdate > TimePerFrame) {
            timeSinceLastUpdate -= TimePerFrame;
            update(TimePerFrame);
        }
        update(timeSinceLastUpdate);
        render();
    }
}
```

On each frame, the `Game::update()` and `Game::render()` methods are called, but when the delta time between two frames is more important than what we want, the `Game::update()` method is called with the maximum value allowed, as many times as necessary.

All these approaches have their strong points and their weak points. Depending on circumstances, one approach will be better than another. But from now on, we will use the minimum time steps approach.

All these solutions are not well adapted to use a physics engine. We will return to this particular point in *Chapter 4, Playing with Physics*. But knowing that it will take two loops: one for the physics and another one for the game logic. Each of these loops can have a frame rate different from each other.

There are other approaches to manage the frame rate of an application. One of the most common is the `sleep()` function, which interrupts the application during a specified time and gives the processor the opportunity to work on other tasks. But this is not a good solution in games and all kinds of applications that need exact timing. SFML provides us with a `sf::RenderWindow::setFramerateLimit()` function that tries to fix the frame rate of the running application by calling `sf::sleep()` internally. This is a good solution, but for testing only.

Another solution is to use the vertical synchronization by calling `void sf::Window::setVerticalSyncEnabled(bool)`. It will limit the number of frames displayed to the refresh rate of the monitor (most of the time 60 Hz, but there is no guarantee). It helps in avoiding some visual artefacts, and limits the frame rate to a good value (but not constant across different computers). V-Sync can occasionally lock too low on some systems. This is why in full production games it can be turned on and off.

# Move our player

Now that we have a clean `game` loop, let's move our `Player` object. For now, let's move it forward and make it turn right and left. We will make it in a way that will not depend on the frame rate. First, let's consider the player.

## The player class

`Player` is a really important class in any kind of game, and changes a lot with the type of game. Here our goal is just to be able to move and rotate it. So the information required is as follows:

- Its shape, size, and color
- Its direction
- Its speed

Let's change the `Player` shape to a square using the SFML class `sf::RectangleShape`. The direction and the speed can be merged into a single object: a mathematical vector (we will speak about this in the next section). SFML provides a nice class for this: `sf::Vector2f`. We will also need to add speed and rotation and set the position of the player, but we will also update it and finally display it on the screen.

Finally, we obtain this class:

```cpp
class Player : public sf::Drawable {
  public:
    Player(const Player&) = delete;
    Player& operator=(const Player&) = delete;
    Player();

    template<typename ... Args>
    void setPosition(Args&& ... args) {
      _shape.setPosition(std::forward<Args>(args)...);
    }

    void update(sf::Time deltaTime);
    bool isMoving;
    int rotation;

  private:
    virtual void draw(sf::RenderTarget& target, sf::RenderStates
states) const override;
    sf::RectangleShape  _shape;
    sf::Vector2f        _velocity;
}
```

As mentioned, the player needs to be displayed on the screen, so we extend it from sf::Drawable. This class simply adds the draw() virtual method to the class that we need to override. To be sure that we override it, we use the new keyword of C++11: override.

 Using override, we are sure that we make an override and not an overload. This is a new keyword from C++11.

Moreover, as in the Game class, we make the player non-copyable by explicitly deleting the default implementation of methods.

Now, let's speak about the Player::setPosition() method. As you can see, its signature is really strange. Here, I use another C++11 feature: the variadic template. As you know, sf::Transformable has two versions of the setPosition() method. The first one takes two float numbers, and the second takes sf::Vector2f as the parameter. Because I don't want to build the two versions, I use a new possibility of C++. I simply forward the arguments to sf::Transformable::setPosition() without knowing them. By using this, we can use both of the sf::Transformable:: setPosition() functions.

First, we declare the parameter type of the function as the following template:

```
template<typename Arg> void setPosition(Arg arg);
```

However, we also want to have a variable number of parameters, so we use the ellipse operator. The result is as follows:

```
template<typename … Args> void setPosition(Args ... args);
```

Since we don't want to fix the type of parameter (constant, left-reference, or right-reference), we use another feature of C++11: the right value reference or, in this context, the forwarding/universal reference. This allows us to catch any kind of type by simply adding `&&`. The final signature of the function now is as follows:

```
template<typename … Args> void setPosition(Args&& ... args);
```

Now, to perfectly forward the parameters to `sf::Transformable::setPosition()`, we simply need to unpack the arguments pack using the ellipse operator and call `std::forward` on each of them:

```
_shape.setPosition(std::forward<Args>(args)...);
```

That's it! We can now use any of the `sf::Transformable::setPosition()` methods. This approach is really powerful to make some generic code, so try to understand it.

The `Player` class also has two public attributes: `isMoving` and `rotation`. These attributes will simply store the inputs' states.

Now take a look to the implementation of the functions:

```
Player::Player() : _shape(sf::Vector2f(32,32))
  {
      _shape.setFillColor(sf::Color::Blue);
      _shape.setOrigin(16,16);
  }
```

Here, we just change the _shape constructor to fit with the `sf::RectangeShape` constructor, and center the origin of the shape to its gravity center:

```
void Player::update(sf::Time deltaTime)
{
    float seconds = deltaTime.asSeconds();
    if(rotation != 0)
    {
        float angle = (rotation>0?1:-1)*180*seconds;
        _shape.rotate(angle);
    }
```

```
    if(isMoving)
    {
        float angle = _shape.getRotation() / 180 * M_PI - M_PI / 2;
        _velocity += sf::Vector2f(std::cos(angle),std::sin(angle)) *
60.f * seconds;
    }
    _shape.move(seconds * _velocity);
}
```

Here is the important part. This function updates our player in the
following manner:

- First we rotate it if necessary.

- Then, if the player is moving, we simply get the angle of rotation of the shape
  to know its direction, and then to its existing velocity, we add some speed
  depending on its direction. Notice that for the moment we don't clamp the
  maximal speed.

- To finish, we just have to move it; this is incredibly easy. We simply need to
  call the `move` method on `shape` with `velocity` as the parameter.

Because each frame is not executed in the same time, we need to multiply all the
values (rotation speed, acceleration, and velocity) by the time since the last call. Here
I choose to use pixels per second as the unit, so we need to multiply the value with
the number of seconds since the last call; `sf::Time` provides this ability:

```
void Player::draw(sf::RenderTarget& target, sf::RenderStates states)
const
{
    target.draw(_shape,states);
}
```

This function is not difficult and should not surprise you.

Now, we need to update the `Game::processEvents()` function to set the values of
`isMoving` and `rotation`:

```
void Game::processEvents()
{
    sf::Event event;

    while(_window.pollEvent(event))
    {
        if (event.type == sf::Event::Closed)
            _window.close();
```

```
        else if (event.type == sf::Event::KeyPressed)
        {
            if (event.key.code == sf::Keyboard::Escape)
                _window.close();
            else if(event.key.code == sf::Keyboard::Up)
                _player.isMoving = true;
            else if (event.key.code == sf::Keyboard::Left)
                _player.rotation = -1;
            else if (event.key.code == sf::Keyboard::Right)
                _player.rotation = 1;
        }
        else if (event.type == sf::Event::KeyReleased)
        {
            if(event.key.code == sf::Keyboard::Up)
                _player.isMoving = false;
            else if (event.key.code == sf::Keyboard::Left)
                _player.rotation = 0;
            else if (event.key.code == sf::Keyboard::Right)
                _player.rotation = 0;
        }
    }
}
```

With this code, we set the value of isMoving to true when the up arrow key is pressed and to false when it is released. The same trick is used to set the rotation depending on the left and right arrows, but here we set the rotation direction, 1 for clockwise, -1 for counterclockwise, and 0 to none. All the computations have already been made in Player::update().

# Managing user inputs

Managing the events received from the user is a really important topic. SFML provides us with two different approaches. The first is by polling the events received from a sf::Window instance, and the other is by checking the state in real time of an entry.

First of all, what is an event?

Generally, an event is an object that is triggered when something changes/happens. They are OS-dependent, but SFML provides us with a nice object to handle them in an OS-independent way. This is the `sf::Event` class. This class deals with a vast number of events, as follows:

- Windows contains four different kinds of events. They are as follows:
    - Close
    - Resize
    - Gain/lose focus
    - The mouse pointer goes in/out of the window

- There are three events for the mouse. They are as follows:
    - Move
    - Key press/release
    - Wheel press, release, or move

- The keyboard contains two events. They are as follows:
    - Keys press/release
    - Text entered

- The joystick is also managed with four events. They are as follows:
    - Connected/disconnected
    - Move
    - Press/release the key
    - Enter text

I suggest you take a look at the SFML documentation for this class at `http://www.sfml-dev.org/tutorials/2.2/window-events.php`. An important thing to have in mind is that `sf::Event` is nothing but a big union, so you have to pay attention to access the right attributes of an event depending on its type.

# Polling events

These kinds of events are stored in a queue by a `sf::Window` instance. To deal with them, we simply need to extract them one by one using the `sf::Window::pollEvent()` method. Its signature is as follows:

```
bool sf::Window::pollEvent(sf::Event& event);
```

This signature is a bit interesting. The return value is set to `true` if an event has been extracted from the queue and `false` in other cases. When an event is extracted, the event parameter is set to correspond to the correct value. In other words, the event parameter is the event that we get when the function returns `true`. The typical use of this is as follows:

```
sf::Event event;
while(_window.pollEvent(event))
{
    // do something with the event
}
```

This is exactly what we've done in our actual application. For the moment, we use the event polling to deal with the user inputs.

These event types are used for specific cases (such as closing the window, using the escape key to exit, pausing the game, and so on), and not to move a player because events are perceived so jerky in a non-real-time. The resulting movement will also be jerky.

# Real-time events

SFML provides us with the possibility to check the state of an entity at any time. This entity can be the mouse, keyboard, or a joystick. Here, we don't use events, but we simply check the position of the mouse, and whether a specific button or key is pressed. This is really different from the events, and is particularly well adapted for the player's actions such as movement, shooting, and so on.

As you have probably noticed, our actual use of event in the `Player` class is wrong. So we need to change it to use real-time events without changing the controls keys. To do this, we will add a `processEvents()` method in the `Player` class that will set the value of `isMoving` and `rotation`. We will also change our `Game::processEvents()` function to call the newly created `Player::processEvents()` method. Also, because `isMoving` and `rotation` will be set inside the `Player` class, we will move them as private attributes.

Here is the signature of the new method:

```
void processEvents();
```

As you can see, this is the exact same signature as `Game::processEvents()`. Its implementation is as follows:

```
void Player::processEvents()
{
    isMoving = sf::Keyboard::isKeyPressed(sf::Keyboard::Up);
```

```
    rotation = 0;
    rotation-= sf::Keyboard::isKeyPressed(sf::Keyboard::Left);
    rotation+= sf::Keyboard::isKeyPressed(sf::Keyboard::Right);
}
```

First, we set the isMoving value, depending on the up arrow state. To do this, we use the sf::Keyboard::isKeyPressed() function. Because this function is a static one, we can directly use it without any object. Take a look at its signature:

```
static bool sf::Keyboard::isKeyPressed(sf::Keyboard::Key);
```

This function returns true if the key is pressed, and false if not. Really simple, isn't it?

Now, let's talk about the rotation. The rotation depends on two different inputs. So, we need to think "What will happen if the user presses both at the same time?". It might sound a bit weird, but yes, some players will do this, so we need to consider it. Here, I use a really simple solution:

- First, I reset the value of rotation
- Then, I add rotation depending on the input state for both the keys

By doing this, if no key is pressed, rotation stays to its initial value, that is, 0. If one of the inputs is pressed, then rotation takes the value of 1 or -1, and if both are pressed, the two inputs will cancel each other out, so everything is fine and we get the result we expected.

Now, let's focus on the Player::update() method. This one is not really different. The only line we have to change is the following:

```
float angle = (rotation>0?1:-1)*180*seconds;
```

Because we now set rotation inside the Player class, we are sure that its value is always accurate, so that we don't need to verify it anymore and can remove it. The new line is reduced to the following:

```
float angle = rotation*180*seconds;
```

Now, let's take a look at the updated Game::processEvents() method:

```
void Game::processEvents()
{
    sf::Event event;
    while(_window.pollEvent(event))
    {
        if (event.type == sf::Event::Closed)//Close window
            _window.close();
```

```
        else if (event.type == sf::Event::KeyPressed) //keyboard input
        {
            if (event.key.code == sf::Keyboard::Escape)
                _window.close();
        }
    }
    _player.processEvents();
}
```

Here, we drastically reduce the code size by removing any event dedicated to the player. The only thing to do is to call the `Player::processEvents()` method instead of managing the player controls.

# Handling user inputs

Now that the events are known better, it could be interesting to be able to bind them to some callback when they occur. The main idea behind this is to allow us to dynamically add functionalities. In a game, you sometimes have the possibility to upgrade some weapons, or to use new ones; one option is to make sure that the usage is allowed before executing it, and another is to add it to the player when he is able to use it. By doing this, we remove a lot of if statements in our code and increase the readability of the latter.

To do this, we need a system that allows us to add functionalities to an entity, and that can be triggered by an event. This event can be in real time or generated by polling a `sf::Window` instance.

# Using the Action class

We will create a new class containing an `sf::Event` instance that needs to be executed. This class will implement functionality to check if the internal `sf::Event` instance is executed. The comparison operators are a good way to do this, but it will not work for real-time events because we have nothing to compare with, as we don't pool them. So we will also need `Action::test()` to check if a real-time event is satisfied. We will also need to know whether the event has to be triggered by pressing or releasing the input, or both.

The code for the `Action` class is as follows:

```
class Action
{
    public:
```

```
        enum Type
        {
            RealTime=1,
            Pressed=1<<1,
            Released=1<<2
        };

        Action(const sf::Keyboard::Key& key,int type=Type::RealTime|T
ype::Pressed);
        Action(const sf::Mouse::Button& button,int type=Type::RealTime
|Type::Pressed);

        bool test()const;

        bool operator==(const sf::Event& event)const;
        bool operator==(const Action& other)const;

    private:
        friend class ActionTarget;
        sf::Event _event;
        int _type;
};
```

Let us follow this code step-by-step:

- First, we define enum that will be used as flags in and by the constructors.
- Then, we make the copy constructor and the copy operator.
- Next are the constructors. For the moment, we need to manage inputs from the mouse and the keyboard. So we make two constructors, one for each type of event.
- The `test()` function will allow us to test whether the event is satisfied in real time, and the comparison operators will allow us to compare the event with others.

We shall now take a look at the implementation:

```
Action::Action(const Action& other) : _type(other._type)
{
    std::memcpy(&_event,&other._event,sizeof(sf::Event));
}
Action& Action::operator=(const Action& other)
{
    std::memcpy(&_event,&other._event,sizeof(sf::Event));
    _type = other._type;
    return *this;
}
```

These two functions simply copy the content of Action to another Action instance. Because the sf::Event class doesn't implement the copy operator/constructor, we use the std::memcpy() function from the C string module. This allows us to copy the entire content of sf::Event simply by knowing its size, which can be known using the sizeof() operator. Notice that this is technically correct in this case only because sf::Event doesn't contain any pointers:

```
Action::Action(const sf::Keyboard::Key& key,int type) : _type(type)
{
    _event.type = sf::Event::EventType::KeyPressed;
    _event.key.code = key;
}
```

Here is the constructor for the keyboard events. The key parameter defines the key to bind, and the type parameter defines the state of the input: real-time, pressed, released, or a combination of them. Because the type value is a flag, it can take the value of Pressed and Released at the same time; this creates a problem because the type of an event can't be sf::Event::EventType::KeyPressed and sf::Event::EventType::KeyReleased at the same time. We need to bypass this limitation.

To do this, set the event type to sf::Event::EventType::KeyPressed no matter what the value of type is, and we will have some special cases to deal with later (in test() and comparison operator):

```
Action::Action(const sf::Mouse::Button& button,int type) : _type(type)
{
    _event.type = sf::Event::EventType::MouseButtonPressed;
    _event.mouseButton.button = button;
}
```

This is the same idea as the previous constructor. The only difference is that event.mouseButton cannot be copied. So here we need to use std::memcpy() again:

```
bool Action::operator==(const sf::Event& event)const
{
    bool res = false;
    switch(event.type)
    {
        case sf::Event::EventType::KeyPressed:
        {
            if(_type & Type::Pressed and _event.type == sf::Event::EventType::KeyPressed)
                res = event.key.code == _event.key.code;
        }break;
        case sf::Event::EventType::KeyReleased:
        {
```

```
                if(_type & Type::Released and _event.type == sf::Event::Ev
entType::KeyPressed)
                        res = event.key.code == _event.key.code;
        }break;
        case sf::Event::EventType::MouseButtonPressed:
        {
                if(_type & Type::Pressed and _event.type == sf::Event::Eve
ntType::MouseButtonPressed)
                        res = event.mouseButton.button == _event.mouseButton.
button;
        }break;
        case sf::Event::EventType::MouseButtonReleased:
        {
                if(_type & Type::Released and _event.type == sf::Event::Ev
entType::MouseButtonPressed)
                        res = event.mouseButton.button == _event.mouseButton.
button;
        }break;
        default: break;
    }
    return res;
}
```

`Action::operator==()` is an interesting function. This function will test if two
events are equivalent. But, because we have previously fixed the value for the
keyboard and the mouse to `sf::Event::EventType::[Key/Button]Pressed`, we
need to check these special cases. These cases are represented by the `if` statements:

```
bool Action::operator==(const Action& other)const
{
    return _type == other._type and other == _event;
}
```

This function is pretty simple, first we check the type, and then, we forward the
comparison to the comparison operator previously defined:

```
bool Action::test()const
{
    bool res = false;
    if(_event.type == sf::Event::EventType::KeyPressed)
    {
        if(_type & Type::Pressed)
            res = sf::Keyboard::isKeyPressed(_event.key.code);
    }
    else if (_event.type == sf::Event::EventType::MouseButtonPressed)
    {
```

```
            if(_type & Type::Pressed)
                res = sf::Mouse::isButtonPressed(_event.mouseButton.
button);
        }
        return res;
    }
```

This function is made for checking real-time events. As I have already mentioned, we only need the mouse and keyboard events. To check them, we use the static functions `sf::Keyboard::isKeyPressed()` and `sf::Mouse::isButtonPressed()`. Here we simply have to check the type of events and the state required, and that's it.

Now that the `Action` class was made, let's move on to the next step: binding them to a functionality.

# Action target

We will now need a system to bind a functionality to an event. So let's think about what a functionality is.

A functionality is a piece of code that has to be executed when a criterion is satisfied. Here the criterion is an action and thanks to our freshly defined class, we can now know whether the event is satisfied or not. But what about the piece of code? If we think a little bit about it, the functionality can be put in a function or method, so here we are: a functionality is nothing but a function. So to store the code, and be able to bind it at runtime, we will use the generic function wrapper from the C++11: the template class `std::function`.

> `std::function` is a generic wrapper for any type of function, method, and lambda. It's a very powerful object to store callbacks. To do this, we will use another new class from the C++11, the template class `std::pair`, and a container. Due to our needs, a `std::::list` will be perfectly fine.

Now we have all the keys in hand to build what we need. We will build a container to store as many actions paired with `std::function` as we want:

```
class ActionTarget
{
    public:
        using FuncType = std::function<void(const sf::Event&)>;
```

```
        ActionTarget();

        bool processEvent(const sf::Event& event)const;
        void processEvents()const;

        void bind(const Action& action,const FuncType& callback);
        void unbind(const Action& action);

    private:
        std::list<std::pair<Action,FuncType>> _eventsRealTime;
        std::list<std::pair<Action,FuncType>> _eventsPoll;
};
```

Let's see what happens step by step:

- Firstly, we define the type of the function that will be managed with the new C++11 use of the `using` keyword. This syntax is equivalent to `typedef` except that it is more explicit.

- Secondly, we define a default constructor and the methods to verify the internal events. We create two of them. The first is for non-real-time events (polling), and the other is for real-time events.

- Then we add a method to bind an event to a function, and another to remove any existing event.

Internally, you can make the choice to separate the real-time and non-real-time events to avoid some `if` statements. The goal is to win some readability and computing power.

Now take a look at the implementation:

```
ActionTarget::ActionTarget()
{
}

bool ActionTarget::processEvent(const sf::Event& event)const
{
    bool res = false;
    for(auto& action : _eventsPoll)
    {
        if(action.first == event)
        {
            action.second(event);
            res = true;
            break;
        }
```

```
        }
        return res;
    }

    void ActionTarget::processEvents()const
    {
        for(auto& action : _eventsRealTime)
        {
            if(action.first.test())
                action.second(action.first._event);
        }
    }
```

The two `ActionTarget::processEvent[s]()` methods are not difficult and simply check the validity of the events by using the functions that have been made in the `Action` class. If the event is satisfied, we call the associated function with the `sf::Event` as a parameter.

Here a new `for` loop, syntax is used. It's the `foreach` style of the C++11 `for` loop coupled with the `auto` keyword. This is both a very powerful and succinct syntax:

```
    void ActionTarget::bind(const book::Action& action,const FuncType&
callback)
    {
        if(action._type & Action::Type::RealTime)
            _eventsRealTime.emplace_back(action,callback);
        else
            _eventsPoll.emplace_back(action,callback)
    }
```

This method adds a new event and its callback to the internal container. To avoid some `if` statements in the `processEvent[s]()` methods, I make the choice to separate the real-time event from the others:

```
    void ActionTarget::unbind(const book::Action& action)
    {
        auto remove_func = [&action](const std::pair<book::Action,FuncTy
pe>& pair) -> bool
        {
            return pair.first == action;
        };

        if(action._type & Action::Type::RealTime)
            _eventsRealTime.remove_if(remove_func);
        else
            _eventsPoll.remove_if(remove_func);
    }
```

At runtime, it could be useful to be able to remove some actions. This is the idea of this function. I use the `std::list::remove_if()` method here to remove all the actions of the internal list that match the parameter. It takes a function such as the parameter, so we create a lambda. The lambda functions are a new feature from the C++11. Their syntax is a little special, as follows:

```
[captured, variables](parameters) -> returnType { definition };
```

Let's go through the preceding syntax in detail:

- A lambda is like any other function, except it doesn't have a name (also named anonymous functions). Because of this, a lambda doesn't know the context and sometimes, like here, you will need some variables from the calling context. These variables have to be specified in the `[]` part. You can prefix them with a = or & symbol depending on whether you want to access them by copy or by reference.

- Second is the parameters part. Nothing is new in this part. The parameter type is fixed by the `std::list::remove_if()` function to the same type of template parameter of the `std::list` used.

- Then it's the return type. It's not an obligation, because this type can be deduced from the return statement, but here I've made the choice to explicitly write it, as a complete example. The return type is also fixed by the `std::list::remove_if()` method to `bool`.

- And finally, between { and } is the implementation of the lambda. This implementation is really simple because all the work has already been done in the `Action` class.

And here we are. We have our complete new `ActionTarget` class ready to be used. There are some new C++ features used in this part (`using`, `foreach`, `auto`, and `lambda`). If you don't understand them, I suggest you learn them by reading the C++11 that can be find on this website : `http://en.cppreference.com/w/cpp/language`. It's really essential you understand what is used here before you read on. So if need be, take as much time as required.

Now that we have built the system to manage the events, let's use it. We will change our player, and extend it from `ActionTarget`. We will need to change the code in the `.hpp` file a little bit. Since the C++ allows us to use the multiple inheritance, let's use it, and change the class from:

```
class Player : public sf::Drawable {…};
```

to

```
class Player : public sf::Drawable , public ActionTarget {…}; .
```

By doing this, the functionalities of the `ActionTarget` class are added to the `Player` class. Now, we need to update two functions: `Player::Player()` and `Player::processEvents()`. Notice, that this change imply a modification on the `isMoving` and `rotation` attributes that are now private members of the `Player` class.

```
Player::Player() : _shape(sf::Vector2f(32,32))
                 ,_isMoving(false)
                 _rotation(0)
{
    _shape.setFillColor(sf::Color::Blue);
    _shape.setOrigin(16,16);

    bind(Action(sf::Keyboard::Up),[this](const sf::Event&){
        _isMoving = true;
    });

    bind(Action(sf::Keyboard::Left),[this](const sf::Event&){
        _rotation-= 1;
     });

    bind(Action(sf::Keyboard::Right),[this](const sf::Event&){
        _rotation+= 1;
     });
}
```

Here, we bind the keyboard keys to some callbacks using lambda functions. As you can see, we don't need to check the state of the input in the function because this has already been done in the `ActionTarget::proccessEvents()` method. The callback is called only when the event is satisfied, in this case, when the key is pressed. So we can directly set the value because we know that the key is pressed.

The idea here is to be able to change the inputs without any change in the callbacks. This will be really interesting to build a custom input configuration in the future:

```
void Player::processEvents()
{
    _isMoving = false;
    _rotation = 0;
    ActionTarget::processEvents();
}
```

In this method, we remove all of the codes that check the inputs states, and delegate this to the `ActionTaget::processEvents()` method. The only new thing to do is reset the variable that can be changed by the events.

There is no difference in the final result of our application, but now we have a good starting point to manage our events, and it simplifies our work.

# Event map

Now that we have defined a system to check our event, it would be great to change the inputs associated to a functionality at runtime. This will allow us to create a system where the user can choose which key/button he wants to associate with a specific action. For the moment, we have hardcoded the inputs.

To do this, we will need something that can associate a key with an action. This is what the `std::map` and `std::unordered_map` classes do. Because `std::unordered_map` is quicker than `std::map` at runtime, we prefer to use it. This class comes from the C++ 11.

As previously mentioned, we need to associate a key with an action, so we will create a new class named `ActionMap` that will contain the association map and offer the possibility to add actions at runtime or get one action, thanks to its key:

```
template<typename T = int>
class ActionMap
{
    public:
        ActionMap(const ActionMap<T>&) = delete;
        ActionMap<T>& operator=(const ActionMap<T>&) = delete;

        ActionMap() = default;

        void map(const T& key,const Action& action);
        const Action& get(const T& key)const;

    private:
        std::unordered_map<T,Action> _map;
};
```

Nothing complex here, we just make a wrapper around the container, and make the class in such a way that it cannot be copied with a default empty constructor. We also make the class as a template to be able to choose any kind of key type. In practice, we will often use an integer, but sometimes, it could be interesting to have a string as the key. This is the reason why the template type is `int` by default. Now, let's look at its implementation:

```
template<typename T>
void ActionMap<T>::map(const T& key,const Action& action)
{
    _map.emplace(key,action);
}
```

```
template<typename T>
const Action& ActionMap<T>::get(const T& key)const
{
    return _map.at(key);
}
```

The implementation is really simple to understand. We simply forward what we want to do to the internal container. Because `std::unordered_map` throws exceptions when we try to make an invalid access, for example, we don't need any test.

> Notice that, because the class is a template, the implementation has to be made in the header file. But, in order to not lose readability in the header, there is another way; put the code in a `.tpl` file (`tpl` is the short form for template word) and include it at the end of the header. By doing this, we separate the declaration from the implementation. This is a good practice, and I recommend you to apply it. The `.inl` file extension is also common (shortcut for inline word) instead of `.tpl`.

If you pay attention, the class is not a static one and can be instantiated. This is so that it will allow us to use multiple `ActionMap` class in our project, for example, one to store the player inputs, and another to store the system inputs. But this approach clashes with our actual `ActionTarget` class, so we need to modify it a little bit.

# Back to action target

Since I want to be most generic as possible in the event system, we need to modify our `ActionTarget` class a bit:

- Firstly, the `ActionTaget` class needs to be linked to `ActionMap`. This will allow us to use multiple `ActionMap` in a single project, and this can be very interesting.

- Moreover, because the action is now stored in `ActionMap`, `ActionTarget` doesn't need to store them anymore, but instead it needs to store the key to get them.

- And finally, because `ActionMap` is a template class, we will need to turn `ActionTaget` into a template class too.

The new header looks like this:

```
template<typename T = int>
class ActionTarget
{
    public:
        ActionTarget(const ActionTarget<T>&) = delete;
        ActionTarget<T>& operator=(const ActionTarget<T>&) = delete;

        using FuncType = std::function<void(const sf::Event&)>;

        ActionTarget(const ActionMap<T>& map);

        bool processEvent(const sf::Event& event)const;
        void processEvents()const;

        void bind(const T& key,const FuncType& callback);
        void unbind(const T& key);

    private:
        std::list<std::pair<T,FuncType>> _eventsRealTime;
        std::list<std::pair<T,FuncType>> _eventsPoll;

        const ActionMap<T>& _actionMap;
};
```

The major change is to turn all the references of the `Action` class to the template type. The action will now be identified by its key. Because we need to access the `Action` instances at runtime, we need to have a way to reach them.

Here, I use the SFML logic: one big object and a frontend class to use it. The big object is `ActionMap` and the frontend is `ActionTarget`. So, we internally store a reference to `ActionMap` used to store the events, and because we don't need to modify it, we make it as constant.

All these changes affect our class implementation. Instead of directly accessing an `Action` instance, we need to get it by calling `ActionMap::get()`, but nothing more difficult than this. The really important changes are made in the `Player` class, because now, we have the possibility to change the inputs at runtime, but we also need some default inputs, so we need to add a function to initialize the inputs.

Since a player doesn't have infinite possible control, we can create enum that will store all the keys that will be used in the code. For the moment, we have only one player, so we can present this function as static. The implication is that ActionMap internally used has to be static as well. This ActionMap will be added as a static attribute of the Player class. This is the new header of the class:

```cpp
class Player : public sf::Drawable , public ActionTarget<int>
{
    public:
        Player(const Player&) = delete;
        Player& operator=(const Player&) = delete;

        Player();

        template<typename ... Args>
        void setPosition(Args&& ... args);

        void processEvents();

        void update(sf::Time deltaTime);

        enum PlayerInputs {Up,Left,Right};
        static void setDefaultsInputs();

    private:
         virtual void draw(sf::RenderTarget& target, sf::RenderStates
    states) const override;

        sf::RectangleShape  _shape;
        sf::Vector2f        _velocity;

        bool _isMoving;
        int _rotation;

        static ActionMap<int> _playeInputs;
};
```

As you can see, the Player::PlayerInputs enum, the Player::setDefaultsInputs() function, and the Player::_playerInputs attribute have been added. We also change the ActionMap type to ActionMap<int>, because we will use the newly created enum as a key; the default type of enum is int. The implementation of the player class does not change, except in the constructor. Instead of directly creating an action and binding it, we first initialize ActionMap (in Player::setDefaultsInputs) and then use the key store in enum to refer to the action.

So here is the new constructor:

```
Player::Player()  : ActionTarget(_playerInputs)
                  ,_shape(sf::Vector2f(32,32))
                  ,_isMoving(false)
                  ,_rotation(0)
{
    _shape.setFillColor(sf::Color::Blue);
    _shape.setOrigin(16,16);

    bind(PlayerInputs::Up, [this](const sf::Event&){
        _isMoving = true;
    });

    bind(PlayerInputs::Left, [this](const sf::Event&){
        _rotation-= 1;
    });

    bind(PlayerInputs::Right, [this](const sf::Event&){
        _rotation+= 1;
    });
}
```

As you can see, we also need to specify the `_playerInputs` parameter of the
`ActionTarget` constructor, and we change all the `Action` constructions to their
associated key:

```
void Player::setDefaultsInputs()
{
    _playerInputs.map(PlayerInputs::Up,Action(sf::Keyboard::Up));
    _playerInputs.map(PlayerInputs::Right,Action(sf::Keyboard::Rig
ht));
    _playerInputs.map(PlayerInputs::Left,Action(sf::Keyboard::Left));
}
```

Here we simply initialize the `_playerInputs` with some default keys. These keys
are similar to the previous ones, but because `_playerInputs` is a static member of
the `Player` class it has to be created somewhere. A good practice is to define it in the
`.cpp` file. So the last change in the `Player.cpp` file is this line:

```
ActionMap<int> Player::_playerInputs;
```

This will create the object as expected.

We also need to initialize `ActionMap` by calling `Player::setDefaultsInputs()`. To do this, simply add this call to `main` before the game creation. The `main` should look like this by now:

```
int main(int argc,char* argv[])
{
    book::Player::setDefaultsInputs();

    book::Game game;
    game.run();

    return 0;
}
```

The final result doesn't change, but I think that you can understand the power of the event system that has been created. It allows us to bind functionalities and change the key binding at runtime, this will be really useful in the future.

The result of the actual application should look like this:

You should also be able to rotate the square using the right and left arrows of your keyboard, and make it move by pressing the up arrow. The next step will be to turn this stupid square into a nice spaceship.

# Keeping track of resources

In general game development, the term **resource** defines an external component that will be loaded at runtime within the application. Most of the time, a resource is a multimedia file such as music and image, but it can also be a script or a configuration file. Throughout this book, the term resource will mostly refer to a multimedia resource.

The resources require more memory, and one of the consequences of this is that all the operations on it run slowly, such as the copy. Another thing is that we don't want to have the same resource loaded multiple times in the memory. To avoid all this, we will use them in a particular way, with the help of a resource manager. Most of the time, a resource is loaded from a file to the hard disk, but there are other ways to load them, for example, from the memory or the network.

# Resources in SFML

The SFML library deals with a great numbers of different resources:

| Graphics module | Audio module |
|---|---|
| Texture | SoundBuffer |
| Image | Music |
| Font | |
| Shader | |

All of these resources have some common points. Firstly, we can't use them directly as an output to the screen or the speakers. We have to use a frontend class that doesn't hold the data, but instead holds a reference to it. One of the implications is that the coping objects are quicker. Secondly, all these resource classes share the same SFML API (Application Programming Interface) with some deviations sometimes. A typical example is loading the resources from the hard disk, which has the following signature:

```
bool loadFomFile(const std::string &filename);
```

This function takes the complete path (relative or absolute) of the file to load, and returns `true` if the loading is successful and `false` if there is an error. It's very important to check the returned value to deal with the possible error, most of the time, an invalid path.

There are other versions of this type of member function that allows us to load the resource from different kinds of media. The function bool loadFromMemory(const void *data, std::size_t size); allows the user to load the resource from a RAM. A typical use of this function is to load the resource from hardcoded data. The other option with the SFML is to load the resource from a custom stream:

```
bool loadFromStream(sf::InputStream& stream);
```

This allows the user to fully define the load process. It can be used to load the data from a compressed or encrypted file, from the network, or from whatever device you want. But for now, we will focus on the file way (loadFromFile()) to design our future resources manager. Before starting to create it, take a look at each SFML resource class.

## The texture class

The sf::Texture class represents an image as a pixel array. Each pixel is an **RGBA (red, green, blue, alpha)** value that defines the color at a specific position of the image. This pixel array is stored on the graphic card, in the video memory so it does not use any RAM. Because sf::Texture is stored in the video memory, the graphic card can access it quickly for each draw, but sf::Texture can't be manipulated (changed) as freely as sf::Image can. Every time we want to change it, we will need to reupload it on the video memory using the sf::Texture::upload() function. These operations are quite slow, so be careful when you use them. There are several common image formats sported by the SFML: .bmp, .png, .tga, .jpg, .gif, .psd, .hdr, and .pic. Notice that the .png images can be transparent, and can have an alpha channel to smooth edges again a transparent background.

The frontend class used to display sf::Texture is sf::Sprite. It's the texture representation with its own transformation, colors, and position. An important thing is that sf::Texture must be alive as long as sf::Sprite that used it is alive in order to avoid undefined behaviors. This is because sf::Sprite doesn't copy the texture data, but instead keeps a reference of it.

# The image class

The `sf::Image` class behaves as the `sf::Texture` class but with some important differences due to its storage. The pixel array is stored in the RAM instead of the graphic card. The implications are multiple. The first implication is that it's possible to modify each pixel of the image without any transfer. The second is that it's possible to save the image back to a file placed on the hard drive. The last is that it's not possible to directly display an image on the screen. We need to perform the following steps:

1.  First, convert it to `sf::Texture`
2.  Then, create `sf::Sprite` referring to the texture
3.  Finally, display this sprite.

Even if the entire image is not required for the display, it's possible to use only a part of it. So there is no waste of memory on the graphic card. The supported file formats are exactly the same for `sf::Texture` and `sf::Image`.

It's important to limit the use of `sf::Image` only when you really need it, for example, to modify a loaded image at runtime, to access any of its pixels, or to split it into multiple `sf::Texture` classes. In other cases, it's advisable to directly use `sf::Texture` for performance issues.

# The font class

The `sf::Font` class allows us to load and manipulate character fonts. Most of the common types of fonts are supported such as `TrueType`, `Type 1`, `CFF`, `OpenType`, `SFNT`, `X11 PCF`, `Windows FNT`, `BDF`, `PFR`, and `Type 42`. The `sf::Font` class holds the data, but it's not possible to use it directly. You will need to use the frontend class `sf::Text`, like `sf::Sprite` for `sf::Texture`. This class has some properties such as the font size, color, position, rotation, and so on. The `sf::Font` class must remain accessible as long as all of `sf::Text` that refer to it are alive.

In SFML 2.1, there is no default font for `sf::Text`, so you need at least one font file to display them in your application. The default system font will not be used at all. Moreover, `sf:Text` is actually an object that inherits from `sf::Drawable`, and is physically represented by an OpenGL texture. You have to pay attention to the fact that updating the text every frame has a processing cost, and text needs to be updated only when it's changed.

# The shader class

A shader is a program that will be executed directly on the graphic card, that is written in a specific language, GLSL, which is very similar to the C. There are two of them:

- **Fragment shaders**: This modifies the geometry of an object
- **Pixel shaders**: This modifies the pixel's value of the scene

Shaders are really powerful, and allow us to apply some real-time manipulations on our scene, such as light. To use them, you only need to specify it on the `RenderTarget.draw(sf::drawable&, sf::shader)` function.

I recommend you read the entire description of `sf::Shader` in the documentation before starting to use them.

# The sound buffer class

The `sf::SoundBuffer` class is used to store a sound effect. This class is especially designed to hold the entire audio sample in the memory as an array of 16 bits signed integers. Use it for short audio samples that require no latency and that can fit in the memory, for example, foot steps or gun shots.

Many audio formats are supported, such as `.ogg`, `.wav`, `.flac`, `.aiff`, `.au`, `.raw`, `.paf`, `.svx`, `.nist`, `.voc`, `.ircam`, `.w64`, `.mat4`, `.mat5 pvf`, `.htk`, `.sds`, `.avr`, `.sd2`, `.caf`, `.wve`, `.mpc2k`, and `.rf64`. Notice that the `.mp3` format is not supported because of its restrictive license.

Like `sf::Texture`, `sf::SoundBuffer` holds data, but does not allow us to play it directly. We need to use the `sf::Sound` class to do this. The `sf::Sound` class provides some common functionalities, such as play, stop, and pause but we can also change its volume, pitch, and position. A `sf::Sound` class refers to `ssf::SoundBuffer` that must stay valid as long as `sf::Sound` is played.

# The music class

The `sf::Music` class is the class used to play music. Unlike `sf::SoundBuffer` that is appropriate for short effects, `sf::Music` is designed to deal with long music themes. Themes are generally much longer than effects, and need a lot of memory to hold them completely. To overcome this, `sf::Music` does not load the entire resource at once, but, instead, streams it. This is really useful for large music files that take hundreds of MBs to avoid saturating the memory. Moreover, `sf::Music` has almost no loading delay.

Unlike other resources, sf::Music does not have any lightweight class. You can directly use it. It allows us to use the same features as sf::SoundBuffer and sf::Sound paired, such as play, pause, stop, request its parameters (channels and sample rate), and change the way it is played (pitch, volume, and 3D position).

As a sound stream, a music file is played in its own thread in order to not block the rest of the program. This means that you can leave the music file alone after calling play(), it will manage itself very well.

# Use case

Earlier in this chapter, I've explained that we will turn the blue square into a nice space ship. It's time to do that. Here is the result that will be obtained:

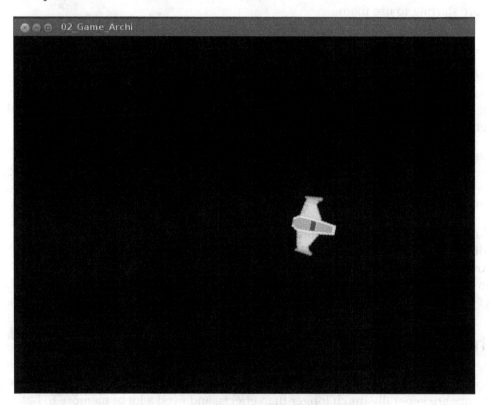

It's not a big change, but it's a starting point for our future game.

To do this, we need to turn `sf::RectangleShape` that represents the `Player` class into `sf::Sprite`. We will also change the `_shape` attribute name into `_ship`; but there is an issue: where is the texture used to store the ship image? To make an attribute of the player of it can be a solution because there is only one player, but we will use another approach: a resources manager.

Before starting to create the manager, let's talk about the **Resource Acquisition Is Initialization (RAII)** idiom.

# RAII idiom

RAII is a principle in which a resource is acquired and released with a class construction and destruction, because these two functions are automatically called. It has the advantage over the manual management to be executed every time, even when some exceptions occur. It's used with the smart pointer classes in the C++11, and can be performed with every type of resource such as files, or in our case, SFML resources.

# Building a resources manager

The goal of a resources manager is to manage the resources and ensure that all the resources are loaded only once to avoid any more copies.

As previously mentioned, we focus on the resources loaded from the hard drive, so a good way to avoid any duplication is to use an identifier for the resource.

We will use `std::unordered_map` again, and build a wrapper around it, as the `ActionMap` class. Because SFML provides a lot of different types of resources, and I don't want to make one for each of them, I will build the resources manager as a template class again. But this time, the template type will be the resource and the key type. We will use the RAII idiom to automate the load and release the resources.

The class looks like this:

```
template<typename RESOURCE,typename IDENTIFIER = int>
class ResourceManager
{
    public:
        ResourceManager(const ResourceManager&) = delete;
        ResourceManager& operator=(const ResourceManager&) = delete;

        ResourceManager() = default;
```

```
            template<typename ... Args>
            void load(const IDENTIFIER& id,Args&& ... args);

            RESOURCE& get(const IDENTIFIER& id)const;

    private:
            std::unordered_map<IDENTIFIER,std::unique_ptr<RESOURCE>> _map;
};
```

We make the class in such a manner that it cannot be copied, and create some functions to load a resource, and another one to get it. Because all the SFML resource classes don't have the exact same parameters for the `loadFromFile()` function (`sf::Shader`), I decided to use a template that will forward the arguments exactly as `Player::setPosition()`.

Moreover, some classes cannot be copied, so we need to use a pointer to store them in a container. Because of the RAII idiom, the choice has been made to use the `std::unique_ptr` template class.

 A new class from the C++11 is `std::unique_ptr` and it is one of the smart pointers. Its internals use the RAII idiom, so we don't need to manage the memory deallocation.

Now the implementation is as follows:

```
template<typename RESOURCE,typename IDENTIFIER>
template<typename ... Args>
void ResourceManager<RESOURCE,IDENTIFIER>::load(const IDENTIFIER&
id,Args&& ... args)
{
    std::unique_ptr<RESOURCE> ptr(new RESOURCE);
    if(not ptr->loadFromFile(std::forward<Args>(args)...))
        throw std::runtime_error("Impossible to load file");
    _map.emplace(id,std::move(ptr));
}
```

A feature from the C++11 is `std::move` and it allows us to use the move constructor instead of the copy constructor. The `std::unique_ptr` template class supports the type of constructor, so using it seems to be a good idea. The idea under the move semantic is to dump a temporary object by taking its content instead of copying it. The result is a gain in performance.

Here, we create a new resource using the template parameter RESOURCE as `std::unique_ptr`. Then we load the resource from the hard drive using the parameter pack args. Finally, we store it internally.

Notice that if the load fails, an exception is thrown rather than returning `false` as value:

```
template<typename RESOURCE,typename IDENTIFIER>
RESOURCE& ResourceManager<RESOURCE,IDENTIFIER>::get(const IDENTIFIER&
id)const
{
    return *_map.at(id);
}
```

This function simply delegates the job to the `std::unordered_map::at()` function by passing the `id` argument to it. The `::at()` method throws an exception when no object is found.

Because our actual `ResourceManager` class uses `loadFromFile()` in the `load()` method, we have a problem with the `sf::Music` class. `LoadFromFile()`, which doesn't exist in the `sf::Music` class and is replaced with `openFromFile()`. So we need to fix that.

To do this, we will use the `partial` specialization. The partial specialization is a technical used in template programming to make some special case, exactly like this one. We need to specialize the `load()` method when `RESOURCE` is set to `sf::Music`. The problem is that we can't do it directly because the `ResourceManager` class has two template parameters, and the other one doesn't need to be fixed. So instead, we have to specialize the entire class by creating a new one:

```
template<typename IDENTIFIER>
class ResourceManager<sf::Music,IDENTIFIER>
{
    public:
        ResourceManager(const ResourceManager&) = delete;
        ResourceManager& operator=(const ResourceManager&) = delete;

        ResourceManager() = default;

        template<typename ... Args>
        void load(const IDENTIFIER& id,Args&& ... args);

        sf::Music& get(const IDENTIFIER& id)const;

    private:
        std::unordered_map<IDENTIFIER,std::unique_ptr<sf::Music>> _
map;
};
```

This class is the replica of the previous one, except that we have removed one template parameter to fix it to `sf::Music`. Here is the implementation:

```
template<typename IDENTIFIER>
template<typename ... Args>
void ResourceManager<sf::Music,IDENTIFIER>::load(const IDENTIFIER&
id,Args&& ... args)
{
    std::unique_ptr<sf::Music> ptr(new sf::Music);

    if(not ptr->openFromFile(std::forward<Args>(args)...))
        throw std::runtime_error("Impossible to load file");
    _map.emplace(id,std::move(ptr));
};

template<typename IDENTIFIER>
sf::Music& ResourceManager<sf::Music,IDENTIFIER>::get(const
IDENTIFIER& id) const
{
    return *_map.at(id);
}
```

Here again, this is exactly the same, except that we have changed `loadFromFile()` to `openFromFile()`.

Finally, one class with a specialization has been constructed to deal with all the SFML resources types, and use the RAII idiom to free memory when required.

The next step is to use this class to change the appearance of the player.

# Changing the player's skin

Now that we have built a nice system to manage any kind of resource, let's use them. As previously mentioned, to change the player's square into a ship, we need to change `sf::RectangleShapethat`, represent the `Player` class in `sf::Sprite`, and then set the texture source of `sf::Sprite` loaded by the texture manager. So we need a texture manager.

If we think about it, all the managers will be global to our application, so we will group them into a static class named `Configuration`. This class will hold all the game configurations and the managers. `ActionMap` can also be stored inside this class, so we will move `ActionMap` inside the player into this new class, and create an `initialize()` method to initialize all the inputs and textures.

This class is really simple, and can't be instantiated, so all the attributes and methods will be static:

```
class Configuration
{
    public:
        Configuration() = delete;
        Configuration(const Configuration&) = delete;
        Configuration& operator=(const Configuration&) = delete;

        enum Textures : int {Player};
        static ResourceManager<sf::Texture,int> textures;

        enum PlayerInputs : int {Up,Left,Right};
        static ActionMap<int> player_inputs;

        static void initialize();

    private:

        static void initTextures();
        static void initPlayerInputs();
};
```

As you can see, the class is not really difficult. We only move the _playerInputs and enum from the Player class and add ResourceManager for textures. Here is the implementation:

```
ResourceManager<sf::Texture,int> Configuration::textures;
ActionMap<int> Configuration::player_inputs;

void Configuration::initialize()
{
    initTextures();
    initPlayerInputs();
}

void Configuration::initTextures()
{
    textures.load(Textures::Player, "media/Player/Ship.png");
}

void Configuration::initPlayerInputs()
{
```

```
player_inputs.map(PlayerInputs::Up,Action(sf::Keyboard::Up));
player_inputs.map(PlayerInputs::Right,Action
    (sf::Keyboard::Right));
player_inputs.map(PlayerInputs::Left,Action
    (sf::Keyboard::Left));
}
```

Here again, the code is simple. We now have just a few changes to make in the player class to draw it as a spaceship. We need to replace `sf::RectangleShape _shape` with `sf::Sprite _ship;`.

In the constructor, we need to set the texture and the origin of the sprite as follows:

```
_ship.setTexture(Configuration::textures.get(Configuration::Textures:
:Player));
_ship.setOrigin(49.5,37.5);
```

Don't forget to call `Configuration::initialize()` from `main()` before anything else. We now have a nice spaceship as a player.

There is a lot of code and different classes to get this result, but if you think about it, this will really help us in the future, and reduce the number of code lines in our final applications.

# Summary

In this chapter, we covered the general game architecture, the input management, and the resources. You also learned about the RAII idiom and some C++11 features such as lambda, variadic templates, smart pointers, move syntax, and perfect forwarding.

All the basic building blocks are now set up, so in the next chapter, we will make complete games by completing the current application to raise it to the asteroid game, and we will also build a Tetris game.

# Making an Entire 2D Game

# 3

In this chapter, we will finally make our first game. In fact, we will build two games, as follows:

- We will build our first game, an Asteroid clone game, by improving our actual application of SFML
- Our next game will be a Tetris clone game

We will also learn some skills such as:

- Entity models
- Board management

We are all fans of old school games, so let's get loaded to create some of them right away. In addition, each of these two games has a completely different architecture. It's really interesting as far as the learning process is concerned.

## Turning our application to an Asteroid clone

**Asteroid** is an arcade "shoot 'em up" game created in 1979 by Atari Inc., and is considered a classic. The player controls a spaceship in an asteroid field with some flying saucers appearing on the screen from time to time, attacking it. The goal of this game is to destroy all the asteroids and saucers by shooting at them. Each level increases the number of asteroids in the field, and the game becomes harder and harder.

To build this game, we will use our actual application as a base, but we need to add a lot of things to it.

# The Player class

The player is represented as a spaceship. The spaceship has the ability to rotate left and right, to shoot, and the spaceship can also give itself a boost. The player can also send the ship into hyperspace, causing it to disappear and reappear in a random location on the screen, at the risk of self-destructing or appearing on top of an asteroid.

The player starts with three lives, and on every 10,000 points, a new life is won. If the player crashes into something, it will be destroyed and the player will lose one life. It will reappear at the starting point, that is, the middle of the screen.

# The levels

Each level starts with some big asteroids in random places that are drifting in various directions. Each level will have an increased number of asteroids. This number is four for the first level and eleven starting from the fifth level.

The board is a bit special because it's a Euclidean torus (see the definition on Wikipedia for more detail: http://en.wikipedia.org/wiki/Torus). The top and the bottom of the screen wrap to meet each other, as do the left and right sides, except that the top right meets the bottom left, and vice versa. The level is finished when there are no more meteors on the screen.

# The enemies

There are two kinds of enemies: meteors and flying saucers. Both of them can destroy you if you crash into them, and both add some points when you destroy them by shooting at them.

# The meteors

There are three types of meteors. Each one has its own size, speed, and a points number that differs from the others. Here is a table that summarizes the different meteors' properties:

| Size | Big | Medium | Small |
| --- | --- | --- | --- |
| Speed | Slow | Medium | Fast |
| Split | 2~3 medium | 2~3 smalls | - |
| Base Points | 20 | 60 | 100 |

Each time a meteor is hit, it is split into a smaller meteor, except for the small ones. The big meteors are also those that represent the starting meteor field of each level.

## The flying saucers

Time to time! A flying saucer appears and tries to disturb the player. There are two saucers, a big one, which does nothing apart from moving, and a small one, that shoots at the player. The higher the score of the player, the higher is the chance that a small saucer appears instead of a big one. Starting from 40,000, only small saucers appear. In addition, the more points the player has, the higher is the precision of the saucers.

# Modifying our application

Now that we have all the information required to build our game, let's start to change it. The first step is to change our world to a Euclidean torus with a fixed size. Here is a representation of a torus taken from the Wikipedia page:

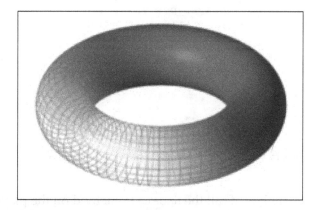

To do this, we will need some information from inside the game, such as the world size. We will add the information inside the Game class as two integer values, height and width:

```
const int _x, const _y;
```

We will initialize them with the constructor. So now, we need parameters for this class:

```
Game(int x=800, int y=600);
```

We will need to change our constructor implementation a bit, as shown in the following code snippet:

```
Game::Game(int x, int y) :
  _window(sf::VideoMode(x,y),"03_Asteroid"),x(x),y(y){
    _player.setPosition(100,100);
}
```

Okay, now we can choose the size of the world, but how do we make it a torus? In reality, it's not complicated. We only need to check the position of each entity after moving them; and if they are out of the world, we correct their positions.

Let's try this with the player, as shown in the following code snippet:

```
void Game::update(sf::Time deltaTime)
{
  _player.update(deltaTime);
  sf::Vector2f player_pos = _player.getPosition();
  if(player_pos.x < 0){
    player_pos.x = _x;
    player_pos.y = _y - player_pos.y;
  } else if (player_pos.x > _x){
    player_pos.x = 0;
    player_pos.y = _y - player_pos.y;
  }
  if(player_pos.y < 0)
  player_pos.y = _y;
  else if(player_pos.y > _y)
  player_pos.y = 0;
    _player.setPosition(player_pos);
}
```

As you can see here, firstly, we call the `update()` method on the player, and then we correct its position if it's out of the world range. We now have an infinite world.

The `Player::getPosition()` method used is as follows:

```
const sf::Vector2f& Player::getPosition()const{return
  _ship.getPosition();}
```

The only sad thing with this is that we modify the player's position inside the `Game` class. It will be better if the player could manage its position itself, isn't it? Wrong! If you think a bit about this, you will understand that the player doesn't care about the world's shape. It's the world's work to be able to adapt the position of its entity, not the contrary.

Here we have two options: keep our code as it is or establish a more flexible system. If we quickly think about what will be required for the managements of the meteors and saucers, the second option seems best. So let's build a more flexible system.

In game development, there are two major design patterns that answer to this. They are as follows:

- The hierarchical entity system
- The entity component system

Each of these patterns answer the problem in a different way. We will see them right after the world class.

# The World class

All our logic is actually made in the Game class. This is a good way, but we can do better. If we think about it, the Game class has to not only process events, create the window, and delegate other classes to the pause and menu systems, but also perform all the entity management.

To be more explicit, the game doesn't have to manage any entity, but can create a world and populate it. Then, all the work is done by the world class.

The world is a container of entities but also of sounds effects. It has a specific size, shape, and rules (such as physics). It can also be displayed on screen. Finally, the class looks similar to the following code snippet:

```cpp
class World : public sf::Drawable
{
  public:
  World(const World&) = delete;
  World& operator=(const World&) = delete;
  World(float x,float y);
  ~World();
  void add(Entity* entity);
  void clear();
  bool isCollide(const Entity& other);
  int size();

  void add(Configuration::Sounds sound_id);

  const std::list<Entity*> getEntities()const;
  int getX()const;
  int getY()const;
  void update(sf::Time deltaTime);
```

```
    private:
    std::list<Entity*>  _entities;
    std::list<Entity*>  _entities_tmp;

    std::list<std::unique_ptr<sf::Sound>> _sounds;
    virtual void draw(sf::RenderTarget& target, sf::RenderStates
    states) const override;

    const int _x;
    const int _y;
};
```

Like the other classes, we make the `World` class non-replicable. We add some functions to add an entity to the world, and some functions to remove them all as well. Because it's possible to have some sounds in the world, we also add a method to add them. It takes an ID from the `Configuration` class, exactly like the IDs for `Textures`. We also add some functions to get information such as the number of entities, the size of the world, and so on.

Now if we take a look at the attributes, we can see two containers for the entities. This is a trick that will make our lives easier. I will explain it in the implementation. The other container is for `sf::Sound` that can be added to the world. I will also explain it in the implementation.

Now, take a look at the implementation. This class is a bit long, and some functions have been reduced to not take a lot of space in this chapter:

```
World::World(float x,float y): _x(x),_y(y){}
World::~World(){clear();}
```

There is no difficulty in these functions. The constructor simply sets the size of the world, and the destructor clears it; as shown in the following code snippet:

```
void World::add(Entity* entity) {
    _entities_tmp.push_back(entity);
}
```

This is another simple function, but we don't add an entity directly to the `_entites` container. Instead, we add it to a temporary container that contains only the entities created during a particular time frame. The reason for doing this will be explained in the `update()` function:

```
void World::clear()
{
   for(Entity* entity :_entities)
   delete entity;
```

```
_entities.clear();
for(Entity* entity :_entities_tmp)
delete entity;
_entities_tmp.clear();
_sounds.clear();
}
```

Here, we clean the entire world by deleting all its entities and sounds. Because we use raw pointers for the entities, we need to delete them explicitly unlike sf::Sound:

```
void World::add(Configuration::Sounds sound_id)
{
    std::unique_ptr<sf::Sound> sound(new
      sf::Sound(Configuration::sounds.get(sound_id)));
    sound->setAttenuation(0);
    sound->play();
    _sounds.emplace_back(std::move(sound));
}
```

This function creates a sf::Sound parameter from a sf::SoundBuffer parameter contained in the Configuration class, initialize it, and play it. Because each sf::Sounds has its own thread, the sf::Sound::play() parameter will not interrupt our main thread. And then, we store it in the appropriate container:

```
bool World::isCollide(const Entity& other)
{
    for(Entity* entity_ptr : _entities)
        if(other.isCollide(*entity_ptr))
            return true;
    return false;
}
```

The World::isCollide() function is a helper to check whether an entity is colliding with another one. This will be used to place the meteors at the beginning of the game:

```
int World::size(){return _entities.size() + _entities_tmp.size();}
int World::getX()const{return _x;}
int World::getY()const {return _y;}
const std::list<Entity*> World::getEntities()const {return
  _entities;}
```

These functions are pretty simple. There are just some getters. The only thing that is particular is `size()` because it returns the total number of entities:

```cpp
void World::update(sf::Time deltaTime)
{
  if(_entities_tmp.size() > 0)
  _entities.merge(_entities_tmp);
  for(Entity* entity_ptr : _entities)
  {
    Entity& entity = *entity_ptr;
    entity.update(deltaTime);
    sf::Vector2f pos = entity.getPosition();
    if(pos.x < 0)
    {
      pos.x = _x;
      pos.y = _y - pos.y;
    } else if (pos.x > _x) {
      pos.x = 0;
      pos.y = _y - pos.y;
    }
    if(pos.y < 0)
    pos.y = _y;
    else if(pos.y > _y)
    pos.y = 0;
    entity.setPosition(pos);
  }
  const auto end = _entities.end();
  for(auto it_i = _entities.begin(); it_i != end; ++it_i)
  {
    Entity& entity_i = **it_i;
    auto it_j = it_i;
    it_j++;
    for(; it_j != end;++it_j)
    {
      Entity& entity_j = **it_j;
      if(entity_i.isAlive() and entity_i.isCollide(entity_j))
      entity_i.onDestroy();
      if(entity_j.isAlive() and entity_j.isCollide(entity_i))
      entity_j.onDestroy();
    }
```

```
    }
    for(auto it = _entities.begin(); it != _entities.end();)
    {
        if(not (*it)->isAlive())
        {
            delete *it;
            it = _entities.erase(it);
        }
        else
        ++it;
    }
    _sounds.remove_if([](const std::unique_ptr<sf::Sound>& sound) ->
        bool {
        return sound->getStatus() != sf::SoundSource::Status::Playing;
    });
}
```

This function is a bit more complicated than the previous version of it. Let's explain it in detail:

1.  We merge the entities' container together into the main container.
2.  We update all entities, and then verify that their positions are correct. If this is not the case, we correct them.
3.  We check the collision between all the entities and dead entities are removed.
4.  Sounds that have been played are removed from the container.

In the update and collision loops, some entities can create others. That's the reason for the _entities_tmp container. In this way, we are sure that our iterator is not broken at any time, and we do not update/collide entities that have not experienced a single frame, as shown in the following code snippet:

```
void World::draw(sf::RenderTarget& target, sf::RenderStates
    states) const
{
    for(Entity* entity : _entities)
    target.draw(*entity,states);
}
```

This function is simple, and forwards its job to all the entities. As you can see, the World class is not really complicated, and manages any kind of entities and all sounds. By doing this, we can remove a lot of tasks from the Game class, and delegate it to the World class.

# The hierarchical entity system

This system is the most intuitive. Each kind of entity is a different class in your code, and all of them are extended from a common virtual class, most of the time called **Entity**. All the logic is made inside the class in the `Entity::update()` function. For our project, the hierarchical tree could be similar to the following figure:

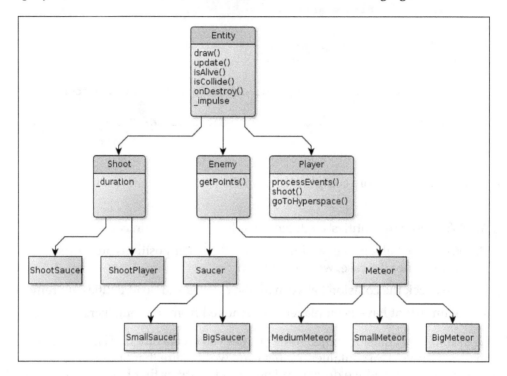

As you can see, there are several abstraction layers. For this project, and because we don't have a lot of different kind of entities, we will use this solution.

# The entity component system

This is a totally different approach. Instead of having each type of entity represented as a class, there is only one class: entity. To this entity, we attach some property such as the position, ability to be draw, a gun, and whatever you want. This system is really powerful, and is a great solution in video games, but is also difficult to build. I will not get into more detail about this system, because I will come back to it in the next chapter. So even if we don't use it right now, don't be frustrated, we will build and use it in the next project.

# Designing our game

Now that we have chosen the entity component system approach and created a world that will be populated by them, let's think about the needs. Following table summarizes the needs:

| Entity | Parent | Specificities |
|---|---|---|
| Entity | | This can move |
| | | This can be drawn |
| | | This can collide with another entity |
| Player | Entity | This can shoot |
| | | This is controlled by inputs |
| | | This can collide with everything except the one it shoots |
| Enemy | Entity | This can be destroyed by shooting |
| | | This gets the player some points when destroyed by shooting |
| Saucer | Enemy | This has a bigger chance to spawn a small saucer when the point number increases |
| | | This can collide with everything except saucer shoots |
| BigSaucer | Saucer | This has a special skin |
| SmallSaucer | Saucer | This can shoot the Player entity |
| | | This has a special skin |
| Meteors | Enemy | This can collide with everything except other meteors |
| BigMeteor | Meteors | This splits into some MediumMeteor when destroyed |
| | | This has a special skin |
| MediumMeteor | Meteors | This splits into SmallMetors when destroyed |
| | | This has a special skin |
| SmallMeteor | Meteors | This has a special skin |
| Shoot | Entity | This lives for a specific time |
| ShootPlayer | Shoot | This can only collide with enemies |
| | | This has a specific skin |
| ShootSaucer | Shoot | This can collide with Meteor and Player |
| | | This has a special skin |

Now that we have all the information needed for each class, let's build them. The final result will look similar to the following:

## Prepare the collisions

In this project we will use a simple collision detection: collision between circles. As just said this is very basic and can be improved a lot, but is sufficient for now. Take a look to the class:

```
class Collision
{
  public:
    Collision() = delete;
    Collision(const Collision&) = delete;
    Collision& operator=(const Collision&) = delete;
    static bool circleTest(const sf::Sprite& first, const sf::Sprite&
second);
};
```

The is no member here, and the class can't be instantiate. The aim of the class is to group some helper function used by other classes. So here, only one collision test is describe that take two sf::Sprite as parameters. Take a look to the implementation.

```
bool Collision::circleTest(const sf::Sprite& first, const sf::Sprite&
second)
{
```

```
sf::Vector2f first_rect(first.getTextureRect().width,
first.getTextureRect().height);
first_rect.x *= first.getScale().x;
first_rect.y *= first.getScale().y;

sf::Vector2f second_rect(second.getTextureRect().width,
second.getTextureRect().height);
second_rect.x *= second.getScale().x;
second_rect.y *= second.getScale().y;

float radius1 = (first_rect.x + first_rect.y) / 4;
float radius2 = (second_rect.x + second_rect.y) / 4;
float xd = first.getPosition().x - second.getPosition().x;
float yd = first.getPosition().y - second.getPosition().y;

return std::sqrt(xd * xd + yd * yd) <= radius1 + radius2;
}
```

The function first computes the radius for each of the sprite. Then it checks if the distance between the two sprites (computed using the Pythagoras theorem) is less than the sum of the tow radius. If it's verify, then there is no collision, on the other side, there is one, even if we don't exactly know the exact point.

# The Entity class

To build our system, we need the base class, so let's start with the Entity class:

```
class Entity :  public sf::Drawable
{
  public:
//Constructors
  Entity(const Entity&) = delete;
  Entity& operator=(const Entity&) = delete;
  Entity(Configuration::Textures tex_id,World& world);
  virtual ~Entity();

//Helpers
  virtual bool isAlive()const;

  const sf::Vector2f& getPosition()const;
  template<typename ... Args>
  void setPosition(Args&& ... args);
  virtual bool isCollide(const Entity& other)const = 0;
```

```
//Updates
  virtual void update(sf::Time deltaTime) = 0;
  virtual void onDestroy();

  protected:
  sf::Sprite _sprite;
  sf::Vector2f _impulse;
  World& _world;
  bool _alive;

  private :
  virtual void draw(sf::RenderTarget& target, sf::RenderStates
  states) const override;
};
```

Let's discuss this class step by step:

1.  Firstly, we make the class noncopyable.

2.  Then we make the destructor virtual. This is a really important point because the Entity class will be used as a polymorphic class. So we need to set the destructor as virtual to be able to destruct the real object and not only it's Entity base.

3.  We also define some helper functions to know if the entity is alive and also to set/get its position. The code is the same as we have in the Player class. We also define some virtual methods that will be overridden in other classes.

4.  The virtual function onDestroy() is important. Its goal is to execute some code before the destruction on the entity by shooting it or whatever. For example, the ability of a Meteor entity to be split will be put in this function, and so will all kind of sounds caused by the destruction of the object.

Now take a look to the implementation of the Entity class:

```
Entity::Entity(Configuration::Textures tex_id,World& world) :
  _world(world),_alive(true)
{
  sf::Texture& texture = Configuration::textures.get(tex_id);
  _sprite.setTexture(texture);
  _sprite.setOrigin(texture.getSize().x/2.f,texture.getSize
    ().y/2.f);
}
```

The constructor sets the texture to the internal sf::Sprite function, and then center the origin of it. We also set the world of the entity, and the alive value:

```
const sf::Vector2f& Entity::getPosition()const {return
  _sprite.getPosition();}
void Entity::draw(sf::RenderTarget& target, sf::RenderStates
  states) const {target.draw(_sprite,states);}
```

These two functions are the exact same as those in the Player class. So no surprises here:

```
bool Entity::isAlive()const {return _alive;}
void Entity::onDestroy(){_alive = false;}
```

These two functions are new. It's simply a helper function. IsAlive() is used to know if an entity have to be removed from the world, and the onDestroy() function is a method that will be called when a collision is detected with another Entity. Nothing complicated for now.

# The Player class

Now that we have the Entity class, let's change the Player class to extend it from Entity:

```
class Player : public Entity , public ActionTarget<int>
{
  public:
  Player(const Player&) = delete;
  Player& operator=(const Player&) = delete;
  Player(World& world);

  virtual bool isCollide(const Entity& other)const;
  virtual void update(sf::Time deltaTime);
  void processEvents();
  void shoot();
  void goToHyperspace();
  virtual void onDestroy();

  private:
  bool _isMoving;
  int _rotation;
  sf::Time _timeSinceLastShoot;
}
```

As you can see, we removed all the functions and attributes related to the position and the display. The `Entity` class already does it for us. And now the implementation of this class is as follows:

```
Player::Player(World& world)  : Entity(Configuration::Textures::Player
,world)
  ,ActionTarget(Configuration::player_inputs),_isMoving(false)
    ,_rotation(0)
{
  //bind ..
  bind(Configuration::PlayerInputs::Shoot, [this](const
    sf::Event&){
    shoot();
  });
  bind(Configuration::PlayerInputs::Hyperspace, [this](const
    sf::Event&){
    goToHyperspace();
  });
}
```

Here we remove all the code that initializes the `_sprite` function, and delegate the job to the `Entity` constructor. We also add two new abilities, to shoot and to go to hyperspace:

```
bool Player::isCollide(const Entity& other)const
{
  if(dynamic_cast<const ShootPlayer*>(&other) == nullptr) {
    return Collision::circleTest(_sprite,other._sprite);
  }
  return false;
}
```

We set the default behavior of the collision. We need to know the real type of the `Entity` as a parameter. To do this we use the virtual table lookup by trying to convert the `Entity` class to a specific pointer type. If this is not possible, `nullptr` is returned by `dynamic_cast()`. There are other approaches to do this, such as double dispatch. But the one used here is the simplest and easy to understand but is a slow operation. Once the real type of entity is known, the collision test is made. In this project, the hit box of each entity is the circle inscribed in its sprite. This is a pretty good approximation:

```
void Player::shoot()
{
  if(_timeSinceLastShoot > sf::seconds(0.3))
  {
```

```
        _world.add(new ShootPlayer(*this));
        _timeSinceLastShoot = sf::Time::Zero;
    }
}
```

This function creates a ShootPlayer instance and adds it to the world. Because we don't want that the player to create a shoot in every frame, we add a timer that is updated in the Player::update() method, as shown:

```
void Player::goToHyperspace()
{
    _impulse = sf::Vector2f(0,0);
    setPosition(random(0,_world.getX()),random(0,_world.getY()));
    _world.add(Configuration::Sounds::Jump);
}
```

This method teleports the player to a random place in the world. It also removes all the impulsion, so the player will not continue to move in its previous direction after a teleportation:

```
void Player::update(sf::Time deltaTime)
{
    float seconds = deltaTime.asSeconds();
    _timeSinceLastShoot += deltaTime;
    if(_rotation != 0)
    {
        float angle = _rotation*250*seconds;
        _sprite.rotate(angle);
    }

    if(_isMoving)
    {
        float angle = _sprite.getRotation() / 180 * M_PI - M_PI / 2;
        _impulse += sf::Vector2f(std::cos(angle),std::sin(angle)) * 300.f
*
        seconds;
    }
    _sprite.move(seconds * _impulse);
}
```

This method updates the position and the rotation of a `Player` according to the different action made by the user. It also updates the time since the last shoot to be able to shoot again.

```
void Player::onDestroy()
{
  Entity::onDestroy();
  Configuration::lives--;
  _world.add(Configuration::Sounds::Boom);
}
```

To better understand the `Entity::onDestroy()` method, remember that this function is called before the destruction (and the call of the destructor) of an `Entity` instance when a collision occurs. So here we call the `onDestroy()` function of the `Entity` base of the class, and then do the special things of the player, such as reduce the number of lives, set the player value to `nullptr`, and finally, add an explosion sound to the world. The other methods of the `Player` class have not changed.

## The Enemy class

We will now create the Enemy class as we have already described, in the table at the beginning of the `Design our game` part:

```
class Enemy : public Entity
{
  public:
  Enemy(const Enemy&) = delete;
  Enemy& operator=(const Enemy&) = delete;
  Enemy(Configuration::Textures tex_id,World& world);

  virtual int getPoints()const = 0;
  virtual void onDestroy();
};
```

This class is pretty small because it doesn't need a lot of new logic compared to the `Player` class. We only need to briefly specify the `onDestroy()` method by adding points to the global score of the game. So we create a `getPoints()` method that will simply return the number of points for an enemy.

```
Enemy::Enemy(Configuration::Textures tex_id,World& world) :
  Entity(tex_id,world)
{
  float angle = random(0.f,2.f*M_PI);
  _impulse = sf::Vector2f(std::cos(angle),std::sin(angle));
}
```

The constructor simply initializes the _impulse vector to a random one, but with the length as 1. This vector will be multiplied by the speed of the Saucers/Meteor entity in their respective constructors:

```
void Enemy::onDestroy()
{
  Entity::onDestroy();
  Configuration::addScore(getPoints());
}
```

This method simply calls the onDestroy() function from the Entity base of the object, and then adds the points won by destroying the object.

# The Saucer class

Now that we have the Enemy class made, we can build the Saucer base class corresponding to our expectations:

```
class Saucer : public Enemy
{
  public:
  Saucer(const Saucer&) = delete;
  Saucer& operator=(const Saucer&) = delete;
  using Enemy::Enemy;

  virtual bool isCollide(const Entity& other)const;
  virtual void update(sf::Time deltaTime);
  virtual void onDestroy();
  static void newSaucer(World& world);
};
```

This class is pretty simple; we just have to specify the method already built in the Entity and Enemy class. Because the class will not specify the constructor, we use the using-declaration to refer to the one from Enemy. Here, we introduce a new function, newSaucer(). This function will randomly create a saucer depending on the player's score and add it to the world.

Now, take a look to the implementation of this class:

```
bool Saucer::isCollide(const Entity& other)const
{
  if(dynamic_cast<const ShootSaucer*>(&other) == nullptr) {
    return Collision::circleTest(_sprite,other._sprite);
  }
  return false;
}
```

The same technique as in `Player::isCollide()` is used here, so no surprises. We specify this function in the `Saucer` base class because the collisions are the same for any of the saucers. It avoids code duplication as follows:

```cpp
void Saucer::update(sf::Time deltaTime)
{
  float seconds = deltaTime.asSeconds();
  Entity* near = nullptr;
  float near_distance = 300;
  for(Entity* entity_ptr : _world.getEntities())
  {
    if(entity_ptr != this and (dynamic_cast<const
      Meteor*>(entity_ptr) or dynamic_cast<const
        ShootPlayer*>(entity_ptr)))
    {
      float x = getPosition().x - entity_ptr->getPosition().x;
      float y = getPosition().y - entity_ptr->getPosition().y;
      float dist = std::sqrt(x*x + y*y);
      if(dist < near_distance) {

          near_distance = dist;
          near = entity_ptr;
      }
    }
  }
  if(near != nullptr)
  {
    sf::Vector2f pos = near->getPosition() - getPosition();
    float angle_rad = std::atan2(pos.y,pos.x);
    _impulse -=
      sf::Vector2f(std::cos(angle_rad),std::sin(angle_rad)) * 300.f
        * seconds;
  } else {
    sf::Vector2f pos = Configuration::player->getPosition() -
      getPosition();
    float angle_rad = std::atan2(pos.y,pos.x);
    _impulse +=
      sf::Vector2f(std::cos(angle_rad),std::sin(angle_rad)) * 100.f
        * seconds;
  }
  _sprite.move(seconds * _impulse);
}
```

This function is pretty long but not really complicated. It manages the movement of the saucer. Let's explain it step by step:

1. We look for the nearest object of the saucer into which it may crash.

2. If there is an object found too close, we add an impulse to the saucer in the opposite direction of this object. The goal is to avoid a crash.

3. Let's now continue with the other functions.

```
void Saucer::onDestroy()
{
    Enemy::onDestroy();
    _world.add(Configuration::Sounds::Boom2);
}
```

4. This function is simple. We simply call the `onDestroy()` method from the `Enemy` base of the class, and then add an explosion sound to the world:

```
void Saucer::newSaucer(World& world)
{
  Saucer* res = nullptr;
  if(book::random(0.f,1.f) > Configuration::getScore()/
    40000.f)
  res = new BigSaucer(world);
  else
  res = new SmallSaucer(world);
  res->setPosition(random(0,1)*world.getX(),
    random(0.f,(float)world.getY()));
  world.add(res);
}
```

5. As previously mentioned, this function creates a saucer randomly and adds it to the world. The more the points the player has, the greater the chance to create a `SmallSaucer` entity. When the score reaches 40,000 `SmallSaucer` is created as explained in the description of the game.

Now that we have created the `Saucer` base class, let's make the `SmallSaucer` class. I'll not explain the `BigSaucer` class because this is the same as the `SmallSaucer` class but simpler (no shooting), as shown in the following code snippet:

```
class SmallSaucer : public Saucer
{
  public :
  SmallSaucer(World& world);
  virtual int getPoints()const;
  virtual void update(sf::Time deltaTime);
```

```
    private:
    sf::Time_timeSinceLastShoot;
};
```

Because we know the skin of the `SmallSaucer` entity, we don't need the texture ID as a parameter, so we remove it from the constructor parameter. We also add an attribute to the class that will store the elapsed time since the last shoot was made, as in `Player` entity.

Now take a look at the implementation:

```
SmallSaucer::SmallSaucer(World& world)  : Saucer(Configuration::Texture
s::SmallSaucer,world)
{
  _timeSinceLastShoot = sf::Time::Zero;
  _world.add(Configuration::Sounds::SaucerSpawn2);
  _impulse *= 400.f;
}
```

This constructor is simple because a great part of the job is already done in the base of the class. We just initialize the impulsion and add a sound to the world when the saucer appears. This will alert the player of the enemy and add some fun to the game:

```
int SmallSaucer::getPoints()const {return 200;}
```

This function simply sets the number of points that are won when the `SmallSaucer` entity is destroyed:

```
void SmallSaucer::update(sf::Time deltaTime)
{
  Saucer::update(deltaTime);
  _timeSinceLastShoot += deltaTime;
  if(_timeSinceLastShoot > sf::seconds(1.5))
  {
    if(Configuration::player != nullptr)
    _world.add(new ShootSaucer(*this));
    _timeSinceLastShoot = sf::Time::Zero;
  }
}
```

This function is fairly simple. Firstly, we just move the saucer by calling the `update()` function from the `Saucer` base, then shoot the player as soon as we can, and that's all.

Here is a screenshot of the saucer behavior:

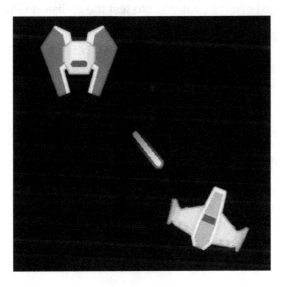

# The Meteor class

Now it's time to build the main enemies of the game: the meteors. We will start by the virtual `Meteor` class. Here is its definition:

```
class Meteor : public Enemy
{
  public:
  Meteor(const Meteor&) = delete;
  Meteor& operator=(const Meteor&) = delete;
  using Enemy::Enemy;

  virtual bool isCollide(const Entity& other)const;
  virtual void update(sf::Time deltaTime);
};
```

As you can see, this class is very short. We only specify the collision rules and the update function that will manage its move. Now, take a look at its implementation:

```
bool Meteor::isCollide(const Entity& other)const
{
  if(dynamic_cast<const Meteor*>(&other) == nullptr) {
    return Collision::circleTest(_sprite,other._sprite);
  }
  return false;
}
```

The collisions are tested with all Entity except the Meteors as it was specified. Here again, we use the circleTest() function to test the collision with the other objects:

```
void Meteor::update(sf::Time deltaTime)
{
  float seconds = deltaTime.asSeconds();
  _sprite.move(seconds * _impulse);
}
```

This function couldn't be more simple. We only move the meteor entity by computing the distance traveled since the last frame. There is nothing complicated to do here because a meteor is straight all the time, so there is no change in its direction.

Now that we have the base of all the meteors, let's make the big one. I will not explain the others because the logic is the same. The following code snippet explains it:

```
class BigMeteor : public Meteor
{
  public :
  BigMeteor(World& world);
  virtual int getPoints()const;
  virtual void onDestroy();
};
```

You can see this class is also very concise. We only need to define the constructor, the number of points earned, and the destruction. And now, the implementation of this class is as follows:

```
BigMeteor::BigMeteor(World& world) :
  Meteor((Configuration::Textures)random
    (Configuration::Textures::BigMeteor1,
      Configuration::Textures::BigMeteor4),world)
{
  _impulse *= 100.f;
}
```

The constructor is not difficult, but the choice of the texture ID is. Because there are several textures possible for a BigMeteor, we choose one of them randomly, as shown in the following code snippet:

```
int BigMeteor::getPoints()const {return 20;h}
void BigMeteor::onDestroy()
{
  Meteor::onDestroy();
  int nb = book::random(2,3);
  for(int i=0;i<nb;++i)
```

```
    {
        MediumMeteor* meteor = new MediumMeteor(_world);
        meteor->setPosition(getPosition());
        _world.add(meteor);
    }
    _world.add(Configuration::Sounds::Explosion1);
}
```

This method is the most important one. It creates some other meteors when a big one is destroyed, and adds them to the world. We also add an explosion sound for more fun during the game.

# The Shoot class

Now that all the enemies are made, let's build the last entity class, the Shoot. A Shoot is very simple. It's nothing but an entity that goes straight, and lives only for a specific time:

```
class Shoot : public Entity
{
    public:
    Shoot(const Shoot&) = delete;
    Shoot& operator=(const Shoot&) = delete;
    using Entity::Entity;
    virtual void update(sf::Time deltaTime);
    protected:
    sf::Time _duration;
};
```

Nothing surprising here, we only add a _duration attribute that will store the elapsed time since the creation of the Shoot class. Now, the implementation of the update function is as follows:

```
void Shoot::update(sf::Time deltaTime)
{
    float seconds = deltaTime.asSeconds();
    _sprite.move(seconds * _impulse);
    _duration -= deltaTime;
    if(_duration < sf::Time::Zero)
    _alive = false;
}
```

This function moves the shoot and adjusts the _duration attribute by removing the elapsed time. If the shoot live time reaches zero, we set it to dead, and the world will do the rest.

Now, let's build the `ShootPlayer` class:

```
class ShootPlayer : public Shoot
{
  public :
  ShootPlayer(const ShootPlayer&) = delete;
  ShootPlayer& operator=(const ShootPlayer&) = delete;
  ShootPlayer(Player& from);

  virtual bool isCollide(const Entity& other)const;
};
```

As you can see, the constructor has changed here. There is no more a `World` instance as a parameter apart from the source that creates the shoot. Let's take a look at the implementation to better understand the reason for this:

```
ShootPlayer::ShootPlayer(Player& from) : Shoot(Configuration::Textures
::ShootPlayer,from._world)
{
  _duration = sf::seconds(5);
  float angle = from._sprite.getRotation() / 180 * M_PI - M_PI /
    2;
  _impulse = sf::Vector2f(std::cos(angle),std::sin(angle)) *
    500.f;
  setPosition(from.getPosition());
  _sprite.setRotation(from._sprite.getRotation());
  _world.add(Configuration::Sounds::LaserPlayer);
}
```

As you can see, the world instance is copied from the source. Moreover, the initial position of the bullet is set to the position of the `Player` class when it is created. We also rotate the bullet as needed, and set its direction. I will not explain the collision function because there is nothing new compared to the previously explained functions.

The `ShootSaucer` class uses the same logic as the `ShootPlayer` class, but there is a change. The accuracy of the saucers changes with the number of points of the player. So we need to add a bit of randomness. Let's take a look to the constructor:

```
ShootSaucer::ShootSaucer(SmallSaucer& from) :
  Shoot(Configuration::Textures::ShootSaucer,from._world)
{
  _duration = sf::seconds(5);
  sf::Vector2f pos = Configuration::player->getPosition() -
    from.getPosition();
```

```
float accuracy_lost = book::random(-
    1.f,1.f)*M_PI/((200+Configuration::getScore())/100.f);
float angle_rad = std::atan2(pos.y,pos.x) + accuracy_lost;
float angle_deg = angle_rad * 180 / M_PI;

_impulse = sf::Vector2f(std::cos(angle_rad),std::sin(angle_rad))
    * 500.f;
setPosition(from.getPosition());
_sprite.setRotation(angle_deg + 90);
_world.add(Configuration::Sounds::LaserEnemy);
}
```

Let's explain this function step by step:

1. We compute the direction vector of the bullet.
2. We add to it a little loss of accuracy depending of the current score.
3. We set the _impulsion vector depending on the computed direction.
4. We set the position and the rotation of the sprite as needed.
5. And finally, we release it to the world.

Now that all the classes have been made, you will be able to play the game. The final result should look like this:

Pretty nice, isn't it?

# Building a Tetris clone

Now that we've created a complete game, let's build another one, a **Tetris** clone. This game is simpler than the previous one and will take less time to build, but is still very interesting. In fact, the internal architecture of this game is really different from the others. This is due to the kind of game that it is: a puzzle. The aim of the game is to fill lines of a grid with pieces made of four squares. Each time a line in completed, it's destroyed, and points are added to the player. Because this is a different kind of game, there are several implications as there is no player or no enemies in this game, only pieces and a board (grid). For this game, I will focus on the game logic only. So I will not reuse the previously made classes such as `Action`, `ActionMap`, `ActionTarget`, `Configuration`, and `ResourceManager` to be more concise. Of course, you can use them to improve the proposed source code.

So, to build this game we will need to build some classes:

- `Game`: This class will be very similar to the `Game` class from the previous project and will manage the rendering

- `Board`: This class will manage all the logic of the game

- `Piece`: This class will represent all the different kinds of tetrimino (pieces formed by four squares)

- `Stats`: This class will be used to show different information to the player

The final game will look like the following screenshot:

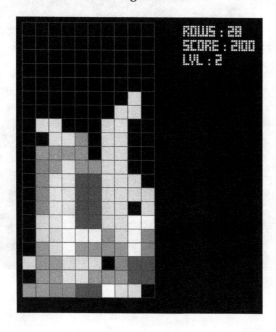

Now that we know how to structure a game, we will directly think about the need of each class.

# The Stats class

This class will be used to display the game information to the player such as the level, the number of rows, and the score. We will also use this class to display the **Game Over** message if it's needed. Because this class will display some information to the screen and can be put anywhere on the render space, we will extend it from `sf::Drawable` and `sf::Transformable`. Here is the header of this class:

```
class Stats : public sf::Transformable,public sf::Drawable
{
  public:
  Stats();
  void addLines(int lines);
  unsigned int getLvl()const;
  void gameOver();

  private:
  virtual void draw(sf::RenderTarget& target,sf::RenderStates
    states=sf::RenderStates::Default) const override;

  unsigned int _nbRows;
  unsigned int _nbScore;
  unsigned int _nbLvl;
  bool _isGameOver;

  sf::Text _textRows;
  sf::Text _textScore;
  sf::Text _textLvl;
  sf::Text _textGameOver;
  sf::Font _font;
};
```

There is no real surprise for this class. We have some `sf::Text` that will be used to display information, and their values as numbers. We also add the point calculation to this class with the `addLines()` function.

As previously mentioned, for the Tetris game, we need to focus on the game logic, so we are not going to use any manager for the font.

Now take a look at the implementation of this class:

```
constexpr int  FONT_SIZE 24;
Stats::Stats() : _nbRows(0), _nbScore(0), _nbLvl(0),
  _isGameOver(false)
{
  _font.loadFromFile("media/fonts/trs-million.ttf");
  _textRows.setFont(_font);
  _textRows.setString("rows : 0");
  _textRows.setCharacterSize(FONT_SIZE);
  _textRows.setPosition(0,0);

  _textScore.setFont(_font);
  _textScore.setString("score : 0");
  _textScore.setCharacterSize(FONT_SIZE);
  _textScore.setPosition(0,FONT_SIZE + 1);

  _textLvl.setFont(_font);
  _textLvl.setString("lvl : 0");
  _textLvl.setCharacterSize(FONT_SIZE);
  _textLvl.setPosition(0,(FONT_SIZE + 1)*2);

  _textGameOver.setFont(_font);
  _textGameOver.setString("Game Over");
  _textGameOver.setCharacterSize(72);
  _textGameOver.setPosition(0,0);
}
```

The constructor of the class set all the attributes to no surprise:

```
void Stats::gameOver(){_isGameOver = true;}
```

Here again, there are no surprises. We just assigned the _isGameOver value to true:

```
void Stats::addLines(int lines)
{
  if(lines > 0)
  {
    _nbRows += lines;
    _textRows.setString("rows : "+std::to_string(_nbRows));
    _textScore.setString("score : "+std::to_string(_nbScore));
    switch (lines)
    {
      case 1 : _nbScore += 40 * (_nbLvl+1);break;
      case 2 : _nbScore += 100 * (_nbLvl+1);break;
```

```
        case 3 :  _nbScore += 300 * (_nbLvl+1);break;
        case 4 :  _nbScore += 1200 * (_nbLvl+1);break;
        default :break;
    }
    _nbLvl = _nbRows / 10;
    _textLvl.setString("lvl : "+std::to_string(_nbLvl));
    }
}
```

This function is a bit more interesting. Its aim is to add points to the global score depending on the number of lines completed. It also corrects the drawable text value and the level. Because a piece is composed of four squares, the maximum number of lines that can be suppressed with one piece is the number four. So in the switch statement, we only need to check these four possibilities:

```
unsigned int Stats::getLvl()const{return _nbLvl;}
void Stats::draw(sf::RenderTarget& target, sf::RenderStates
    states) const
{
    if(not _isGameOver)
    {
        states.transform *= getTransform();
        target.draw(_textRows,states);
        target.draw(_textScore,states);
        target.draw(_textLvl,states);
    }
    else
    target.draw(_textGameOver,states);
}
```

As all the other `sf::Drawable::draw()` functions, this function draws the object on the screen. If the game is complete, we print the **Game Over** message, in other cases, we print the game score, number of completed rows, and the current level.

In conclusion, this class is very simple and its job is to display all the game information on the screen.

# The Piece class

Now, let's build the first important class of this game, the `Piece` class. In Tetris, there are seven different tetrimino. I will not build seven different classes but only one. The idea is to show you another way to make your entities.

But, what is a piece exactly? If you think about it, you will find that a piece can be represented as an array of numbers. Moreover, a piece can be rotated. There are three ways to do this: calculate the rotation at runtime, pre-calculate the rotation at the startup or predefine them in the code. Because in our game, each piece is known when we create the game, we will choose the last way: hard code all the rotation. It could look bad, but in reality it's not, and it will simplify a lot our implementation as you will see later in this chapter, but keep in mind that it's not a fantastic idea to hard code items in every game.

Now let's take a look at the class:

```cpp
class Piece
{
  public:
  static const unsigned short int NB_ROTATIONS = 4; //< number of
     rotations
  static const unsigned short int MATRIX_SIZE = 4; //< size of the
    matrix
  static const unsigned int PIVOT_Y = 1;
  static const unsigned int PIVOT_X = 2;
  enum TetriminoTypes {O=0,I,S,Z,L,J,T,SIZE}; //< different kind
    of pieces
  static const sf::Color TetriminoColors[TetriminoTypes::SIZE];
     //< different colors for each kind of piece
  static const char
     TetriminoPieces[TetriminoTypes::SIZE]
       [NB_ROTATIONS][MATRIX_SIZE][MATRIX_SIZE];//< store all the
         different shapes

  Piece(const Piece&) = delete;
  Piece& operator=(const Piece&) = delete;
  Piece(TetriminoTypes type,short int rotation);
  TetriminoTypes getType()const;
  void setRotation(short int rotation); //< set the rotation
  short int getRotation()const;
  void setPosition(int x,int y);//< set the position in the
  //board

  int getPosX()const;
  int getPosY()const;
  sf::Time getTimeSinceLastMove()const;

  private:
  const TetriminoTypes _type; //< the piece type
  short int _rotation; //< the piece rotation
```

```
int _positionX; //< position in the board
int _positionY;//< position in the board
sf::Clock _clockSinceLastMove;
};
```

This class is a bit long. Let's explain it step by step:

1.  We will define some constant variables that will be used for configuration purposes.
2.  We will define an enum function with all the different tetrimino pieces.
3.  We will define an array of color. Each cell will represent the color of a tetrimino previously defined in the enum function.
4.  The next line is particular. This defines all the different tetrimino rotations. Because each piece is a 2D array, we also need this information.
5.  The other functions are more common: constructor, getter, and setter.
6.  We will define some private attributes that store the state of the piece.

Now is the funny part, the implementation of all of this. Because of the choices made, the implementation will differ a lot with the previous entity in the **Asteroid** game:

```
const sf::Color Piece::TetriminoColors[Piece::TetriminoTypes::SIZE]= {
  sf::Color::Blue,
  sf::Color::Red,
  sf::Color::Green,
  sf::Color::Cyan,
  sf::Color::Magenta,
  sf::Color::White,
  sf::Color(195,132,58)
}
```

This array stores all the different colors for each tetrimino defined by the TetriminoTypes **enum**:

```
const char Piece::TetriminoPieces[Piece::TetriminoTypes::SIZE]
[Piece::NB_ROTATIONS][Piece::MATRIX_SIZE][Piece::MATRIX_SIZE] = {
    { // O
        {
            {0,0,0,0},
            {0,1,2,0},
            {0,1,1,0},
            {0,0,0,0}
        },
        //...
        {
```

```
                    {0,0,0,0},
                    {0,1,2,0},
                    {0,1,1,0},
                    {0,0,0,0}
                }
            },
            {//I
                {
                    {0,0,0,0},
                    {1,1,2,1},
                    {0,0,0,0},
                    {0,0,0,0}
                },
                {
                    {0,0,1,0},
                    {0,0,2,0},
                    {0,0,1,0},
                    {0,0,1,0}
                },
                {
                    {0,0,0,0},
                    {1,1,2,1},
                    {0,0,0,0},
                    {0,0,0,0}
                },
                {
                    {0,0,1,0},
                    {0,0,2,0},
                    {0,0,1,0},
                    {0,0,1,0}
                }
            },
            //...
        };
```

At first glance, this is a very special array but turns out it's not really. In fact, each different piece is defined in the first cell of the array, the second cell represents all the different rotations of this piece and the rest is the representation of the piece rotation as a 2D array. The 0 value represents empty, 2 represents the center of the piece, and 1 represents the other piece of the tetrimino. I've not put all the code because it is pretty long, but you can take a look at it if needed at 03_Simple_2D_game/Tetris/ src/SFML-Book/Piece.cpp.

```
Piece::Piece(TetriminoTypes type,short int rotation) :
    _type(type), _rotation(rotation), _positionX(0), _positionY(0)
        {assert(rotation >= 0 and rotation < NB_ROTATIONS);}
```

The `assert` function is a macro that will raise an error and exit the program if the expression such as parameter is false. You can remove it by adding #define NDEBUG to your code/compiler option to disable this function.

The `assert()` function is useful to do checks in the debug mode only. Use it when you want to be sure that a specific case is respected at run time.

The constructor of the `Piece` class is simple, but we can easily send wrong parameter values to it. So I decided to show you the assert functionality, as follows:

```
Piece::TetriminoTypes Piece::getType()const {return _type;}

short int Piece::getRotation()const {return _rotation;}

int Piece::getPosX()const {return _positionX;}

int Piece::getPosY()const {return _positionY;}
sf::Time Piece::getTimeSinceLastMove()const {return
  _clockSinceLastMove.getElapsedTime();}

void Piece::setRotation(short int rotation)
{
  assert(rotation >= 0 and rotation < NB_ROTATIONS);
  _rotation = rotation;
  _clockSinceLastMove.restart();
}

void Piece::setPosition(int x,int y)
{
  _positionX = x;
  _positionY = y;
  _clockSinceLastMove.restart();
}
```

All of these functions are getters and setters, and they are simple. The only particular thing is the `setPosition/Rotation()` functions because it also resets the internal clock. Since the clock stores the time since the last movement of the piece, in reality it should not sock you.

# The Board class

Now, that all the pieces are made, let's build the class that will manage them, the **Board**.

This class will be represented as a grid (array) that stores colors (piece). So internally, this class is nothing but an array of integers. Each cell will store the kind of piece because the kind of piece determines its color (see the `Piece` class). Now take a look at the header of this class:

```
class Board : public sf::Transformable, public sf::Drawable
{
  public:
  static const int DEFAULT_BOARD_COLUMNS = 10;
  static const int DEFAULT_BOARD_LINE = 20;
  static const int DEFAULT_CELL_X = 24;
  static const int DEFAULT_CELL_Y = 24;

  Board(int columns=DEFAULT_BOARD_COLUMNS, int
    line=DEFAULT_BOARD_LINE, int cell_x=DEFAULT_CELL_X, int
      cell_y=DEFAULT_CELL_Y);
  ~Board();

  void spawn(Piece& piece);
  bool move(Piece& piece, int delta_x, int delta_y);
  bool isFallen(const Piece& piece);
  void drop(Piece& piece);
  bool rotateLeft(Piece& piece);
  bool rotateRight(Piece& piece);
  bool isGameOver();
  int clearLines(const Piece& piece); //< clear all possible lines

  private:
  bool rotate(Piece& piece, int rotation);
  void draw(const Piece& piece);
  void clear(const Piece& piece);
  virtual void draw(sf::RenderTarget& target, sf::RenderStates
    states=sf::RenderStates::Default) const override;
  void flood(const Piece& piece, int value);

        void flood(int grid_x, int grid_y, int piece_x, int
piece_y, Piece::Tetrimino_Types type, int rotation, bool visited[]
[Piece::MATRIX_SIZE], int value);
        void flood(int grid_x, int grid_y, int piece_x, int
piece_y, Piece::Tetrimino_Types type, int rotation, bool visited[]
```

```
[Piece::MATRIX_SIZE],bool& flag);

        void clearLine(int y); //< clear a line

        const int _columns;
        const int _lines;
        const int _cellX;
        const int _cellY;

        bool _isGameOver;

        sf::VertexArray _grid;//< grid borders
        int* _gridContent;//< lines * columns
};
```

In the Board class we firstly define some configuration variable. This class is drawable and transformable, so we extend it from the corresponding SFML class. Then we create the constructor that take the size of the board as parameters and some methods to add, move and manage a Piece. We also add some private methods that will help use to in the implementation of the publics, and we store the size of the board internally, such as the grid. Because the size is not known at compile time, we need to build the grid at runtime, so the grid is a pointer to an array. We also add a sf::VertexArray that will contain the graphical grid to display on the screen.

Now that the class has been explained, let's implement it.

```
constexpr int  CELL_EMPTY -1;
Board::Board(int columns,int lines,int cell_x,int cell_y): _
columns(columns),_lines(lines),_cellX(cell_x),_cellY(cell_y), _
gridContent(nullptr),_isGameOver(false)
{
    _gridContent = new int[_lines*_columns];
    std::memset(_gridContent,CELL_EMPTY,_lines*_columns*sizeof(int));

    sf::Color gridColor(55,55,55);
    _grid = sf::VertexArray(sf::Lines,(_lines+1+_columns+1)*2);
    for(int i=0;i<=_lines;++i)
    {
        _grid[i*2] = sf::Vertex(sf::Vector2f(0,i*_cellY));
        _grid[i*2+1] = sf::Vertex(sf::Vector2f(_columns*_cellX,i*_
cellY));

        _grid[i*2].color = gridColor;
        _grid[i*2+1].color = gridColor;
    }
```

```
        for(int i=0;i<=columns;++i)
        {
            _grid[(_lines+1)*2 + i*2] = sf::Vertex(sf::Vector2f(i*_
cellX,0));
            _grid[(_lines+1)*2 + i*2+1] = sf::Vertex(sf::Vector2f(i*_
cellX,_lines*_cellY));

            _grid[(_lines+1)*2 + i*2].color = gridColor;
            _grid[(_lines+1)*2 + i*2+1].color = gridColor;
        }
    }
```

The constructor initialize all the attributes but also create the grids content and border. Because the grid content and border are a one dimension arrays, we need to make some trick to access to the right cell instead of using the usual "[][]" operator.

```
Board::~Board() {delete _gridContent;}

void Board::draw(sf::RenderTarget& target, sf::RenderStates states)
const
{
    states.transform *= getTransform();

    for(int y=0; y<_lines; ++y)
        for(int x=0; x<_columns; ++x) {
            if(_gridContent[y*_columns + x] != CELL_EMPTY) {
                sf::RectangleShape rectangle(sf::Vector2f(_cellX,_
cellY));
                rectangle.setFillColor(Piece::TetriminoColors[_
gridContent[y*_columns + x]]);
                rectangle.setPosition(x*_cellX,y*_cellY);
                target.draw(rectangle,states);
            }
        }
    target.draw(_grid,states);
}
```

The draw method is not complex. For each cell, there is some data in it, we construct a rectangle of the right size at the right place, with the right color, and display it. And then we display the grid border.

```
void Board::spawn(Piece& piece)
{
    piece.setPosition(_columns/2,0);
    for(int x=0;x<_columns;++x)
        if(_gridContent[x] != CELL_EMPTY) {
```

```
            _isGameOver = true;
            break;
        }
    draw(piece);
}
```

This function simply sets the initial position of a piece on the board, and adds it to the grid. It also checks if the game is over or not, by the following code snippet:

```
bool Board::move(Piece& piece, int delta_x, int delta_y)
{
  delta_x += piece.getPosX();
  delta_y + piece.getPosY();
  clear(piece);
  bool visited[Piece::MATRIX_SIZE][Piece::MATRIX_SIZE] =
    {{false}};
  bool movable = true
  flood(delta_x,delta_y, (int)Piece::PIVOT_X, (int)Piece::PIVOT_Y,
  piece.getType(),piece.getRotation(),
  visisted, movable);
  if (movable)
  piece.setPosition(delta_x,delta_y);
  draw(piece);
  return movable;
}
```

This function is a bit more complicated, so let's explain it step by step:

1. We will delete the `Piece` class from the board so that it doesn't collide with itself.

2. We will check if we can move the piece and set its new position if we can.

3. We will read the piece to the board

The flood algorithm will be explained later:

```
bool Board::isFallen(const Piece& piece)
{
  clear(piece);
  bool vision[Piece::MATRIX_SIZE][Piece::MATRIX_SIZE] = {{false}};
  bool fallen = true;
  flood(piece.getPosX(),piece.getPosY()+1
  (int)Piece::PIVOT_X,(int)Piece::PIVOT_Y,
  piece.getType(),piece.getRotation(),
  visited,fallen);
  draw(piece)
  return fallen;
}
```

This functionality works as the previously mentioned function with just one exception. It only checks if the piece can move down and not in all directions, as shown in the previous code snippet:

```
void Board::drop(Piece& piece) {while(move(piece,0,1));}
```

This function is a special action that moves the piece as we can to the down. This is a special action in the Tetris game, called "Hard drop".

```
bool Board::rotateLeft(Piece& piece)
{
  int rotation = piece.getRotation();
  if(rotation > 0)
  --rotation;
  else
  rotation = Piece::NB_ROTATIONS - 1;
  return rotate(piece,rotation);
}

bool Board::rotateRight(Piece& piece)
{
  int rotation = piece.getRotation();
  if(rotation < Piece::NB_ROTATIONS -1)
  ++rotation;
  else
  rotation = 0;
  return rotate(piece,rotation);
}
```

These two functions rotate the piece to a specific direction. As there are only four different rotations (NB_ROTATIONS), we need to adjust the new rotation value using a circular check:

```
bool Board::isGameOver(){return _isGameOver;}
bool Board::rotate(Piece& piece,int rotation)
{
  assert(rotation >= 0 and rotation < Piece::NB_ROTATIONS);
  clear(piece);
  bool visited[Piece::MATRIX_SIZE][Piece::MATRIX_SIZE] =
    {{false}};
  bool rotable = true;
  flood((int)piece.getPosX(),(int)piece.getPosY(),
  (int)Piece::PIVOT_X,(int)Piece::PIVOT_Y,
  piece.getType(),rotation,
```

```
  visited,rotable);
  if(rotable)
  piece.setRotation(rotation);
  draw(piece);
  return rotable;
}
```

Like the other functions, this one checks whether we can rotate a piece or not, and return the value. This function does not change the content of the grid:

```
void Board::draw(const Piece&
  piece){flood(piece,piece.getType());}
void Board::clear(const Piece& piece){flood(piece,CELL_EMPTY);}
```

These two functions are very close. Each one modifies the grid with a specific value, to set or remove a piece from the internal grid:

```
void Board::flood(const Piece& piece,int value)
{
  bool visited[Piece::MATRIX_SIZE][Piece::MATRIX_SIZE] =
    {{false}};
  flood((int)piece.getPosX(),
  (int)piece.getPosY(),(int)Piece::PIVOT_X,
  (int)Piece::PIVOT_Y,
  piece.getType(),piece.getRotation(),
  visited,value);
}

void Board::flood(int grid_x,int grid_y,int piece_x,int
  piece_y,Piece::TetriminoTypes type,int rotation,bool visited[]
[Piece::MATRIX_SIZE],int value)
{
  if(piece_x < 0 or piece_x >= Piece::MATRIX_SIZE
  or piece_y < 0 or piece_y > Piece::MATRRIX_SIZE
    Pieces[type][rotation][piece_y][piece_x] == 0)
  return;
visited[piece_y][piece_x] = true;
  _gridContent[grid_y*_columns + grid_x] = value;
  flood(grid_x, grid_y-1, piece_x, piece_y-1, type, rotation,
    visited, value);
  flood(grid_x+1, grid_y, piece_x+1, piece_y, type, rotation,
    visited, value);
  flood(grid_x, grid_y+1, piece_x, piece_y+1, type, rotation,
    visited, value);
```

```
    flood(grid_x-1, grid_y, piece_x-1, piece_y, type, rotation,
        visited, value);
}


void Board::flood(int grid_x,int grid_y,int piece_x,int
    piece_y,Piece::TetriminoTypes type,int rotation,bool visited[]
[Piece::MATRIX_SIZE],bool& flag)
{
    if(piece_x < 0 or piece_x >= Piece::MATRIX_SIZE
    or piece_y < 0 or piece_y >= Piece::MATRIX_SIZE
    or visited[piece_y][piece_x] == true
    or Piece::TetriminoPieces[type][rotation][piece_y][piece_x] ==
        0)
    return;
    visited[piece_y][piece_x] = true;
    if(grid_x < 0 or grid_x >= (int)_columns
    or grid_y < 0 or grid_y >= (int)_lines
    or _gridContent[grid_y*_columns + grid_x] != CELL_EMPTY) {
        flag = false;
        return;
    }
    flood(grid_x, grid_y-1, piece_x, piece_y-1, type, rotation,
        visited, flag);
    flood(grid_x+1, grid_y, piece_x+1, piece_y, type, rotation,
        visited, flag);
    flood(grid_x, grid_y+1, piece_x, piece_y+1, type, rotation,
        visited, flag);
    flood(grid_x-1, grid_y, piece_x-1, piece_y, type, rotation,
        visited, flag);
}
```

This `flood` function is an implementation of the `flood` algorithm. It allows us to fill the array with a value, depending of another array. The second array is the shape to fill in the first one. In our case, the first array is the grid, and the second the piece, as shown in the following code snippet:

```
void Board::clearLine(int yy)
{
    assert(yy < _lines);
    for(int y=yy; y>0; --y)
    for(int x=0; x<_columns; ++x)
    _gridContent[y*_columns + x] = _gridContent[(y-1)*_columns + x];
}
int Board::clearLines(const Piece& piece)
{
    int nb_delete = 0;
```

```
     clear(piece);
     for(int y=0; y<_lines; ++y)
     {
        int x =0;
        for(;_gridContent[y*_columns + x] != CELL_EMPTY and
          x<_columns; ++x);
        if(x == _columns) {
           clearLine(y);
           ++nb_delete;
        }
     }
     draw(piece);
     return nb_delete;
  }
```

This function simply removes all the completed lines, and lowers all the upper lines to simulate gravity.

Now, the board class is made, and we have all that we need to build the game. So let's do it.

# The Game class

The Game class is very similar to the Game class from Asteroid. Its purpose is the same and all the internal logic is similar as well, as shown in the following code snippet:

```
class Game
{
  public:
  Game(); //< constructor
  void run(int minimum_frame_per_seconds);

  private:
  void processEvents();//< Process events
  void update(sf::Time deltaTime); //< do some updates
  void render();//< draw all the stuff
  void newPiece();

  sf::RenderWindow _window; //< the window used to display the
    game
  std::unique_ptr<Piece> _currentPiece; //< the current piece
  Board _board; //< the game board
  Stats _stats; //< stats printer
  sf::Time _nextFall;
};
```

As you can see, we don't change the logic of the Game class, but we add it some private functions and attributes to correspond to the different kind of games. A window is still required, but we add the current piece reference, the board (that replaces the world), and a stats printer. We also need a way to store the next fall of a piece.

Now take a look at the implementation of this class:

```
Game::Game()  : _window(sf::VideoMode(800, 600),"SFML
  Tetris"),_board()
{
  rand_init()
  _board.setPosition(10,10);
  _stats.setPosition(300,10);
  newPiece();
}
```

The constructor initializes the different attributes of the class, and sets the position of the different drawable object. It also creates the first piece to start the game. We don't manage any menu here:

```
void Game::run(int minimum_frame_per_seconds)
{
  sf::Clock clock;
  sf::Time timeSinceLastUpdate;
  sf::Time TimePerFrame =
    sf::seconds(1.f/minimum_frame_per_seconds);
  while (_window.isOpen())
  {
    processEvents();
    timeSinceLastUpdate = clock.restart();
    while (timeSinceLastUpdate > TimePerFrame)
    {
      timeSinceLastUpdate -= TimePerFrame;
      update(TimePerFrame);
    }
    update(timeSinceLastUpdate);
    render();
  }
}
void Game::processEvents()
{
```

```
  sf::Event event;
  while(_window.pollEvent(event))
  {
    if (event.type == sf::Event::Closed)//Close window
    _window.close();
    else if (event.type == sf::Event::KeyPressed) //keyboard input
    {
      if (event.key.code == sf::Keyboard::Escape) {
        _window.close();
      } else if (event.key.code == sf::Keyboard::Down) {
        _board.move(*_currentPiece,0,1);
      } else if (event.key.code == sf::Keyboard::Up) {
        _board.move(*_currentPiece,0,-1);
      } else if (event.key.code == sf::Keyboard::Left) {
        _board.move(*_currentPiece,-1,0);
      } else if (event.key.code == sf::Keyboard::Right) {
        _board.move(*_currentPiece,1,0);
      } else if (event.key.code == sf::Keyboard::Space) {
        _board.drop(*_currentPiece);
        newPiece();
      } else if (event.key.code == sf::Keyboard::S) {
        _board.rotateRight(*_currentPiece);
      } else if (event.key.code == sf::Keyboard::D) {
        _board.rotateLeft(*_currentPiece);
      }
    }
  }
}
void Game::update(sf::Time deltaTime)
{
  if(not _board.isGameOver())
  {
  _stats.addLines(_board.clearLines(*_currentPiece));
  _nextFall += deltaTime;
  if((not _board.isFallen(*_currentPiece)) and (_currentPiece-
    >getTimeSinceLastMove() > sf::seconds(1.f)))
  newPiece();
  sf::Time max_time = sf::seconds(std::max(0.1,0.6-
    0.005*_stats.getLvl()));
  while(_nextFall > max_time)
  {
```

```
        _nextFall -= max_time;
        _board.move(*_currentPiece,0,1);
    }
    } else {
        _stats.gameOver();
    }
}
```

This function is not complicated but is interesting, because all the logic of the game is here. Let's see this in the following steps:

1.  The first step is to clear lines and update the score.

2.  Then, we will check whether we need to spawn another piece or not

3.  We will calculate the time needed by the current level to force a movement downward and apply it if necessary.

4.  Of course, if the game is over, we don't do all this stuff, but tell the stats printer that the game is over:

    ```
    void Game::render()
    {
        _window.clear();
        if(not _board.isGameOver())
        _window.draw(_board);
        _window.draw(_stats);
        _window.display();
    }
    ```

5.  Here again, there is nothing new. We just draw all that can be drawn depending on the situation:

    ```
    void Game::newPiece()
    {
        _currentPiece.reset(new
        Piece((Piece::TetriminoTypes)random
          (0,Piece::TetriminoTypes::SIZE-1),0));
        _board.spawn(*_currentPiece);
    }
    ```

6.  This last function creates a piece at random, and adds it to the grid, which will set its default position.

And here we are. The game is finished!

# Summary

As you surely noticed, there are some common points with the previous game we made, but not a lot. The main idea of showing you this game, is that there is no "super technique" that will work in every kind of game. You have to adapt your internal architecture and logic depending on the kind of game you want to build. I hope you understand that.

In the next chapter, you will learn how to use a physics engine, and add it in the Tetris game to build a new kind of game.

# 4
# Playing with Physics

In the previous chapter, we built several games, including a Tetris clone. In this chapter, we will add physics into this game and turn it into a new one. By doing this, we will learn:

- What is a physics engine
- How to install and use the Box2D library
- How to pair the physics engine with SFML for the display
- How to add physics in the game

In this chapter, we will learn the magic of physics. We will also do some mathematics but relax, it's for conversion only. Now, let's go!

## A physics engine – késako?

In this chapter, we will speak about physics engine, but the first question is "what is a physics engine?" so let's explain it.

A physics engine is a software or library that is able to simulate Physics, for example, the Newton-Euler equation that describes the movement of a rigid body. A physics engine is also able to manage collisions, and some of them can deal with soft bodies and even fluids.

There are different kinds of physics engines, mainly categorized into real-time engine and non-real-time engine. The first one is mostly used in video games or simulators and the second one is used in high performance scientific simulation, in the conception of special effects in cinema and animations.

As our goal is to use the engine in a video game, let's focus on real-time-based engine. Here again, there are two important types of engines. The first one is for 2D and the other for 3D. Of course you can use a 3D engine in a 2D world, but it's preferable to use a 2D engine for an optimization purpose. There are plenty of engines, but not all of them are open source.

# 3D physics engines

For 3D games, I advise you to use the `Bullet` physics library. This was integrated in the Blender software, and was used in the creation of some commercial games and also in the making of films. This is a really good engine written in C/C++ that can deal with rigid and soft bodies, fluids, collisions, forces… and all that you need.

# 2D physics engines

As previously said, in a 2D environment, you can use a 3D physics engine; you just have to ignore the depth (Z axes). However, the most interesting thing is to use an engine optimized for the 2D environment. There are several engines like this one and the most famous ones are Box2D and Chipmunk. Both of them are really good and none of them are better than the other, but I had to make a choice, which was Box2D. I've made this choice not only because of its C++ API that allows you to use overload, but also because of the big community involved in the project.

# Physics engine comparing game engine

Do not mistake a physics engine for a game engine. A physics engine only simulates a physical world without anything else. There are no graphics, no logics, only physics simulation. On the contrary, a game engine, most of the time includes a physics engine paired with a render technology (such as OpenGL or DirectX). Some predefined logics depend on the goal of the engine (RPG, FPS, and so on) and sometimes artificial intelligence. So as you can see, a game engine is more complete than a physics engine. The two mostly known engines are Unity and Unreal engine, which are both very complete. Moreover, they are free for non-commercial usage.

So why don't we directly use a game engine? This is a good question. Sometimes, it's better to use something that is already made, instead of reinventing it. However, do we really need all the functionalities of a game engine for this project? More importantly, what do we need it for? Let's see the following:

- A graphic output
- Physics engine that can manage collision

Nothing else is required. So as you can see, using a game engine for this project would be like killing a fly with a bazooka. I hope that you have understood the aim of a physics engine, the differences between a game and physics engine, and the reason for the choices made for the project described in this chapter.

# Using Box2D

As previously said, Box2D is a physics engine. It has a lot of features, but the most important for the project are the following (taken from the Box2D documentation):

- **Collision**: This functionality is very interesting as it allows our tetrimino to interact with each other
    - Continuous collision detection
    - Rigid bodies (convex polygons and circles)
    - Multiple shapes per body

- **Physics**: This functionality will allow a piece to fall down and more
    - Continuous physics with the time of impact solver
    - Joint limits, motors, and friction
    - Fairly accurate reaction forces/impulses

As you can see, Box2D provides all that we need in order to build our game. There are a lot of other features usable with this engine, but they don't interest us right now so I will not describe them in detail. However, if you are interested, you can take a look at the official website for more details on the Box2D features (`http://box2d.org/about/`).

It's important to note that Box2D uses meters, kilograms, seconds, and radians for the angle as units; SFML uses pixels, seconds, and degrees. So we will need to make some conversions. I will come back to this later.

# Preparing Box2D

Now that Box2D is introduced, let's install it. You will find the list of available versions on the Google code project page at `https://code.google.com/p/box2d/downloads/list`. Currently, the latest stable version is 2.3. Once you have downloaded the source code (from compressed file or using SVN), you will need to build it.

# Build

Here is the good news, Box2D uses CMake as build process so you just have to follow the exact same steps as the SFML build described in the first chapter of this book and you will successfully build Box2D. If everything is fine, you will find the example project at this place: `path/to/Box2D/build/Testbed/Testbed`. Now, let's install it.

# Install

Once you have successfully built your Box2D library, you will need to configure your system or IDE to find the Box2D library and headers. The newly built library can be found in the `/path/to/Box2D/build/Box2D/` directory and is named `libBox2D.a`. On the other hand, the headers are located in the `path/to/Box2D/Box2D/` directory. If everything is okay, you will find a `Box2D.h` file in the folder.

On Linux, the following command adds Box2D to your system without requiring any configuration:

```
sudo make install
```

# Pairing Box2D and SFML

Now that Box2D is installed and your system is configured to find it, let's build the physics "hello world": a falling square.

It's important to note that Box2D uses meters, kilograms, seconds, and radian for angle as units; SFML uses pixels, seconds, and degrees. So we will need to make some conversions.

Converting radians to degrees or vice versa is not difficult, but pixels to meters… this is another story. In fact, there is no way to convert a pixel to meter, unless if the number of pixels per meter is fixed. This is the technique that we will use.

So let's start by creating some utility functions. We should be able to convert radians to degrees, degrees to radians, meters to pixels, and finally pixels to meters. We will also need to fix the pixel per meter value. As we don't need any class for these functions, we will define them in a namespace converter. This will result as the following code snippet:

```
namespace converter
{
    constexpr double PIXELS_PER_METERS = 32.0;
```

```
constexpr double PI = 3.14159265358979323846;

template<typename T>
constexpr  T pixelsToMeters(const T& x){return x/PIXELS_PER_
METERS;};

template<typename T>
constexpr T metersToPixels(const T& x){return x*PIXELS_PER_
METERS;};

template<typename T>
constexpr T degToRad(const T& x){return PI*x/180.0;};

template<typename T>
constexpr T radToDeg(const T& x){return 180.0*x/PI;}
}
```

As you can see, there is no difficulty here. We start to define some constants and then the convert functions. I've chosen to make the function template to allow the use of any number type. In practice, it will mostly be double or int. The conversion functions are also declared as constexpr to allow the compiler to calculate the value at compile time if it's possible (for example, with constant as a parameter). It's interesting because we will use this primitive a lot.

# Box2D, how does it work?

Now that we can convert SFML unit to Box2D unit and vice versa, we can pair Box2D with SFML. But first, how exactly does Box2D work?

Box2D works a lot like a physics engine:

1.  You start by creating an empty world with some gravity.
2.  Then, you create some object patterns. Each pattern contains the shape of the object position, its type (static or dynamic), and some other characteristics such as its density, friction, and energy restitution.
3.  You ask the world to create a new object defined by the pattern.
4.  In each game loop, you have to update the physical world with a small step such as our world in the games we've already made.

Because the physics engine does not display anything on the screen, we will need to loop all the objects and display them by ourselves.

Let's start by creating a simple scene with two kinds of objects: a ground and square. The ground will be fixed and the squares will not. The square will be generated by a user event: mouse click.

This project is very simple, but the goal is to show you how to use Box2D and SFML together with a simple case study. A more complex one will come later.

We will need three functionalities for this small project to:

- Create a shape
- Display the world
- Update/fill the world

Of course there is also the initialization of the world and window. Let's start with the main function:

1. As always, we create a window for the display and we limit the FPS number to 60. I will come back to this point with the `displayWorld` function.

2. We create the physical world from Box2D, with gravity as a parameter.

3. We create a container that will store all the physical objects for the memory clean purpose.

4. We create the ground by calling the `createBox` function (explained just after).

5. Now it is time for the minimalist `game` loop:
    - Close event managements
    - Create a box by detecting that the right button of the mouse is pressed

6. Finally, we clean the memory before exiting the program:

```
int main(int argc,char* argv[])
{
    sf::RenderWindow window(sf::VideoMode(800, 600, 32), "04_
Basic");
    window.setFramerateLimit(60);
    b2Vec2 gravity(0.f, 9.8f);
    b2World world(gravity);
```

```
    std::list<b2Body*> bodies;
    bodies.emplace_back(book::createBox(world,400,590,800,20,b2_
staticBody));

    while(window.isOpen()) {
        sf::Event event;
        while(window.pollEvent(event)) {
            if (event.type == sf::Event::Closed)
                window.close();
        }
        if (sf::Mouse::isButtonPressed(sf::Mouse::Left)) {
            int x = sf::Mouse::getPosition(window).x;
            int y = sf::Mouse::getPosition(window).y;
            bodies.emplace_back(book::createBox(world,x,y,32,32));
        }
        displayWorld(world,window);
    }

    for(b2Body* body : bodies) {
        delete static_cast<sf::RectangleShape*>(body-
>GetUserData());
        world.DestroyBody(body);
    }
    return 0;
}
```

For the moment, except the Box2D world, nothing should surprise you so let's continue with the box creation.

This function is under the book namespace.

```
b2Body* createBox(b2World& world,int pos_x,int pos_y, int size_x,int
size_y,b2BodyType type = b2_dynamicBody)
{
    b2BodyDef bodyDef;
    bodyDef.position.Set(converter::pixelsToMeters<double>(pos_x),
                    converter::pixelsToMeters<double>(pos_y));
    bodyDef.type = type;
    b2PolygonShape b2shape;
    b2shape.SetAsBox(converter::pixelsToMeters<double>(size_x/2.0),
                    converter::pixelsToMeters<double>(size_y/2.0));
```

```
    b2FixtureDef fixtureDef;
    fixtureDef.density = 1.0;
    fixtureDef.friction = 0.4;
    fixtureDef.restitution= 0.5;
    fixtureDef.shape = &b2shape;

    b2Body* res = world.CreateBody(&bodyDef);
    res->CreateFixture(&fixtureDef);

    sf::Shape* shape = new sf::RectangleShape(sf::Vector2f(size_x,siz
e_y));
    shape->setOrigin(size_x/2.0,size_y/2.0);
    shape->setPosition(sf::Vector2f(pos_x,pos_y));

    if(type == b2_dynamicBody)
        shape->setFillColor(sf::Color::Blue);
    else
        shape->setFillColor(sf::Color::White);

    res->SetUserData(shape);

    return res;
}
```

This function contains a lot of new functionalities. Its goal is to create a rectangle of a specific size at a predefined position. The type of this rectangle is also set by the user (dynamic or static). Here again, let's explain the function step-by-step:

1.  We create `b2BodyDef`. This object contains the definition of the body to create. So we set the position and its type. This position will be in relation to the gravity center of the object.

2.  Then, we create `b2Shape`. This is the physical shape of the object, in our case, a box. Note that the `SetAsBox()` method doesn't take the same parameter as `sf::RectangleShape`. The parameters are half the size of the box. This is why we need to divide the values by two.

3.  We create `b2FixtureDef` and initialize it. This object holds all the physical characteristics of the object such as its density, friction, restitution, and shape.

4.  Then, we properly create the object in the physical world.

5.  Now, we create the display of the object. This will be more familiar because we will only use SFML. We create a rectangle and set its position, origin, and color.

6. As we need to associate and display SFML object to the physical object, we use a functionality of Box2D: the `SetUserData()` function. This function takes `void*` as a parameter and internally holds it. So we use it to keep track of our SFML shape.

7. Finally, the body is returned by the function. This pointer has to be stored to clean the memory later. This is the reason for the body's container in `main()`.

Now, we have the capability to simply create a box and add it to the world. Now, let's render it to the screen. This is the goal of the `displayWorld` function:

```
void displayWorld(b2World& world, sf::RenderWindow& render)
{
    world.Step(1.0/60, int32(8), int32(3));
    render.clear();
    for (b2Body* body=world.GetBodyList(); body!=nullptr; body=body-
>GetNext())
    {
        sf::Shape* shape = static_cast<sf::Shape*>(body-
>GetUserData());
        shape->setPosition(converter::metersToPixels(body-
>GetPosition().x),
        converter::metersToPixels(body->GetPosition().y));
        shape->setRotation(converter::radToDeg<double>(body-
>GetAngle()));
        render.draw(*shape);
    }
    render.display();
}
```

This function takes the physics world and window as a parameter. Here again, let's explain this function step-by-step:

1. We update the physical world. If you remember, we have set the frame rate to 60. This is why we use 1,0/60 as a parameter here. The two others are for precision only. In a good code, the time step should not be hardcoded as here. We have to use a clock to be sure that the value will always be the same. Here, it has not been the case to focus on the important part: physics. And more importantly, the physics loop should be different from the display loop as already said in *Chapter 2*, *General Game Architecture, User Inputs, and Resource Management*. I will come back to this point in the next section.

2.  We reset the screen, as usual.

3.  Here is the new part: we loop the body stored by the world and get back the SFML shape. We update the SFML shape with the information taken from the physical body and then render it on the screen.

4.  Finally, we render the result on the screen.

That's it. The final result should look like the following screenshot:

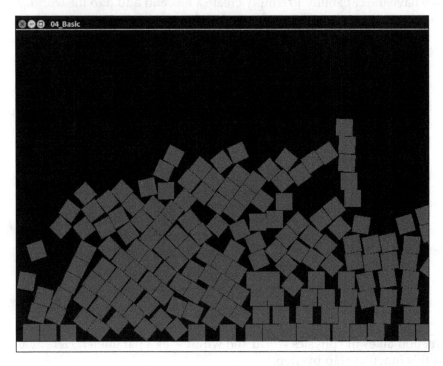

As you can see, it's not really difficult to pair SFML with Box2D. It's not a pain to add it. However, we have to take care of the data conversion. This is the real trap. Pay attention to the precision required (`int`, `float`, `double`) and everything should be fine.

Now that you have all the keys in hand, let's build a real game with physics.

# Adding physics to a game

Now that Box2D is introduced with a basic project, let's focus on the real one. We will modify our basic Tetris to get Gravity-Tetris alias Gravitris. The game control will be the same as in Tetris, but the game engine will not be. We will replace the board with a real physical engine.

With this project, we will reuse a lot of work previously done. As already said, the goal of some of our classes is to be reusable in any game using SFML. Here, this will be made without any difficulties as you will see. The classes concerned are those you deal with user event `Action`, `ActionMap`, `ActionTarget` — but also `Configuration` and `ResourceManager`. Because all these classes have already been explained in detail in the previous chapters, I will not waste time to explain them again in this one.

There are still some changes that will occur in the `Configuration` class, more precisely, in the enums and `initialization` methods of this class because we don't use the exact same sounds and events that were used in the Asteroid game. So we need to adjust them to our needs.

Enough with explanations, let's do it with the following code:

```
class Configuration
{
    public:
        Configuration() = delete;
        Configuration(const Configuration&) = delete;
        Configuration& operator=(const Configuration&) = delete;

        enum Fonts : int {Gui};
        static ResourceManager<sf::Font,int> fonts;

        enum PlayerInputs : int { TurnLeft,TurnRight, MoveLeft,
MoveRight,HardDrop};
        static ActionMap<int> playerInputs;

        enum Sounds : int {Spawn,Explosion,LevelUp,};
        static ResourceManager<sf::SoundBuffer,int> sounds;

        enum Musics : int {Theme};
        static ResourceManager<sf::Music,int> musics;
```

```
        static void initialize();

    private:
        static void initTextures();
        static void initFonts();
        static void initSounds();
        static void initMusics();
        static void initPlayerInputs();
};
```

As you can see, the changes are in the enum, more precisely in Sounds and PlayerInputs. We change the values into more adapted ones to this project. We still have the font and music theme. Now, take a look at the initialization methods that have changed:

```
void Configuration::initSounds()
{
    sounds.load(Sounds::Spawn, "media/sounds/spawn.flac");
    sounds.load(Sounds::Explosion, "media/sounds/explosion.flac");
    sounds.load(Sounds::LevelUp, "media/sounds/levelup.flac");
}
void Configuration::initPlayerInputs()
{
    playerInputs.map(PlayerInputs::TurnRight,Action(sf::Keyboard::
Up));
    playerInputs.map(PlayerInputs::TurnLeft,Action(sf::Keyboard::Do
wn));
    playerInputs.map(PlayerInputs::MoveLeft,Action(sf::Keyboard::Le
ft));
    playerInputs.map(PlayerInputs::MoveRight,Action(sf::Keyboard::Rig
ht));
    playerInputs.map(PlayerInputs::HardDrop,Action(sf::Keyboard::Spa
ce,
    Action::Type::Released));
}
```

No real surprises here. We simply adjust the resources to our needs for the project. As you can see, the changes are really minimalistic and easily done. This is the aim of all reusable modules or classes. Here is a piece of advice, however: keep your code as modular as possible, this will allow you to change a part very easily and also to import any generic part of your project to another one easily.

# The Piece class

Now that we have the configuration class done, the next step is the `Piece` class. This class will be the most modified one. Actually, as there is too much change involved, let's build it from scratch. A piece has to be considered as an ensemble of four squares that are independent from one another. This will allow us to split a piece at runtime. Each of these squares will be a different fixture attached to the same body, the piece.

We will also need to add some force to a piece, especially to the current piece, which is controlled by the player. These forces can move the piece horizontally or can rotate it.

Finally, we will need to draw the piece on the screen.

The result will show the following code snippet:

```
constexpr int BOOK_BOX_SIZE = 32;
constexpr int BOOK_BOX_SIZE_2 = BOOK_BOX_SIZE / 2;
class Piece : public sf::Drawable
{
    public:
        Piece(const Piece&) = delete;
        Piece& operator=(const Piece&) = delete;

        enum TetriminoTypes {O=0,I,S,Z,L,J,T,SIZE};
        static const sf::Color TetriminoColors[TetriminoTypes::SIZE];

        Piece(b2World& world,int pos_x,int pos_y,TetriminoTypes type,float rotation);
        ~Piece();
        void update();
        void rotate(float angle);
        void moveX(int direction);
        b2Body* getBody()const;

    private:
        virtual void draw(sf::RenderTarget& target, sf::RenderStates states) const override;
        b2Fixture* createPart((int pos_x,int pos_y,TetriminoTypes type); ///< position is relative to the piece int the matrix coordinate (0 to 3)
        b2Body * _body;
        b2World& _world;
};
```

Some parts of the class don't change such as the `TetriminoTypes` and `TetriminoColors` enums. This is normal because we don't change any piece's shape or colors. The rest is still the same.

The implementation of the class, on the other side, is very different from the precedent version. Let's see it:

```
Piece::Piece(b2World& world,int pos_x,int pos_y,TetriminoTypes
type,float rotation)  :  _world(world)
{
    b2BodyDef bodyDef;
    bodyDef.position.Set(converter::pixelsToMeters<double>(pos_x),
    converter::pixelsToMeters<double>(pos_y));
    bodyDef.type = b2_dynamicBody;
    bodyDef.angle = converter::degToRad(rotation);
    _body = world.CreateBody(&bodyDef);

    switch(type)
    {
        case TetriminoTypes::O : {
            createPart((0,0,type); createPart((0,1,type);
            createPart((1,0,type); createPart((1,1,type);
        }break;
        case TetriminoTypes::I : {
            createPart((0,0,type); createPart((1,0,type);
            createPart((2,0,type); createPart((3,0,type);
        }break;
        case TetriminoTypes::S : {
            createPart((0,1,type); createPart((1,1,type);
            createPart((1,0,type); createPart((2,0,type);
        }break;
        case TetriminoTypes::Z : {
            createPart((0,0,type); createPart((1,0,type);
            createPart((1,1,type); createPart((2,1,type);
        }break;
        case TetriminoTypes::L : {
            createPart((0,1,type); createPart((0,0,type);
            createPart((1,0,type); createPart((2,0,type);
        }break;
        case TetriminoTypes::J : {
            createPart((0,0,type); createPart((1,0,type);
            createPart((2,0,type); createPart((2,1,type);
        }break;
```

```
        case TetriminoTypes::T : {
            createPart((0,0,type); createPart((1,0,type);
            createPart((1,1,type); createPart((2,0,type);
        }break;
        default:break;
    }
    body->SetUserData(this);
    update();
}
```

The constructor is the most important method of this class. It initializes the physical body and adds each square to it by calling `createPart()`. Then, we set the user data to the piece itself. This will allow us to navigate through the physics to SFML and vice versa. Finally, we synchronize the physical object to the drawable by calling the `update()` function:

```
Piece::~Piece()
{
    for(b2Fixture* fixture=_body->GetFixtureList();fixture!=nullptr;
    fixture=fixture->GetNext())
{
        sf::ConvexShape* shape = static_
cast<sf::ConvexShape*>(fixture->GetUserData());
        fixture->SetUserData(nullptr);
        delete shape;
    }
    _world.DestroyBody(_body);
}
```

The destructor loop on all the fixtures attached to the body, destroys all the SFML shapes and then removes the body from the world:

```
b2Fixture* Piece::createPart((int pos_x,int pos_y,TetriminoTypes type)
{
    b2PolygonShape b2shape;
    b2shape.SetAsBox(converter::pixelsToMeters<double>(BOOK_BOX_
SIZE_2),
    converter::pixelsToMeters<double>(BOOK_BOX_SIZE_2)
    ,b2Vec2(converter::pixelsToMeters<double>(BOOK_BOX_
SIZE_2+(pos_x*BOOK_BOX_SIZE)),
converter::pixelsToMeters<double>(BOOK_BOX_SIZE_2+(pos_y*BOOK_BOX_
SIZE)))),0);
```

```
        b2FixtureDef fixtureDef;
        fixtureDef.density = 1.0;
        fixtureDef.friction = 0.5;
        fixtureDef.restitution= 0.4;
        fixtureDef.shape = &b2shape;

        b2Fixture* fixture = _body->CreateFixture(&fixtureDef);

        sf::ConvexShape* shape = new sf::ConvexShape((unsigned int)
    b2shape.GetVertexCount());
        shape->setFillColor(TetriminoColors[type]);
        shape->setOutlineThickness(1.0f);
        shape->setOutlineColor(sf::Color(128,128,128));
        fixture->SetUserData(shape);

        return fixture;
    }
```

This method adds a square to the body at a specific place. It starts by creating a physical shape as the desired box and then adds this to the body. It also creates the SFML square that will be used for the display, and it will attach this as user data to the fixture. We don't set the initial position because the constructor will do it.

```
    void Piece::update()
    {
        const b2Transform& xf = _body->GetTransform();

        for(b2Fixture* fixture = _body->GetFixtureList(); fixture !=
    nullptr;
        fixture=fixture->GetNext())
        {
            sf::ConvexShape* shape = static_
    cast<sf::ConvexShape*>(fixture->GetUserData());
            const b2PolygonShape* b2shape = static_
    cast<b2PolygonShape*>(fixture->GetShape());
            const uint32 count = b2shape->GetVertexCount();
            for(uint32 i=0;i<count;++i)
            {
                b2Vec2 vertex = b2Mul(xf,b2shape->m_vertices[i]);
                shape->setPoint(i,sf::Vector2f(converter::metersToPixels(
    vertex.x),
                converter::metersToPixels(vertex.y)));
            }
        }
    }
```

This method synchronizes the position and rotation of all the SFML shapes from the physical position and rotation calculated by Box2D. Because each piece is composed of several parts—fixture—we need to iterate through them and update them one by one.

```
void Piece::rotate(float angle) {
    body->ApplyTorque((float32)converter::degToRad(angle),true);
}
void Piece::moveX(int direction) {
    body->ApplyForceToCenter(b2Vec2(converter::pixelsToMeters(directi
on),0),true);
}
```

These two methods add some force to the object to move or rotate it. We forward the job to the Box2D library.

```
b2Body* Piece::getBody()const {return _body;}

void Piece::draw(sf::RenderTarget& target, sf::RenderStates states)
const
{
    for(const b2Fixture* fixture=_body->GetFixtureList();fixture!=null
ptr; fixture=fixture->GetNext())
    {
        sf::ConvexShape* shape = static_
cast<sf::ConvexShape*>(fixture->GetUserData());
        if(shape)
            target.draw(*shape,states);
    }
}
```

This function draws the entire piece. However, because the piece is composed of several parts, we need to iterate on them and draw them one by one in order to display the entire piece. This is done by using the user data saved in the fixtures.

# The World class

Now that we have built our pieces, let's make a world that will be populated by them. This class will be very similar to the one previously made in the Tetris clone. But now, the game is based on physics. So we need to separate the physics and the display updates. To do this, two update methods will be used.

The big change is that the board is no longer a grid, but a physical world. Because of this, a lot of internal logic will be changed. Now, let's see it:

```cpp
class World : public sf::Drawable
{
    public:
        World(const World&) = delete;
        World& operator=(const World&) = delete;

        World(int size_x,int size_y);
        ~World();
        void update(sf::Time deltaTime);
        void updatePhysics(sf::Time deltaTime);
        Piece* newPiece();
        int clearLines(bool& del,const Piece& current);
        void updateGravity(int level);
        void add(Configuration::Sounds sound_id);
        bool isGameOver()const;

    private:
        virtual void draw(sf::RenderTarget& target, sf::RenderStates
    states) const override;
        b2World _physicalWorld;
        void createWall(int pos_x, int pos_y, int size_x, int size_y);
        const int _x;
        const int _y;
        std::list<std::unique_ptr<sf::Sound>> _sounds;
};
```

We make the class non-replicable, with size as a parameter. As you can see, there are now two `update` methods. One for the physics and another one for the SFML objects. We still have some methods specific for the game such as `newPiece()`, `clearLines()`, `isGameOver()`, a new one relative to the `updateGravity()` physic, and a method to add sounds to our world. This method directly comes from the Meteor game by copying and pasting it.

Now that the class is introduced, take a look at its implementation. The following constructor initializes the physical world with a default gravity and adds some walls to it:

```cpp
World::World(int size_x,int size_y) : _physicalWorld(b2Vec2(0.f,
1.5f)),_x(size_x), _y(size_y)
{
```

```
    createWall(0,0,BOOK_BOX_SIZE,_y*BOOK_BOX_SIZE);
    createWall(BOOK_BOX_SIZE*(_x+1.2),0,BOOK_BOX_SIZE,_y*BOOK_BOX_
SIZE);
    createWall(0,BOOK_BOX_SIZE*_y,BOOK_BOX_SIZE*(_x+2.2),BOOK_BOX_
SIZE);
}
```

The destructor removes all the SFML shapes attached to the bodies still present in the world:

```
World::~World()
{
    for (b2Body* body=_physicalWorld.GetBodyList(); body!=nullptr;)
    {
        b2Body* next = body->GetNext();
        if(body->GetType() == b2_dynamicBody)
            delete static_cast<Piece*>(body->GetUserData());
        else
            delete static_cast<sf::RectangleShape*>(body-
>GetUserData());
        body = next;
    }
}
```

The following method synchronizes the physical bodies with the SFML objects that display it. It also removes all the sounds effects that are finished, as already explained in the previous chapter:

```
void World::update(sf::Time deltaTime)
{
    for (b2Body* body=_physicalWorld.GetBodyList(); body!=nullptr;
    body=body->GetNext())
    {
        if(body->GetType() == b2_dynamicBody){
            Piece* piece = static_cast<Piece*>(body->GetUserData());
            piece->update();
        }
    }
    _sounds.remove_if([](const std::unique_ptr<sf::Sound>& sound) ->
bool {
            return sound->getStatus() != sf::SoundSource::Status::Playi
ng;
        });
}
```

Now, we construct a class inside the `World.cpp` file because we don't need the class anywhere else. This class will be used to query the physical world by getting all the fixtures inside an area. This will be used more, especially to detect the completed lines:

```
Class _AABB_callback  : public b2QueryCallback
{
    public :
        std::<b2Fixture*> fixtures;

        virtual bool ReportFixture(b2Fixture* fixture) override {
            if(fixture->GetBody()->GetType() == b2_dynamicBody)
                fixtures.emplace_back(fixture);
            return true;
        }
};
```

The following method clears the completed lines by querying the world, especially with the made class. Then, we count the number of fixtures (squares) on each line; if this number satisfies our criteria, we delete all the fixtures and the line. However, by doing this, we could have some bodies with no fixture. So, if we remove the last fixture attached to a body, we also remove the body. Of course, we also remove all the SFML shapes corresponding to those deleted objects. Finally, for more fun, we add some sounds to the world if needed:

```
int World::clearLines(bool& del,const Piece& current)
{
    int nb_lines = 0;
    _AABB_callback callback;
    del = false;
    for(int y=0;y<=_y;++y)
{ //loop on Y axies
        b2AABB aabb; //world query
        //set the limit of the query
        aabb.lowerBound = b2Vec2(converter::pixelsToMeters<double>(0),
        converter::pixelsToMeters<double>((y+0.49)*BOOK_BOX_SIZE));
        aabb.upperBound = b2Vec2(converter::pixelsToMeters<double>(_x*
BOOK_BOX_SIZE),
            converter::pixelsToMeters<double>((y+0.51)*BOOK_BOX_
SIZE));
        //query the world
        _physicalWorld.QueryAABB(&callback,aabb);
```

```
                if((int)callback.fixtures.size() >= _x)
{
            for(b2Fixture* fixture : callback.fixtures)
{
                b2Body* body = fixture->GetBody();
                del |= body == current.getBody();

                if(body->GetFixtureList()->GetNext() != nullptr)
                {//no more fixture attached to the body
                    sf::ConvexShape* shape = static_
cast<sf::ConvexShape*>(fixture->GetUserData());
                    body->DestroyFixture(fixture);
                    delete shape;
                } else {
                    Piece* piece = static_cast<Piece*>(body-
>GetUserData());
                    delete piece;
                }
                fixture = nullptr;
            }
            ++nb_lines;
        }
        callback.fixtures.clear();
    }
    if(nb_lines > 0)
        add(Configuration::Sounds::Explosion);
    return nb_lines;
}
```

The following function sets the gravity depending on the current level. Bigger the level, stronger is the gravity:

```
void World::updateGravity(int level) {
    physical_world.SetGravity(b2Vec2(0,1.5+(level/2.0)));
}
```

The following function is directly taken from the Asteroid clone, and was already explained. It just adds sound to our world:

```
void World::add(Configuration::Sounds sound_id)
{
    std::unique_ptr<sf::Sound> sound(new
sf::Sound(Configuration::sounds.get(sound_id)));
    sound->setAttenuation(0);
    sound->play();
    _sounds.emplace_back(std::move(sound));
}
```

This method checks if the game is over with a simple criterion, "are there any bodies out of the board?":

```cpp
bool World::isGameOver()const
{
    for (const b2Body* body=_physicalWorld.GetBodyList();
body!=nullptr;
    body=body->GetNext())
    {
        if(body->GetType() == b2_staticBody)
            continue;
        if(body->GetPosition().y < 0)
            return true;
    }
    return false;
};
```

This function updates only the physical world by forwarding the job to Box2D:

```cpp
void World::updatePhysics(sf::Time deltaTime)
{
    float seconds = deltaTime.asSeconds();
    _physicalWorld.Step(seconds,8,3);
}
```

Now, we create a piece and set its initial position to the top of our board. We also add a sound to alert the player about this:

```cpp
Piece* World::newPiece()
{
    add(Configuration::Sounds::Spawn);
    return new Piece(_physicalWorld,_x/2*BOOK_BOX_SIZE, BOOK_BOX_
SIZE,static_cast<Piece::TetriminoTypes>( random(0, Piece::TetriminoTyp
es::SIZE-1)), random(0.f,360.f));
}
```

The `draw()` function is pretty simple. We iterate on all the bodies still alive in the world and display the SFML object attached to them:

```cpp
void World::draw(sf::RenderTarget& target, sf::RenderStates states)
const
{
    for (const b2Body* body=_physicalWorld.GetBodyList();
body!=nullptr;body=body->GetNext())
    {
        if(body->GetType() == b2_dynamicBody){
```

```
            Piece* piece = static_cast<Piece*>(body->GetUserData());
            target.draw(*piece,states);
        } else {//static body
            sf::RectangleShape* shape = static_
cast<sf::RectangleShape*>(body->GetUserData());
            target.draw(*shape,states);
        }
    }
}
```

The following functions are helpful. Its aim is to create a static body that will represent a wall. All the functionalities used were already explained in the first part of this chapter, so nothing should surprise you:

```
void World::creatWeall(int pos_x, int pos_y,int size_x,int size_y)
{
    b2BodyDef bodyDef;
    bodyDef.position.Set(converter::pixelsToMeters<double>(pos_x),
    converter::pixelsToMeters<double>(pos_y));
    bodyDef.type = b2_staticBody;

    b2PolygonShape b2shape;
    double sx = converter::pixelsToMeters<double>(size_x)/2.0;
    double sy = converter::pixelsToMeters<double>(size_y)/2.0;
    b2shape.SetAsBox(sx,sy,b2Vec2(sx,sy),0);

    b2FixtureDef fixtureDef;
    fixtureDef.density = 1.0;
    fixtureDef.friction = 0.8;
    fixtureDef.restitution= 0.1;
    fixtureDef.shape = &b2shape;

    b2Body* body = _physicalWorld.CreateBody(&bodyDef);
    body->CreateFixture(&fixtureDef);

    sf::Shape* shape = new sf::RectangleShape(sf::Vector2f(size_x,size_y));
    shape->setOrigin(size_x/2.0,size_y/2.0);
    shape->setPosition(sf::Vector2f(pos_x+size_x/2.0,pos_y+size_y/2.0));
    shape->setFillColor(sf::Color(50,50,50));
    body->SetUserData(shape);
}
```

# The Game class

Now, we have a world that can be populated by some pieces, let's build the last important class—the Game class.

There is a big change in this class. If you remember, in *Chapter 2, General Game Architecture, User Inputs, and Resource Management,* I said that a game with physics should use two game loops instead of one. The reason for this is that most of the physical engine works well with a fixed time step. Moreover, this can avoid a really bad thing. Imagine that your physical engine takes 0.01 second to compute the new position of all the bodies in your world, but the delta time passed as argument to your update function is fewer. The result will be that your game will enter in a death state and will finally freeze.

The solution is to separate the physics from the rendering. Here, the physics will run at 60 FPS and the game at a minimum of 30 FPS. The solution presented here is not perfect because we don't separate the computation in different threads, but this will be done later, in the sixth chapter.

Take a look at the Game header file:

```
class Game: public ActionTarget<int>
{
    public:
        Game(const Game&) = delete;
        Game& operator=(const Game&) = delete;
        Game(int x,int y,int word_x=10,int word_y=20);
        void run(int minimum_frame_per_seconds=30,int phyiscs_frame_
per_seconds=60);

    private:
        void processEvents();
        void update(const sf::Time& deltaTime,const sf::Time&
timePerFrame);
        void updatePhysics(const sf::Time& deltaTime,const sf::Time&
timePerFrame);
        void render();

        sf::RenderWindow _window;
        int _moveDirection;
        int _rotateDirection;
        Piece* _currentPiece;
        World _world;
        Stats _stats;
        sf::Time timeSinceLastFall;
};
```

No surprises here. The usual methods are present. We just duplicate the `update` function, one for logic and the other for physics.

Now, let's see the implementation. The constructor initializes `World` and binds the player inputs. It also creates the initial piece that will fall on the board:

```
Game::Game(int X, int Y,int word_x,int word_y) : ActionTarget(Config
uration::playerInputs), _window(sf::VideoMode(X,Y),"04_Gravitris"),_
currentPiece(nullptr), _world(word_x,word_y)
{
    bind(Configuration::PlayerInputs::HardDrop,[this](const
sf::Event&){
        _currentPiece = _world.newPiece();
        timeSinceLastFall = sf::Time::Zero;
    });
    bind(Configuration::PlayerInputs::TurnLeft,[this](const
sf::Event&){
        _rotateDirection-=1;
    });
    bind(Configuration::PlayerInputs::TurnRight,[this](const
sf::Event&){
        _rotateDirection+=1;
    });
    bind(Configuration::PlayerInputs::MoveLeft,[this](const
sf::Event&){
        _moveDirection-=1;
    });
    bind(Configuration::PlayerInputs::MoveRight,[this](const
sf::Event&){
        _moveDirection+=1;
    });
    _stats.setPosition(BOOK_BOX_SIZE*(word_x+3),BOOK_BOX_SIZE);
    _currentPiece = _world.newPiece();
}
```

The following function has nothing new except that the two `update()` functions are called instead of one:

```
void Game::run(int minimum_frame_per_seconds, int physics_frame_per_
seconds)
{
    sf::Clock clock;
    const sf::Time timePerFrame = sf::seconds(1.f/minimum_frame_per_
seconds);
```

```
    const sf::Time timePerFramePhysics = sf::seconds(1.f/physics_
frame_per_seconds);

    while (_window.isOpen())
    {
        sf::Time time = clock.restart();
        processEvents();
        if(not _stats.isGameOver())
    {
            updatePhysics(time,timePerFramePhysics);
            update(time,timePerFrame);
        }
        render();
    }
}
```

The following function updates the logic of our game:

```
void Game::update(const sf::Time& deltaTime,const sf::Time&
timePerFrame)
{
    sf::Time timeSinceLastUpdate = sf::Time::Zero;

    timeSinceLastUpdate+=deltaTime;
    timeSinceLastFall+=deltaTime;
    if(timeSinceLastUpdate > timePerFrame)
    {
        if(_currentPiece != nullptr)
        {
            _currentPiece->rotate(_rotateDirection*3000);
            _currentPiece->moveX(_moveDirection*5000);

            bool new_piece;
            int old_level =_stats.getLevel();
            _stats.addLines(_world.clearLines(new_piece,*_
currentPiece));
            if(_stats.getLevel() != old_level) //add sound
                _world.add(Configuration::Sounds::LevelUp);

            if(new_piece or timeSinceLastFall.asSeconds() >
std::max(1.0,10-_stats.getLevel()*0.2))
                {//create new piece
                    _currentPiece = _world.newPiece();
```

```
                    timeSinceLastFall = sf::Time::Zero;
            }
        }
        _world.update(timePerFrame);
        _stats.setGameOver(_world.isGameOver());
        timeSinceLastUpdate = sf::Time::Zero;
    }
    _rotateDirection=0;
    _moveDirection=0;
}
```

Here is the step-by-step evaluation of the preceding code:

1.  We start by updating some time value by adding the `deltaTime` parameter to them.

2.  Then, we apply some forces to the current piece if needed.

3.  We update the world by cleaning all the complete lines and also update the score.

4.  If needed, we create a new piece that will replace the current one.

Now, take a look at the physics:

```
void Game::updatePhysics(const sf::Time& deltaTime,const sf::Time&
timePerFrame)
{
    static sf::Time timeSinceLastUpdate = sf::Time::Zero;
    timeSinceLastUpdate+=deltaTime;
    _world.updateGravity(_stats.getLevel());

    while (timeSinceLastUpdate > timePerFrame)
    {
        _world.updatePhysics(timePerFrame);
        timeSinceLastUpdate -= timePerFrame;
    }
}
```

This function updates all the physics, including the gravity that changes with the current level. Here again, nothing is too complicated.

The `processEvents()` and `render()` functions don't change at all, and are exactly the same as in the first Tetris.

As you can see, the `Game` class doesn't change a lot and is very similar to the one previously made. The two loops—logics and physics—are the only real changes that occur.

# The Stats class

Now, the last thing to build is the `Stats` class. However, we have already made it in the previous version of Tetris, so just copy and paste it. A little change has been made for the game over, by adding a getter and setter. That's it.

Now, you have all the keys in hand to build your new Tetris with sounds and gravity. The final result should look like the following screenshot:

# Summary

Since the usage of a physics engine has its own particularities such as the units and game loop, we have learned how to deal with them. Finally, we learned how to pair Box2D with SFML, integrate our fresh knowledge to our existing Tetris project, and build a new funny game.

In the next chapter, we will learn how to add a user interface to our game in order to interact with the user easily, by creating our own game user interface or by using an existing one.

# 5
# Playing with User Interfaces

In the previous chapters, we have learned how to build some simple games. This chapter will show you how to improve those games by adding a user interface to them. This chapter will cover two different possibilities of user interface:

- Creating your own objects
- Using a library that already exists–**Simple and Fast Graphical User Interface (SFGUI)**

By the end of this chapter, you should be able to create simple to complex interfaces to communicate with the player.

## What is a GUI?

A **Graphical User Interface** (**GUI**) is a mechanism that allows the user to visually interact with a software through graphical objects such as icons, text, buttons, and so on. Internally, a GUI handles some events and binds them to functions, mostly called callbacks. These functions define the reaction of the program.

There are a lot of different common objects that are always present in a GUI, such as buttons, windows, labels, and layouts. I don't think I need to explain to you what a button, window, or label is, but I will explain to you in short what a layout is.

A layout is an invisible object that manages the arrangements of the graphical objects on the screen. Simply put, its goal is to take care of the size and the position of the objects by managing a part of them. It's like a table that makes sure none of these objects are on top of the others, and which adapts their size to fill the screen as proportionately as possible.

# Creating a GUI from scratch

Now that the GUI terms have been introduced, we will think about how to build it one by one using SFML. This GUI will be added to the Gravitris project, and the result will be similar to the following two screenshots:

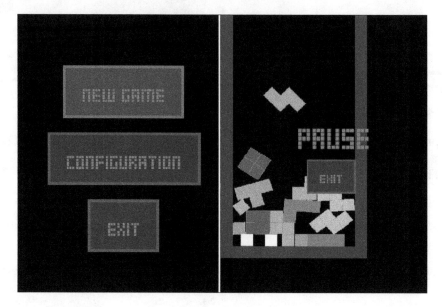

These show you the starting menu of the game and the pause menu during the game.

To build this GUI, only four different objects have been used: TextButton, Label, Frame, and VLayout. We will now see how to structure our code to be as flexible as possible to be able to extend this GUI in future if needed.

# Class hierarchy

As already said, we will need to build different components for the GUI. Each one has its own characteristics and features that can be slightly different from the others. Following are some characteristics of these components:

- TextButton: This class will represent a button that can trigger an "on click" event when clicked on. Graphically, it's a box with text inside it.

- Label: This accepts simple text that can be displayed on the screen.

- `Frame`: This class is an invisible container that will contain some object through a layout. This object will also be attached to an SFML window and will fill the entire window. This class can also process events (like catching the resize of the window, the click of the *Esc* key, and so on).

- `Vlayout`: This class's functionality has already been explained–it displays objects vertically. This class has to be able to adjust the positions of all the objects attached to it.

Because we want to build a GUI reusable and it needs to be as flexible as possible, we need to think bigger than our 4 classes to build it. For example, we should be able to easily add a container, switch to a horizontal layout or grid layout, make use of sprite buttons and so on. Basically, we need a hierarchy that allows the addition of new components easily. Here is a possible solution:

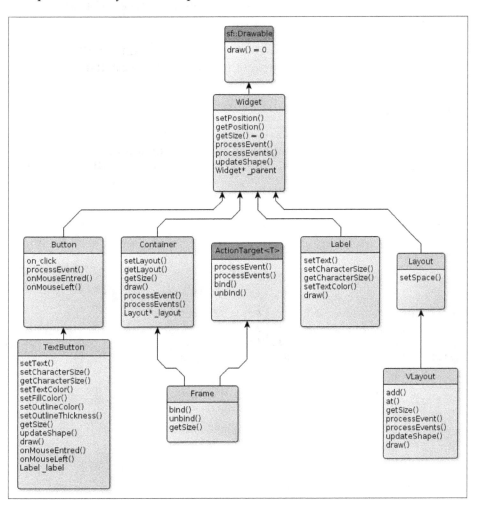

In this hierarchy, each green box represents an external class of the GUI.

In the GUI system, each component is a `Widget`. This class is the base of all the other components and defines the common methods to interact with them. We also define some virtual classes, such as `Button`, `Container`, and `Layout`. Each of these classes adapts the `Widget` class and adds the possibility of growing our system without too much effort. For example, adding an `HLayout` class will be made possible by extending it from `Layout`. Other examples include some specific buttons such as `RadioButton` and `CheckBox`, which use the `Button` class.

In this hierarchy, the `Frame` class extends the `ActionTarget` class. The idea is to be able to use the bind methods of `ActionTarget` to catch some events such as when working in some window and the *Esc* key is pressed.

Now that the hierarchy has been shown to you, we will continue with the implementation of the different classes. Let's start from the base: the `Widget` class.

## The Widget class

As already explained, this class is the common trunk of all the other GUI components. It provides some common methods with default behaviors that can be customized or improved on. A `Widget` class not only has a position and can be moved, but also has the ability to be displayed on screen. Take a look at its header source:

```
class Widget : public sf::Drawable
{
  public:
  Widget(Widget* parent=nullptr);
  virtual ~Widget();

  void setPosition(const sf::Vector2f& pos);
  void setPosition(float x,float y);
  const sf::Vector2f& getPosition()const;
  virtual sf::Vector2f getSize()const = 0;

  protected:
  virtual bool processEvent(const sf::Event& event,const
    sf::Vector2f& parent_pos);
  virtual void processEvents(const sf::Vector2f& parent_pos);
  virtual void updateShape();

  Widget* _parent;
  sf::Vector2f _position;
};
```

This first class is simple. We define a construct and a virtual destructor. The virtual destructor is very important because of the polymorphism usage inside the GUI logic. Then we define some getters and setters on the internal variables. A widget can also be attached to another one that is contained in it so we keep a reference to it for updating purposes. Now take a look at the implementation for a better understanding:

```
Widget::Widget(Widget* parent) : _parent(parent){}
Widget::~Widget(){}
void Widget::setPosition(const sf::Vector2f& pos) {_position =
  pos;}
void Widget::setPosition(float x,float y)
{
  _position.x = x;
  _position.y = y;
}
const sf::Vector2f& Widget::getPosition()const {return _position;}
bool Widget::processEvent(const sf::Event& event,const sf::Vector2f&
parent_pos) {return false;}
void Widget::processEvents(const sf::Vector2f& parent_pos) {}
```

Up to this point, nothing should surprise you. We only defined some getters/setters and coded the default behavior for event handling.

Now have a look at the following function:

```
void Widget::updateShape()
{
  if(_parent)
  _parent->updateShape();
}
```

This function, unlike the others we saw, is important. Its goal is to propagate the update request through the GUI tree. For example, from a button with a change in its size due to a text change, to its layout, to the container. By doing this, we are sure that each component will be updated without further efforts.

# The Label class

Now that the `Widget` class has been introduced, let's build our first widget, a label. This is the simplest widget that we can build. So we will learn the logic of GUI through it. The result will be as follows:

For doing this we will run the following code:

```
class Label : public Widget
{
  public:
  Label(const std::string& text, Widget* parent=nullptr);
  virtual ~Label();

  void setText(const std::string& text);
  void setCharacterSize(unsigned int size);
  unsigned int getCharacterSize()const;
  void setTextColor(const sf::Color& color);
  virtual sf::Vector2f getSize()const override;

  private:
  sf::Text _text;
  virtual void draw(sf::RenderTarget& target, sf::RenderStates
    states) const override;
};
```

As you can see this class is nothing other than a box around `sf::Text`. It defines some methods taken from the `sf::Text` API with the exact same behavior. It also implements the requirements of `Widget` class such as the `getSize()` and `draw()` methods. Now let's have a look at the implementation:

```
Label::Label(const std::string& text, Widget* parent) :
  Widget(parent)
{
  _text.setFont(Configuration::fonts.get
    (Configuration::Fonts::Gui));
  setText(text);
  setTextColor(sf::Color(180,93,23));
}
```

The constructor initializes the text from a parameter, sets the default font taken from the Configuration class, and sets a color.

```
Label::~Label() {}
void Label::setText(const std::string& text)
{   _text.setString(text);
    updateShape();
}
void Label::setCharacterSize(unsigned int size)
{
    _text.setCharacterSize(size);
    updateShape();
}
```

These two functions forward their jobs to sf::Text and request for an update because of the possible change of size.

```
unsigned int Label::getCharacterSize()const {return
    _text.getCharacterSize();}

void Label::setTextColor(const sf::Color& color)
    {_text.setColor(color);}

sf::Vector2f Label::getSize()const
{
    sf::FloatRect rect = _text.getGlobalBounds();
    return sf::Vector2f(rect.width,rect.height);
}
```

SFML already provides a function to get the size of a sf::Text parameter, so we use it and convert the result into the excepted one as shown by the following code snippet:

```
void Label::draw(sf::RenderTarget& target, sf::RenderStates
    states) const
{
    states.transform.translate(_position);
    target.draw(_text,states);
}
```

This function is simple, but we need to understand it. Each widget has its own position, but is relative to the parent. So when we display the object, we need to update the sf::RenderStates parameter by translating the transform matrix by the relative position, and then draw all the stuff needed. It's simple, but important.

# The Button class

Now, we will build another `Widget` class that is very useful: the `Button` class. This class will be a virtual one because we want to be able to build several button classes. But there are common functions shared by all the button classes, such as the "on click" event. So, the goal of this class is to group them. Take a look to the header of this class:

```
class Button : public Widget
{
  public:
    using FuncType = std::function<void(const sf::Event&
      event,Button& self)>;
    static FuncType defaultFunc;
    Button(Widget* parent=nullptr);

    virtual ~Button();
    FuncType onClick;

  protected:
    virtual bool processEvent(const sf::Event& event,const
      sf::Vector2f& parent_pos)override;
    virtual void onMouseEntered();
    virtual void onMouseLeft();

  private:
    enum Status {None =0,Hover = 1};
    int _status;
};
```

As usual, we declare the constructor and the destructor. We also declare an `onClick` attribute, which is an `std::function` that will be triggered when the button is pushed. This is our callback. The callback type is kept as `typedef` and we also declare a default empty function for convenience. Now, take a look at the implementation:

```
Button::FuncType Button::defaultFunc = [](const
  sf::Event&,Button&)->void{};
```

With the help of the following code snippet, we declare an empty function that will be used as the default for the `onClick` attribute. This function does nothing:

```
Button::Button(Widget* parent) : Widget(parent),
  onClick(defaultFunc), _status(Status::None) {}
```

We build the constructor that forwards its parameter to its parent class and also sets the onClick value to the default empty function previously defined to avoid undefined performance when the callback is not initialized by the user, as shown in the following code snippet:

```
Button::~Button() {}
bool Button::processEvent(const sf::Event& event,const
sf::Vector2f& parent_pos)
{
  bool res = false;
  if(event.type == sf::Event::MouseButtonReleased)
  {
    const sf::Vector2f pos = _position + parent_pos;
    const sf::Vector2f size = getSize();
    sf::FloatRect rect;
    rect.left = pos.x;
    rect.top = pos.y;
    rect.width = size.x;
    rect.height = size.y;
    if(rect.contains(event.mouseButton.x,event.mouseButton.y))
{
      onClick(event,*this);
        res = true;
    }
  } else if (event.type == sf::Event::MouseMoved) {
    const sf::Vector2f pos = _position + parent_pos;
    const sf::Vector2f size = getSize();
    sf::FloatRect rect;
    rect.left = pos.x;
    rect.top = pos.y;
    rect.width = size.x;
    rect.height = size.y;
    int old_status = _status;
    _status = Status::None;
    const sf::Vector2f
    mouse_pos(event.mouseMove.x,event.mouseMove.y);
    if(rect.contains(mouse_pos))
      _status=Status::Hover;
    if((old_status & Status::Hover) and not (_status &
      Status::Hover))
        onMouseLeft();
    else if(not (old_status & Status::Hover) and (_status &
      Status::Hover))
        onMouseEntered();
  }
  return res;
}
```

This function is the heart of our class. It manages the events by triggering some callbacks when some criteria are satisfied. Let's take a look at it step by step:

1. If the event received as the parameter is a click, we have to check whether it happens in the button area. If so, we trigger our onClick function.

2. On the other hand, if the event is caused by moving the pointer, we verify if the mouse pointer is hovering over the button. If so, we set the status value to Hover, and here is the trick:

3. If this flag was newly defined to Hover, then we call the onMouseEntered() method, which can be customized.

4. If the flag was previously defined to Hover but is not set to it anymore, it's because the mouse left the area of the button, so we call another method: onMouseLeft().

 The value returned by the processEvent() method will stop the propagation of the event on the GUI if it's set to true. Returning false will continue the propagation of the event, so it's also possible to use an event without stopping its propagation; on the mouse moving away, for example. But in this case, we simply can't click on multiple widget objects at the same time, so we stop if needed.

I hope the logic of the processEvent() function is clear, because our GUI logic is based on it.

Following two functions are the default empty behavior of the button with a mouse move event. Of course, we will customize them in the specialized Button classes:

```
void Button::onMouseEntered() {}
void Button::onMouseLeft() {}
```

## The TextButton class

This class will extend our previously defined Button class. The result will be a rectangle on the screen with text inside it, just as shown in the following screenshot:

Now take a look at the implementation. Remember that our `Button` class extends from `sf::Drawable`:

```
class TextButton : public
{
  public:
  TextButton(const std::string& text, Widget* parent=nullptr);
  virtual ~TextButton();

  void setText(const std::string& text);
  void setCharacterSize(unsigned int size);

  void setTextColor(const sf::Color& color);
  void setFillColor(const sf::Color& color);
  void setOutlineColor(const sf::Color& color);
  void setOutlineThickness(float thickness);
  virtual sf::Vector2f getSize()const override;

  private:
  sf::RectangleShape _shape;
  Label _label;
  void updateShape()override;
  virtual void draw(sf::RenderTarget& target, sf::RenderStates
    states) const override;
  sf::Color _fillColor;
  sf::Color _outlineColor;
  virtual void onMouseEntered()override;
  virtual void onMouseLeft()override;
};
```

This class extends the `Button` class and adds a rectangle shape and a label to it. It also implements the `onMouseEntered()` and `onMouseLeft()` functions. These two functions will change the color of the button, making them a bit lighter:

```
TextButton::TextButton(const std::string& text,Widget* parent)  :
  Button(parent), _label(text,this)
{
  setFillColor(sf::Color(86,20,19));
  setOutlineThickness(5);
  setOutlineColor(sf::Color(146,20,19));
}
```

The constructor initializes the different colors and the initial text:

```
TextButton::~TextButton() {}
void TextButton::setText(const std::string& text)
  {_label.setText(text);}
void TextButton::setCharacterSize(unsigned int size)
  {_label.setCharacterSize(size);}
```

```
void TextButton::setTextColor(const sf::Color& color)
  {_label.setTextColor(color);}

void TextButton::setFillColor(const sf::Color& color)
{
  _fillColor = color;
  _shape.setFillColor(_fillColor);
}

void TextButton::setOutlineColor(const sf::Color& color)
{
  _outlineColor = color;
  _shape.setOutlineColor(_outlineColor);
}

void TextButton::setOutlineThickness(float thickness)
  {_shape.setOutlineThickness(thickness);}

sf::Vector2f TextButton::getSize()const
{
  sf::FloatRect rect = _shape.getGlobalBounds();
  return sf::Vector2f(rect.width,rect.height);
}
```

All these functions set the different attributes by forwarding the job. It also calls the updateShape() method to update the container:

```
void TextButton::updateShape()
{
  sf::Vector2f label_size = _label.getSize();
  unsigned int char_size = _label.getCharacterSize();
  _shape.setSize(sf::Vector2f(char_size*2 + label_size.x
    ,char_size*2 + label_size.y));
  _label.setPosition(char_size,char_size);
  Widget::updateShape();
}
```

The following function updates the shape by resizing it using the size from the internal label and adding some padding to it:

```
void TextButton::draw(sf::RenderTarget& target, sf::RenderStates
states) const
{
  states.transform.translate(_position);
  target.draw(_shape,states);
  target.draw(_label,states);
}
```

This method has the same logic as Label. It moves `sf::RenderStates` to the position of the button and draws all the different `sf::Drawable` parameters:

```
void TextButton::onMouseEntered()
{
  const float light = 1.4f;
  _shape.setOutlineColor(sf::Color(_outlineColor.r*light,
  _outlineColor.g*light,
  _outlineColor.b*light));
  _shape.setFillColor(sf::Color(_fillColor.r*light,
  _fillColor.b*light,
  _fillColor.b*light));
}

void TextButton::onMouseLeft()
{
  _shape.setOutlineColor(_outlineColor);
  _shape.setFillColor(_fillColor);
}
```

These two functions change the color of the button when the cursor is hovering over it and reset the initial color when the cursor leaves it. This is useful for the user, because he knows which button will be clicked easily.

As you can see, implementation of a `TextButton` is pretty short, all thanks to the changes made in the parent classes, `Button` and `Widget`.

## The Container class

This class is another type of `Widget` and will be abstract. A `Container` class is a `Widget` class that will store other widgets through a `Layout` class. The purpose of this class is to group all the common operations between the different possible `Container` classes, even as in our case, we only implement a `Frame` container.

```
class Container   : public Widget
{
  public:
  Container(Widget* parent=nullptr);
  virtual ~Container();

  void setLayout(Layout* layout);
  Layout* getLayout()const;

  virtual sf::Vector2f getSize()const override;

  protected:
  virtual void draw(sf::RenderTarget& target, sf::RenderStates
    states) const override;
```

```
virtual bool processEvent(const sf::Event& event,const
    sf::Vector2f& parent_pos)override;
virtual void processEvents(const sf::Vector2f&
    parent_pos)override;

private:
Layout* _layout;
};
```

As usual, we define the constructor and destructor. We also add accessors to the internal Layout class. We will also implement the draw() method and the event processing. Now take a look at the implementation in the following code snippet:

```
Container::Container(Widget* parent) : Widget(parent),
    _layout(nullptr) {}
Container::~Container()
{
    if(_layout != nullptr and _layout->_parent == this) {
        _layout->_parent = nullptr;
        delete _layout;
    }
}
```

The destructor deletes the internal Layout class, but only if the parent of the Layout class is the current container. This avoids double free corruption and respects the RAII idiom:

```
void Container::setLayout(Layout* layout)
{
    if(_layout != nullptr and _layout->_parent == this) {
        _layout->_parent = nullptr;
    }
    if((_layout = layout) != nullptr) {
        _layout->_parent = this;
        _layout->updateShape();
    }
}
```

The previous function sets the layout of the container and deletes it from the memory if needed. Then it takes ownership of the new layout and updates the internal pointer to it.

```
Layout* Container::getLayout()const {return _layout;}
sf::Vector2f Container::getSize()const
{
    sf::Vector2f res(0,0);
    if(_layout)
```

```
    res = _layout->getSize();
    return res;
}
void Container::draw(sf::RenderTarget& target, sf::RenderStates
    states) const
{
    if(_layout)
    target.draw(*_layout,states);
}
```

The three previous functions do the usual job, just as with the other `Widget`s:

```
bool Container::processEvent(const sf::Event& event,const
    sf::Vector2f& parent_pos)
{
    bool res = false;
    if(and _layout)
        res = _layout->processEvent(event,parent_pos);
    return res;
}
void Container::processEvents(const sf::Vector2f& parent_pos)
{
    if(_layout)
        _layout->processEvents(parent_pos);
}
```

These two previous functions process for the events. Because a `Layout` class doesn't have any event to deal with, it forwards the job to all the internal `Widget` classes. If an event is processed by a `Widget` class, we stop the propagation, because logically no other widget should be able to deal with it.

# The Frame class

Now that the basic container has been constructed, let's extend it with a special one. The following `Widget` class will be attached to `sf::RenderWindow` and will be the main widget. It will manage the render target and the events by itself. Take a look at its header:

```
class Frame : public Container, protected ActionTarget<int>
{
    public:
    using ActionTarget<int>::FuncType;
    Frame(sf::RenderWindow& window);
    virtual ~Frame();

    void processEvents();
```

```
        bool processEvent(const sf::Event& event);

        void bind(int key,const FuncType& callback);
        void unbind(int key);

        void draw();
        virtual sf::Vector2f getSize()const override;

        private:
        sf::RenderWindow& _window;

        virtual bool processEvent(const sf::Event& event,const
            sf::Vector2f& parent_pos)override;
        virtual void processEvents(const sf::Vector2f&
            parent_pos)override;
};
```

As you can see, this class is a bit more complex than the previous `Widget`. It extends the `Container` class to be able to attach a `Layout` class to it. Moreover, it also extends the `ActionTarget` class, but as protected. This is an important point. In fact, we want to allow the user to bind/unbind events, but we don't want to allow them to cast the `Frame` to an `ActionTarget`, so we hide it to the user and rewrite all the methods of the `ActionTarget` class. This is why there is a protected keyword.

The class will also be able to extract events from its parent windows; this explains why we need to keep a reference to it, as seen here:

```
Frame::Frame(sf::RenderWindow& window) : Container(nullptr),
   ActionTarget(Configuration::gui_inputs), _window(window) {}
Frame::~Frame(){}

void Frame::draw() {_window.draw(*this);}

void Frame::bind(int key,const FuncType& callback)
   {ActionTarget::bind(key,callback);}

void Frame::unbind(int key) {ActionTarget::unbind(key);}

sf::Vector2f Frame::getSize()const
{
   sf::Vector2u size = _window.getSize();
   return sf::Vector2f(size.x,size.y);
}
```

All these methods are simple and don't require a lot of explanation. You simply initialize all the attributes with the constructor and forward the job to the attributes stored inside the class for the others, as done here:

```
void Frame::processEvents()
{
    sf::Vector2f parent_pos(0,0);
    processEvents(parent_pos);
}
bool Frame::processEvent(const sf::Event& event)
{
    sf::Vector2f parent_pos(0,0);
    return processEvent(event,parent_pos);
}
```

These two overload functions are exposed to the user. It forwards the job to the override functions inherited from `Widget` by constructing the missing ones or the already known arguments.

```
bool Frame::processEvent(const sf::Event& event,const
  sf::Vector2f& parent_pos)
{
  bool res = ActionTarget::processEvent(event);
  if(not res)
  res = Container::processEvent(event,parent_pos);
  return res;
}

void Frame::processEvents(const sf::Vector2f& parent_pos)
{
  ActionTarget::processEvents();
  Container::processEvents(parent_pos);
  sf::Event event;
  while(_window.pollEvent(event))
  Container::processEvent(event,parent_pos);
}
```

On the other hand, these two functions process to the event management of the `ActionTarget` and `Container` bases of the class, but also take in charge the polling event from its parent window. In this case, all event management will be automatic.

The `Frame` class is now over. As you can see, it's not a complex task, thanks to our hierarchical tree and because we reused code here.

# The Layout class

Now that all the widgets that will be rendered on the screen are building, let's build the class that will be in charge of their arrangement:

```cpp
class Layout : protected Widget
{
  public:
    Layout(Widget* parent=nullptr);
    virtual ~Layout();

    void setSpace(float pixels);

    protected:
    friend class Container;
    float _space;
};
```

As you can see, the abstract class is very simple. The only new feature is the ability to set spacing. We don't have any add(Widget*) method, for example. The reason is that the argument will be slightly different depending on the kind of Layout used. For example, we just need a Widget class as argument for the layout with a single column or line, but the situation is completely different for a grid. We need two other integers that represent the cell in which the widget can be placed. So, no common API is designed here. As you will see, the implementation of this class is also very simple and doesn't require any explanation. It follows the logic of the Widget class we previously created.

```cpp
Layout::Layout(Widget* parent): Widget(parent), _space(5) {}

Layout::~Layout() {}
void Layout::setSpace(float pixels)
{
    if(pixels >= 0) {
        _space = pixels;
        updateShape();
    }
    else
        throw std::invalid_argument("pixel value must be >= 0");
}
```

# The VLayout class

This Layout class will be more complex than the previous ones. This one contains the full implementation of a vertical layout, which automatically adjusts its size and the alignment of all its internal objects:

```
class VLayout : public Layout
{
  public:
  VLayout(const VLayout&) = delete;
  VLayout& operator=(const VLayout&) = delete;
  VLayout(Widget* parent = nullptr);
  ~Vlayout();

  void add(Widget* widget);
  Widget* at(unsigned int index)const;
  virtual sf::Vector2f getSize()const override;

  protected:
  virtual bool processEvent(const sf::Event& event,const
    sf::Vector2f& parent_pos) override;
  virtual void processEvents(const sf::Vector2f& parent_pos)
    override;

  private:
  std::vector<Widget*> _widgets;
  virtual void updateShape() override;
  virtual void draw(sf::RenderTarget& target, sf::RenderStates
    states) const override;
};
```

The class will implement all the requirements from the widget and will also add the features to add widgets in it. So there are some functions to implement. To keep a trace of the widgets attached to the Layout class, we will internally store them in a container. The choice of the std::vector class makes sense here because of the random access of the elements for the at() method and the great number access through the container. So the only reason for the choice is performance, since an std::list will also be able to do the same job. Now, let's have a look at the implementation:

```
VLayout::VLayout(Widget* parent) : Layout(parent) {}
VLayout::~VLayout()
{
    for(Widget* widget : _widgets) {
        if(widget->_parent == this)
            delete widget;
    }
}
```

The destructor will free the memory from the objects attached to the Layout class, with the same criteria as the ones explained in the Container class:

```
void VLayout::add(Widget* widget)
{
  widget->_parent = this;
  _widgets.emplace_back(widget);
  updateShape();
}
Widget* VLayout::at(unsigned int index)const {return
  _widgets.at(index);}
```

These two previous functions add the possibility to add and get access to the widget stored by the class instance. The add() method additionally takes ownership of the added object:

```
sf::Vector2f VLayout::getSize()const
{
  float max_x = 0;
  float y = 0;
  for(Widget* widget : _widgets)
  {
    sf::Vector2f size = widget->getSize();
    if(size.x > max_x)
    max_x = size.x;
    y+= _space + size.y;
  }
  return sf::Vector2f(max_x+_space*2,y+_space);
}
```

This method calculates the total size of the layout, taking into account the spacing. Because our class will display all the objects in a single column, the height will be their total size and the width the maximal of all the objects. The spacing has to be taken into account each time.

```
bool VLayout::processEvent(const sf::Event& event,const sf::Vector2f&
parent_pos)
{
  for(Widget* widget : _widgets)
  {
    if(widget->processEvent(event,parent_pos))
    return true;
  }
    return false ;
}
```

```
void VLayout::processEvents(const sf::Vector2f& parent_pos)
{
  for(Widget* widget : _widgets)
  widget->processEvents(parent_pos);
}
```

These two previous methods forward the job to all the stored widget , but we stop the propagation when it's needed.

```
void VLayout::updateShape()
{
  float max_x = (_parentparent->getSize().x:0);
  for(Widget* widget : _widgets) {
  sf::Vector2f size = widget->getSize();
  float widget_x = size.x;
  if(widget_x > max_x)
  max_x = widget_x;
}

  float pos_y = _space;
  if(_parent)
  pos_y = (_parent->getSize().y - getSize().y)/2.f;
  for(Widget* widget : _widgets)
{

    sf::Vector2f size = widget->getSize();
    widget->setPosition((max_x-size.x)/2.0,pos_y);
    pos_y += size.y + _space;
  }
  Widget::updateShape();
}
```

This method is the most important for this class. It resets the different positions of all the objects by calculating it based on all the other widgets. The final result will be a column of widgets centered vertically and horizontally.

```
void VLayout::draw(sf::RenderTarget& target, sf::RenderStates states)
const
{
  for(Widget* widget : _widgets)
  target.draw(*widget,states);
}
```

This last function asks each `Widget` to render itself by forwarding the parameter. This time, we don't need to translate states because the position of the layout is the same as its parent.

The entire class has now been built and explained. It's now time for the user to use them and add a menu to our game.

# Adding a menu to the game

Now that we have all the pieces in place to build a basic menu, let's do it with our fresh GUI. We will build two of them. The main, game-opening one and the pause menu. This will show you the different usage possibilities of our actual GUI.

If you have understood what we have done until now well, you would have noticed that the base component of our GUI is Frame. All the other widgets will be displayed on the top of it. Here is a schema that summarizes the GUI tree hierarchy:

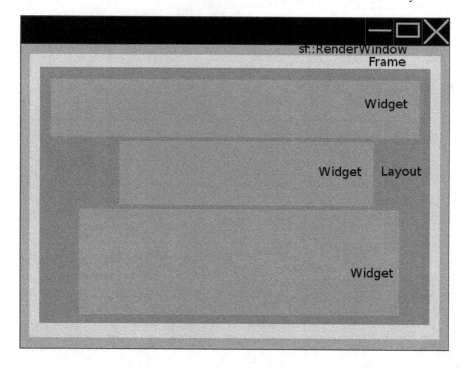

Each color represents a different type of component. The trunk is **sf::RenderWindow** and then we have a **Frame** attached to it with its **Layout**. And finally we have some different **Widget**. Now that the usage has been explained, let's create our main menu.

# Building the main menu

To build the main menu, we will need to add an attribute to the Game class. Let's call it _mainMenu.

```
gui::Frame _mainMenu;
```

We then create an enum function with different possibilities of values in order to know the currently displayed status:

```
enum Status
  {StatusMainMenu,StatusGame,StatusConfiguration,StatusPaused,
    StatusExit} _status
```

Now let's create a function to initialize the menu:

```
void initGui();
```

This function will store the entire GUI construction, except from the constructor that is calling. Now that we have all that we need in the header file, let's move on to the implementation of all this stuff.

First of all, we need to update the constructor by adding in the initialization of _mainMenu and _status. It should look like this:

```
Game::Game(int X, int Y,int word_x,int word_y) :
ActionTarget(Configuration::player_inputs),
_window(sf::VideoMode(X,Y),"05_Gui"), _current_piece(nullptr),
_world(word_x,word_y), _mainMenu(_window),
_status(Status::StatusMainMenu)
{
  //...
  initGui();
}
```

Now we need to implement the initGui() function as follows:

```
void Game::initGui()
{
  book::gui::VLayout* layout = new book::gui::VLayout;
  layout->setSpace(25);
  book::gui::TextButton* newGame = new book::gui::TextButton("New
    Game");
  newGame->onClick = [this](const sf::Event&, book::gui::Button&
    button){
  initGame();
  _status = Status::StatusGame;
};
```

```
layout->add(newGame);
book::gui::TextButton* configuration = new
    book::gui::TextButton("Configuration");
configuration->onClick = [this](const sf::Event&,
    book::gui::Button& button){
    _status = Status::StatusConfiguration;
};

layout->add(configuration);
book::gui::TextButton* exit = new book::gui::TextButton("Exit");
exit->onClick = [this](const sf::Event&, book::gui::Button&
    button){
    _window.close();
};
layout->add(exit);
_mainMenu.setLayout(layout);
_mainMenu.bind(Configuration::GuiInputs::Escape,[this](const
      sf::Event& event){
      this->_window.close();
    });
}
```

Let's discuss this function step by step:

1.  We create a `Vlayout` class and set its spacing.

2.  We create a button with `New Game` as its label.

3.  We set the `onClick` callback function that initializes the game.

4.  We add the button to the layout.

5.  With the same logic, we create two other buttons with different callbacks.

6.  Then we set the layout to the `_mainMenu` parameter.

7.  And we finally add an event directly to the frame that will handle the *Esc* key. This key is defined in the `GuiInputs` enum contained in the `Configuration` class, which was constructed as `PlayerInputs`.

Now that our menu is created, we need to make some little changes in the existing `run()`, `processEvents()`, and `render()` methods. Let's start with `run()`. The modification is negligible. In fact, we just have to add a condition for the call of the update methods, adding verification on the `_status` variable. The new line is now as follows:

```
if(_status == StatusGame and not _stats.isGameOver())
```

The next function is `processEvents()`, which will require a little more modification, but not too much. In fact, we need to call `_mainMenu::processEvent(const f::Event&)` and `_mainMenu::processEvents()`, but only when the game is in `StatusMainMenu` mode. The new method is now as follows:

```
void Game::processEvents()
{
  sf::Event event;
  while(_window.pollEvent(event))
  {
    if (event.type == sf::Event::Closed)
    _window.close();
    else if (event.type == sf::Event::KeyPressed and
      event.key.code == sf::Keyboard::Escape and _status ==
        Status::StatusGame)
    _status = StatusPaused;
    else
    {
      switch(_status)
      {
        case StatusMainMenu: _mainMenu.processEvent(event);break;
        case StatusGame : ActionTarget::processEvent(event);break;
        default : break;
      }
    }
  }
  switch(_status)
  {
    case StatusMainMenu: _mainMenu.processEvents();break;
    case StatusGame :  ActionTarget::processEvents();break;
    default : break;
  }
}
```

As you can see, the modification is not too complicated, and easily understandable.

And now, the last change in the `render()` method. The logic is the same, a switch on the `_status` value.

```
void Game::render()
{
  _window.clear();
  switch(_status)
  {
    case StatusMainMenu: _window.draw(_mainMenu);break;
```

```
        case StatusGame :
        {
if(not _stats.isGameOver())
  _window.draw(_world);
  _window.draw(_stats);
    }break;
    default : break;
  }
_window.display();
}
```

As you can see, we have been able to add a menu to our game without too much effort. The result should be like the figure shown here:

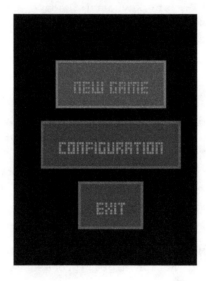

Now, let's build the second menu.

# Building the pause menu

The pause menu will be constructed just like the previous one, so I will skip the constructor part and directly move on to the initGui() function:

```
void Game::initGui()
{
  //...
  book::gui::VLayout* layout = new book::gui::VLayout;
  layout->setSpace(50);
  book::gui::Label* pause = new book::gui::Label("Pause");
  pause->setCharacterSize(70);
```

```
layout->add(pause);
book::gui::TextButton* exit = new book::gui::TextButton("Exit");
exit->onClick = [this](const sf::Event&, book::gui::Button&
  button)
{
  _status = StatusMainMenu;
};

layout->add(exit);
_pauseMenu.setLayout(layout);
_pauseMenu.bind(Configuration::GuiInputs::Escape,[this](const
  sf::Event& event){
_status = StatusGame;
});
}
```

The logic is exactly the same as the one used for the previous menu, but here we use a `Label` and a `TextButton` class. The callback of the button will also change the `_status` value. Here, again, we catch the *Esc* key. The result is to leave this menu. In the `processEvents()`, we only need to add one line to the first switch:

```
case StatusPaused : _pauseMenu.processEvent(event);break;
```

And add another line to the second switch:

```
case StatusPaused : _pauseMenu.processEvents();break;
```

And that's it. We are done with this function.

The next step is the `render()` function. Here again it will be very quick. We add a case in the switch statement as follows:

```
case StatusPaused :
{
    if(not _stats.isGameOver())
        _window.draw(_world);
    _window.draw(_pauseMenu);
}break;
```

The request to draw `_world` means to set the current game state in the background on the menu. This is useless, but pretty cool, so why not?

The final result is the second screenshot shown at the beginning of this chapter. Have a look at what appears on my screen:

# Building the configuration menu

This menu will in fact be implemented in the second part (by using SFGUI), but we need a way to exit the configuration menu. So we simply have to create a _ configurationMenu as the two others and bind the Escape event to set the status to the main menu. The code in the initGui() to add is shown as follows:

```
_configurationMenu.bind(Configuration::GuiInputs::Escape, [this]
  (const sf::Event& event){
    _status = StatusMainMenu;
});
```

I'm sure you are now able to update the processEvents() and render() functions by yourself using your new skills.

That's all concerning our home-made GUI. Of course, you can improve it as you wish. That's one of its advantages.

If you are interested in making improvements, take a look to the external library made regrouping all our custom game framework at http://github.com/Krozark/SFML-utils/.

The next step is to use an already made GUI with more complex widgets. But keep in mind that if you only need to show menus like those presented here, this GUI is enough.

# Using SFGUI

SFGUI is an open source library that implements a complete GUI system based on the top of SFML. Its goal is to provide a rich set of widgets and to be easily customizable and extensible. It also uses modern C++, so it's easy to use in any SFML project without too much effort.

The following screenshot shows the SFGUI in action with the test example provided with the source:

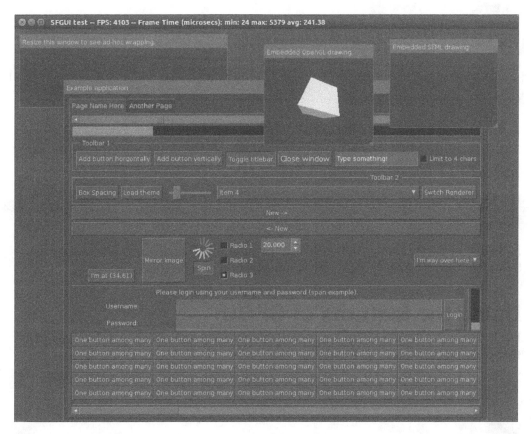

# Installing SFGUI

The first step is to download the source code. You will find it on the official website of the library: http://sfgui.sfml-dev.de/. The current version is 0.2.3 (Feb 20, 2014). You will need to build SFGUI by yourself, but as usual, it comes with the cmake file to help with the build. That is perfect, because we already know how to use it.

Sometimes, you could have a problem like the one shown in the following screenshot during the build step:

```
CMake Error at CMakeLists.txt:26 (find_package):
  By not providing "FindSFML.cmake" in CMAKE_MODULE_PATH this project has
  asked CMake to find a package configuration file provided by "SFML", but
  CMake did not find one.

  Could not find a package configuration file provided by "SFML" (requested
  version 2) with any of the following names:

    SFMLConfig.cmake
    sfml-config.cmake

  Add the installation prefix of "SFML" to CMAKE_PREFIX_PATH or set
  "SFML_DIR" to a directory containing one of the above files.  If "SFML"
  provides a separate development package or SDK, be sure it has been
  installed.
```

In this case, you have to set the CMAKE_MODULE_PATH variable to /path/to/SFML/ cmake/Modules using the add entry parameter. This should fix the problem.

 For other similar problems, take a look at this page: http://sfgui. sfml-dev.de/p/faq#findsfml. It should be helpful.

Now that SFGUI is configured, you need to build it and finally install it exactly as SFML and Box2D. You should now be pretty familiar with this.

# Using the features of SFGUI

I will not go too deep into the usage of SFGUI in this book. The goal is to show you that you don't always need to reinvent the wheel when a good one already exists.

SFGUI use a lot of C++11 features, such as `shared_pointers`, `std::functions`, and some others that have already been covered in this book, and uses the RAII idiom as well. As you already know how to work with these features, you will not be lost when it comes to using SFGUI optimally.

First of all, to use SFGUI objects, you must instantiate one object before all the others: `sfg::SFGUI`. This class holds all the information needed for the rendering. Except from this point, the library can be used pretty much like ours. So let's try it.

# Building the starting level

We will add a menu to our game that will allow us to choose the starting level. The goal of this section is to add a simple form that takes a number as parameter and sets it as the starting level of the game. The final result will look like this:

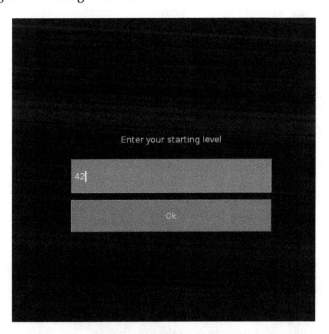

Before starting with SFGUI, we need to make an update to our `Stats` class. In fact, this class doesn't allow us to start at a specific level, so we need to add that functionality. This will be done by adding a new attribute to it as follows:

```
unsigned int _initialLvl;
```

We will also need a new method:

```
void setLevel(int lvl);
```

That's it for the header. Now we need to initialize _initialLvl to 0 by default. And then change the calculation of the current level in the addLines() function. To do this, go to the following line:

```
_nbLvl = _nbRows / 10;
```

Change the preceding line to the following:

```
_nbLvl = _initialLvl + (_nbRows / 10);
```

And finally, we will need to update or implement the assessors on the current level as follows:

```
void Stats::setLevel(int lvl)
{
  _initialLvl = lvl;
  _textLvl.setString("lvl : "+std::to_string(lvl));
}

int Stats::getLevel()const
{
  return _initialLvl + _nbLvl;
}
```

And that's it for the update on this class. Now let's go back to SFGUI.

We will use only three different visual objects to build the needed form: label, text input, and button. But we will also use a layout and a desktop, which is the equivalent of our Frame class. All the initialization will be done in the initGui() function, just as before.

We also need to add two new attributes to our game:

```
sfg::SFGUI _sfgui;
sfg::Desktop _sfgDesktop;
```

The reason for adding _sfgui was previously explained. We add _sfDesktop for the exact same reason we add Frame to contain the objects.

Now take a look at the code needed to create the form:

```
void Game::initGui()
{
  //...
  auto title = sfg::Label::Create("Enter your starting level");
  auto level = sfg::Entry::Create();
  auto error = sfg::Label::Create();
```

```
auto button = sfg::Button::Create( "Ok" );
button->GetSignal( sfg::Button::OnLeftClick ).Connect(
  [level,error,this]() {
    int lvl = 0;
    std::stringstream sstr(static_cast<std::string>(level-
      >GetText()));
    sstr >> lvl;
    if(lvl < 1 or lvl > 100)
    error->SetText("Enter a number from 1 to 100.");
    else
    {
      error->SetText("");
      initGame();
      _stats.setLevel(lvl);
      _status = Status::StatusGame;
    }
  }
);

auto table = sfg::Table::Create();
table->SetRowSpacings(10);
table->Attach(title,sf::Rect<sf::Uint32>(0,0,1,1));
table->Attach(level,sf::Rect<sf::Uint32>(0,1,1,1));
table->Attach(button,sf::Rect<sf::Uint32>(0,2,1,1));
table->Attach(error,sf::Rect<sf::Uint32>(0,3,1,1));
table->SetAllocation(sf::FloatRect((_window.getSize().x-
  300)/2,
(_window.getSize().y-200)/2,
300,200));
_sfgDesktop.Add(table);
}
```

Okay, a lot of new features here, so I will explain them step by step:

1. First of all, we create the different components needed for this form.

2. Then we set the callback of the button on a press event. This callback does a lot of things:

    ° We get back the text entered by the user

    ° We convert this text to an integer using `std::stringstream`

    ° We check the validity of the input

    ° If the input is not valid, we display an error message

    ° On the other hand, if it is valid, we reset the game, set the starting level, and start the game

3. Until all the objects are created, we add them into a layout one by one.

4. We change the size of the layout and center it on the window.

5. Finally, we attach the layout to the desktop.

As all the object are created and stored into `std::shared_` we don't need to keep a trace of them. SFGUI does it for us.

Now that the form is created, we have the same challenges as with our GUI: events and rendering. Good news, the logic is the same! However, we do have to code the `processEvents()` and `render()` functions again.

In the `processEvents()` method, we only need to complete the first switch as shown in the following code snippet:

```
case StatusConfiguration :
{
  _configurationMenu.processEvent(event);
  _sfgDesktop.HandleEvent(event);
}break;
```

As you can see, the logic is the same as our GUI, so the reasoning is clear.

And finally, the rendering. Here, again, the switch has to be completed by using the following code snippet:

```
case StatusConfiguration:
{
  _sfgDesktop.Update(0.0);
  _sfgui.Display(_window);
  _window.draw(_configurationMenu);
}break;
```

The new thing is the `Update()` call. This is for animations. Since in our case, we don't have any animation, we can put 0 as the parameter. It would be good practice to add this in the `Game::update()` function, but it's okay for our needs–and it also avoids changes.

You should now be able to use this new form in the configuration menu.

Of course, in this example, I have just shown you a little piece of SFGUI. It packs in many more features, and if you are interested, I would suggest you to take a look at the documentation and the examples given with the library. It's very interesting.

# Summary

Congratulations, you have now finished this chapter and have gained the ability to communicate with your player in a good way. You are now able to create some buttons, use labels, and add callbacks to some event triggers set off by the user. You also know the basics to create your own GUI and how to use SFGUI.

In the next chapter, we will learn how to use the full power of the CPU by using more than one thread, and see its implications in game programming.

**6**

# Boost Your Code Using Multithreading

In this chapter, we will gain skills about:

- How to run multiple parts of your program in parallel
- How to protect memory access to avoid data race
- How to incorporate those functionalities into Gravitris

At the end of this chapter, you will be able to use all the power offered by the CPU of the computer, by paralyzing your code in a smart way. But first, let's describe the theory.

## What is multithreading?

In computer science, a software can be seen as a stream with a start and exit point. Each software starts its life with the `main()` function in C/C++. This is the entry point of your program. Until this point, you are able to do whatever you want; including creating new routine streams, cloning the entire software, and starting another program. The common point with all these examples is that another stream is created and has its own life, but they are not equivalent.

## The fork() function

This functionality is pretty simple. Calling `fork()` will duplicate your entire running process to a new one. The new process that is created is totally separated from its parent (new PID, new memory area as the exact copy of its parent), and will start just after the `fork()` call. The return value of the `fork()` function is the only difference between the two executions.

Following is an example of the `fork()` function:

```
int main()
{
  int pid = fork();
  if(pid == -1)
    std::cerr<<"Error when calling fork()"<<std::endl;
  else if (pid == 0)
    std::cout<<"I'm the child process"<<std::endl;
  else
    std::cout<<"I'm the parent process"<<std::endl;
  return 0;
}
```

As you can see, it is very simple to use, but there are also some limitations with this use. The most important one concerns the sharing of memory. Because each process has its own memory area, you are not able to share some variables between them. A solution to this is to use files as sockets, pipes, and so on. Moreover, if the parent process dies, the child will still continue its own life without paying attention to its parent.

So this solution is interesting only when you don't want to share anything between your different executions, even their states.

# The exec() family functions

The `exec()` family functions (`execl()`, `execlp()`, `execle()`, `execv()`, `execvp()`, `execvpe()`) will replace the entire running program with another one. When paired with `fork()`, these functions become very powerful. Following is an example of these functions:

```
int main()
{
  int pid = fork();
  if(pid == -1)
  =  std::cerr<<"Error when calling fork()"<<std::endl;
  else if (pid == 0) {
    std::cout<<"I'm the child process"<<std::endl;
  }
  else {
    std::cout<<"I'm the parent process"<<std::endl;
    execlp("Gravitris", "Gravitris", "arg 1", "arg 2",NULL);
    std::cout<<"This message will never be print, except if
      execl() fail"<<std::endl;
  }
  return 0;
}
```

This little code snippet will create two different processes as previously mentioned. Then, the child process will be replaced by an instance of Gravitris. As a call of any of the exec() family functions replace the entire running stream with a new one, all the code under the exec call will not be executed, except if an error occurs.

# Thread functionality

Now, we will speak about threads. The threads' functionalities are very close to the fork ones, but with some important differences. A thread will create a new stream to your running process. Its starting point is a function that is specified as a parameter. A thread will also be executed in the same context as its parent. The main implication is that the memory is the same, but it's not the only one. If the parent process dies, all its threads will die too.

These two points can be a problem if you don't know how to deal with them. Let's take an example of the concurrent memory access.

Let's say that you have a global variable in your program named var. The main process will then create a thread. This thread will then write into var and at the same time, the main process can write in it too. This will result in an undefined behavior. There are different solutions to avoid this behavior and the common one is to lock the access to this variable with a mutex.

To put it simply, a mutex is a token. We can try to take (lock) it or release it (unlock). If more than one process wants to lock it at the same time, the first one will effectively lock it and the second process will be waiting until the unlock function is called on the mutex by the first one. To sum up, if you want to access to a shared variable by more than one thread, you have to create a mutex for it. Then, each time you want to access it, lock the mutex, access the variable, and finally unlock the mutex. With this solution, you are sure that you don't make any data corrupt.

The second problem concerns the synchronization of the end of the execution of your thread with the main process. In fact, there is a simple solution for this. At the end of the main stream, you need to wait until the end of all the running threads. The stream will be blocked as long as any threads remain alive and consequently will not die.

Here is an example of usage of a thread's functionality:

```
#include <SFML/System.hpp>
static sf::Mutex mutex;
static int i = 0;

void f()
{
```

```
        sf::Lock guard(mutex);
        std::cout<<"Hello world"<<std::endl;
        std::cout<<"The value of i is "<<(++i)<<" from f()"<<std::endl;
    }

    int main()
    {
        sf::Thread thread(f);
        thread.launch();
        mutex.lock();
        std::cout<<"The value of i is "<<(++i)<<" from main"<<std::endl;
        mutex.unlock();
        thread.wait();
        return 0;
    }
```

Now that the theory has been explained, let's explain what is the motivation to use multithreading.

# Why do we need to use the thread functionality?

Nowadays, computers in general have a CPU that is able to deal with several threads at the same time. Most of the time 4-12 calculation units are present in a CPU. Each of these units are able to do a task independently from the others.

Let's pretend that your CPU has only four calculation units.

If you take the example of our previous games, all the work was done in a single thread. So only one core is used over the four present. This is a shame, because all the work is done by only one component, and the others are simply not used. We can make it better by splitting our code into several parts. Each of these parts will be executed into a different thread, and the job will be shared between them. Then, the different threads will be executed into a different core (with a maximum of four in our case). So the work is now done in parallel.

Creating several threads offers you the possibility to exploit all the power offered by the computer, allowing you to spend more time on some functionalities such as artificial intelligence.

Another way of usage is when you use some blocking functions such as waiting for a message from the network, playing music, and so on. The problem here is that the running process will be in wait for something, and can't continue its execution. To deal with this, you can simply create a thread and delegate a job to it. This is exactly how `sf::Music` works. There is an internal thread that is used to play music. This is the reason why our games do not freeze when we play a sound or music. Each time a thread is created for this task, it appears transparent to the user. Now that the theory has been explained, let's use it in practice.

# Using threads

In *Chapter 4, Playing with Physics*, we have introduced physics to our game. For this functionality, we have created two game loops: one for logic and another one for physics. Until now, the executions of the physics loop and the other one were made in the same process. Now, it's time to separate their execution into distinct threads.

We will need to create a thread, and protect our variables using a `Mutex` class. There are two options:

- Using object from the standard library
- Using object from the SFML library

Here is a table that summarizes the functionalities needed and the conversion from a standard C++ library to SFML.

The `thread` class:

| Library | Header | Class | Start | Wait |
|---------|--------|-------|-------|------|
| C++ | `<thread>` | `std::thread` | Directly after construction | `::join()` |
| SFML | `<SFML/System.hpp>` | `sf::Thread` | `::launch()` | `::wait()` |

The `mutex` class:

| Library | Header | Class | Lock | Unlock |
|---------|--------|-------|------|--------|
| C++ | `<mutex>` | `std::mutex` | `::lock()` | `::unlock()` |
| SFML | `<SFML/System.hpp>` | `sf::Mutex` | `::lock()` | `::unlock()` |

There is a third class that can be used. It automatically calls `mutex::lock()` on construction and `mutex::unlock()` on destruction, in respect of the RAII idiom. This class is called a lock or guard. Its use is simple, construct it with mutex as a parameter and it will automatically lock/unlock it. Following table explains the details of this class:

| Library | Header | Class | Constructor |
|---------|--------|-------|-------------|
| C++ | `<mutex>` | `std::lock_guard` | `std::lock_guard(std::mutex&)` |
| SFML | `<SFML/System.hpp>` | `sf::Lock` | `sf::Lock(sf::Mutex&)` |

As you can see both libraries offer the same functionalities. The API changed a bit for the `thread` class, but nothing really important.

In this book, I will use the SFML library. There is no real reason for this choice, except that it allows me to show you a bit more of the SFML possibilities.

Now that the class has been introduced, let's get back to the previous example to apply our new skills as follows:

```
#include <SFML/System.hpp>
static sf::Mutex mutex;
static int i = 0;

void f()
{
  sf::Lock guard(mutex);
  std::cout<<"Hello world"<<std::endl;
  std::cout<<"The value of i is "<<(++i)<<" from f()"<<std::endl;
}

int main()
{
  sf::Thread thread(f);
  thread.launch();
  mutex.lock();
  std::cout<<"The value of i is "<<(++i)<<" from main"<<std::endl;
  mutex.unlock();
  thread.wait();
  return 0;
}
```

There are several parts in this simple example. The first part initializes the global variables. Then, we create a function named `f()` that prints **"Hello world"** and then prints another message. In the `main()` function, we create a thread attached to the `f()` function, we launch it, and print the value of `i`. Each time, we protect the access of the shared variable with a mutex (the two different approaches are used).

The print message from the `f()` function is unpredictable. It could be **"The value of i is 1 from f()"** or **"The value of i is 2 from f()"**. We are not able to say which one of the `f()` or `main()` prints will be made first, so we don't know the value that will be printed. The only point that we are sure of is that there is no concurrent access to `i` and the thread will be ended before the `main()` function, thanks to the `thread.wait()` call.

Now that the class that we needed have been explained and shown, let's modify our games to use them.

# Adding multithreading to our games

We will now modify our Gravitris to paralyze the physics calculations from the rest of the program. We will need to change only two files: `Game.hpp` and `Game.cpp`.

In the header file, we will not only need to add the required header, but also change the prototype of the `update_physics()` function and finally add some attributes to the class. So here are the different steps to follow:

1. Add `#include <SFML/System.hpp>`, this will allow us to have access to all the classes needed.

2. Then, change the following code snippet:

    ```
    void updatePhysics(const sf::Time& deltaTime,const
      sf::Time& timePerFrame);
    ```

    to:

    ```
    void updatePhysics();
    ```

    The reason is that a thread is not able to pass any parameters to its wrapped function so we will use another solution: member variables.

3. Add the following variables into the Game class as private:

    ```
    sf::Thread _physicsThread;
    sf::Mutex _mutex;
    bool _isRunning;
    int _physicsFramePerSeconds;
    ```

    All these variables will be used by the physics thread, and the `_mutex` variable will ensure that no concurrent access to one of those variables is made. We will also need to protect the access to the `_world` variable for the same reasons.

4. Now that the header contains all the requirements, let's turn to the implementation.

5. First of all, we will not only need to update our constructor to initialize the `_physicsThread` and `_isRunning` variables, but also protect the access to `_world`.

```
Game::Game(int X, int Y,int word_x,int word_y) :
  ActionTarget(Configuration::player_inputs),
  _window(sf::VideoMode(X,Y),"06_Multithreading"),
  _current_piece(nullptr), _world(word_x,word_y),
  _mainMenu(_window),_configurationMenu(_window),
  _pauseMenu(_window),
  _status(Status::StatusMainMenu),
  _physicsThread(&Game::update_physics,this),
  _isRunning(true)
{
  bind(Configuration::PlayerInputs::HardDrop, [this](const
    sf::Event&){
      sf::Lock lock(_mutex);
      _current_piece = _world.newPiece();
      timeSinceLastFall = sf::Time::Zero;
  });
}
```

6. In the constructor, we will not only initialize the new member variables, but also protect our `_world` variable used in one of the callbacks. This lock is important to be sure that no data race occurs randomly during the execution.

7. Now that the constructor has been updated, we need to change the `run()` function. The goal is to run the physics thread. There are not a lot of changes to make. See it by yourself:

```
void Game::run(int minimum_frame_per_seconds, int
  physics_frame_per_seconds)
{
  sf::Clock clock;
  const sf::Time timePerFrame =
    sf::seconds(1.f/minimum_frame_per_seconds);
  const sf::Time timePerFramePhysics =
    sf::seconds(1.f/physics_frame_per_seconds);
  _physics_frame_per_seconds = physics_frame_per_seconds;
  _physicsThread.launch();

  while (_window.isOpen())
  {
    sf::Time time = clock.restart();
    processEvents();
    if(_status == StatusGame and not _stats.isGameOver()){
      updatePhysics(time,timePerFramePhysics);
      update(time,timePerFrame);
```

```
        }
        render();
    }
    _isRunning = false;
    _physicsThread.wait();
}
```

8.  Now that the main game loop has been updated, we need to make a small change in the update() method to protect the member _world variable.

```
void Game::update(const sf::Time& deltaTime,const sf::Time&
timePerFrame)
{
    static sf::Time timeSinceLastUpdate = sf::Time::Zero;
    timeSinceLastUpdate+=deltaTime;
    timeSinceLastFall+=deltaTime;
    if(timeSinceLastUpdate > timePerFrame)
    {
        sf::Lock lock(_mutex);
        if(_current_piece != nullptr)
        {
            _currentPiece->rotate(_rotateDirection*3000);
            _currentPiece->moveX(_moveDirection*5000);
            bool new_piece;
            {
                int old_level =_stats.getLevel();
                _stats.addLines
                    (_world.clearLines(new_piece,*_currentPiece));
                if(_stats.getLevel() != old_level)
                _world.add(Configuration::Sounds::LevelUp);
            }
            if(new_piece or timeSinceLastFall.asSeconds() >
                std::max(1.0,10-_stats.getLevel()*0.2))
                {
                    _current_piece = _world.newPiece();
                    timeSinceLastFall = sf::Time::Zero;
                }
        }
        _world.update(timePerFrame);
        _stats.setGameOver(_world.isGameOver());
        timeSinceLastUpdate = sf::Time::Zero;
    }
    _rotateDirection=0;
    _moveDirection=0;
}
```

9.  As you can see there is only one modification. We just need to protect the access to the `_world` variable, that's it. Now, we need to change the `updatePhysics()` function. This one will be changed a lot as shown in the following code snippet:

```
void Game::updatePhysics(const sf::Time& deltaTime,const
  sf::Time& timePerFrame)
void Game::updatePhysics()
{
  sf::Clock clock;
  const sf::Time timePerFrame =
    sf::seconds(1.f/_physics_frame_per_seconds);
  static sf::Time timeSinceLastUpdate = sf::Time::Zero;

  while (_isRunning)
  {
    sf::Lock lock(_mutex);
    timeSinceLastUpdate+=deltaTime;
    timeSinceLastUpdate+= clock.restart();
    _world.updateGravity(_stats.getLevel());

    while (timeSinceLastUpdate > timePerFrame)
    {
      if(_status == StatusGame and not _stats.isGameOver())
      _world.update_physics(timePerFrame);
      timeSinceLastUpdate -= timePerFrame;
    }
  }
}
```

We need to change the signature of this function because we are not able to give it some parameters through the thread. So we add an internal clock for this function, with its own loop. The rest of the function follows the logic developed in the `update()` method. Of course, we also use the mutex to protect the access to all the variables used. Now, the physics is able to be updated independently from the rest of the game.

10. There are now little changes to be made in other functions where `_world` is used such as `initGame()` and `render()`. Each time, we will need to lock the access of this variable using the mutex.

11. The changes are as follows concerning the `initGame()` function:

```
void Game::initGame()
{
  sf::Lock lock(_mutex);
  timeSinceLastFall = sf::Time::Zero;
  _stats.reset();
```

```
    _world.reset();
    _current_piece = _world.newPiece();
}
```

12. And now take a look at the `render()` function after it is updated:

```cpp
void Game::render()
{
  _window.clear();
  switch(_status)
  {
    case StatusMainMenu:
    {
      _window.draw(_mainMenu);
    }break;
    case StatusGame :
    {
      if(not _stats.isGameOver())
      {
        sf::Lock lock(_mutex);
        _window.draw(_world);
      }
      _window.draw(_stats);
    }break;
    case StatusConfiguration:
    {
      _sfg_desktop.Update(0.0);
      _sfgui.Display(_window);
      _window.draw(_configurationMenu);
    }break;
    case StatusPaused :
    {
      if(not _stats.isGameOver())
      {
        sf::Lock lock(_mutex);
        _window.draw(_world);
      }
      _window.draw(_pauseMenu);
    }break;
    default : break;
  }
  _window.display();
}
```

13. As you can see, the changes made were really minimalistic, but required to avoid any race conditions.

Now that all the changes have been made in the code, you should be able to compile the project and test it. The graphical result will stay unchanged, but the usage of the different cores of your CPU has changed. Now, the project uses two threads instead of only one. The first one used for the physics and another one for the rest of the game.

# Summary

In this chapter, we covered the use of multithreading and applied it to our existing Gravitris project. We have learned the reason for this, the different possible uses, and the protection of the shared variables.

In our actual game, multithreading is a bit overkill, but in a bigger one for instance with hundreds of players, networking, and real-time strategies; it becomes a *must have*.

In the next chapter, we will build an entire new game and introduce new things such as the isometric view, component system, path finding, and more.

# 7
# Building a Real-time Tower Defense Game from Scratch – Part 1

Now that you have all the basic tools, it's time for us to build something new. What about a mix of a **Real Time Strategy** (**RTS**) and a tower defense? And what about making it a multiplayer game? You like these ideas? Great! This is exactly what we will start building.

As this project is much more consequent than all the others, it will be split in two parts. The first one will focus on the game mechanism and logic, and the second on the multiplayer layer. So, in this chapter we will do the following:

- Create animations
- Build and use a generic map system with tile model and dynamic loading
- Build an entity system
- Make the game's logic

This project will reuse a lot of the components made previously, such as `ActionTarget`, `ResourceManager`, our GUI, and the game loop. To allow you to reuse these components easily for future projects, they have been gathered into a single framework (`SFML-utils`) that has been separated from the code in this book. This framework is available on the GitHub website at `https://github.com/Krozark/SFML-utils`, due to which these components have been moved from the book namespace to `SFML-utils`. Moreover, the map and entity systems that will be explained in this chapter are also part of this framework.

The final result of this chapter will look as follows:

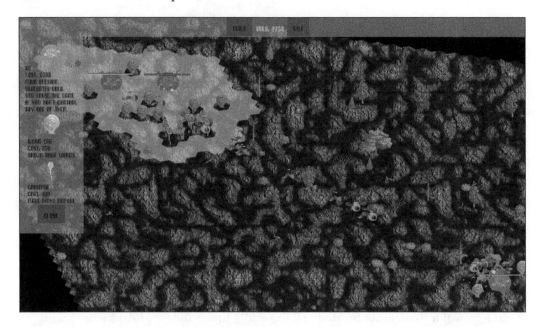

# The goal of the game

First of all, let's explain our goal. As we said previously, we will build a new game that will be a mix of a real-time strategy game and tower defense.

The idea is that each team starts with some money/gold and a main building named GQ. When a team loses all its GQ, it loses the game. The money can be spent to build other buildings with different abilities, or to upgrade them. For example, some of the buildings will spawn warriors who will attack the enemies; other buildings will only defend the surrounding area. There is also a restriction concerning the area where new buildings can be made. In fact, you can only place a new building around your team's existing buildings. This keeps you from placing a big tower in the center of the enemy camp at the start of the game. It's also important to notice that once a building is built, you don't control its behavior just as you don't control the different warriors spawn by it.

Also, each time an enemy is destroyed, some gold is added to your gold stock, allowing you to build more towers, thus increasing your power to defeat your enemies.

Now that the game has been introduced, let's list our needs:

- **Resources and event management**: These two features have been created previously, so we will just reuse them.

- **GUI**: This feature has also been developed already in *Chapter 5, Playing with User Interfaces*. We will reuse it as is.

- **Animation**: In SFML, there is no class to manage animated sprites in SFML, but for our game, we will need this functionality. So we will build it and add it to our framework.

- **Tile map**: This functionality is very important and has to be as flexible as possible to allow us to reuse it in many other projects.

- **Entity manager**: If you remember, this was introduced in *Chapter 3, Making an Entire 2D Game*. Now it's time for us to really see it. This system will avoid a complex inheritance tree.

As you can see, this project is a bit more challenging than the previous one due its complexity, but it will also be much more interesting.

# Building animations

In all our previous games, all the different entities displayed on the screen were static; at least they were not animated. For a more attractive game, the simplest thing to do is add some animations and different entities on the player. For us, this will be applied on the different buildings and warriors.

As we use a sprite-based game and not real-time animation based on bone movement, we need some textures with the animations that are already prepared. So, our textures will look as shown in the following figure:

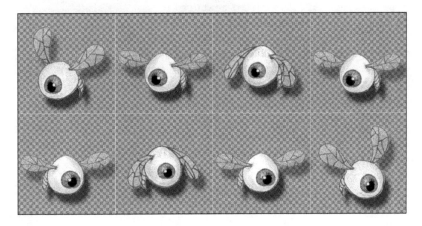

Note that the green grid is not a part of the image and is only shown here for information; the background is transparent in reality.

This type of texture is called a sprite sheet. In this example, the image can be split in two lines of four columns. Each line represents a direction of movement, namely left and right. Each cell of these lines represents a step of the future animation.

The aim of the work for this part is to be able to display a sprite using this sheet as an animation frame.

We will follow the design of the SFML by building two classes. The first one will store the animations and the second one will be used to display works such as sf::Texture and sf::Sprite. These two classes are named as Animation and AnimatedSprite.

# The Animation class

The Animation class only stores all the required data, for example, the textures and the different frames.

As this class is a kind of resource, we will use it through our ResourceManager class.

Here is the header of the class:

```
class Animation
{
  public:
  Animation(sf::Texture* texture=nullptr);
  ~Animation();

  void setTexture(sf::Texture* texture);
  sf::Texture* getTexture()const;

  Animation& addFrame(const sf::IntRect& rect);
  Animation& addFramesLine(int number_x,int number_y,int line);
  Animation& addFramesColumn(int number_x,int number_y,int
    column);
  size_t size()const;
  const sf::IntRect& getRect(size_t index)const;

  private:
  friend class AnimatedSprite;
  std::vector<sf::IntRect> _frames;
  sf::Texture* _texture;
};
```

As you can see, this class is nothing but a container for a texture and some rectangles. To simplify the usage of this class, some helper functions have been created, namely `addFramesLines()` and `addFramesColumn()`. Each of these functions add a complete line or column to the internal `_frames` list. The implementation of this class is also very simple and is as follows:

```
Animation::Animation(sf::Texture* texture) : _texture(texture){}

Animation::~Animation(){}

void Animation::setTexture(sf::Texture* texture){ _texture =
    texture;}

sf::Texture* Animation::getTexture() const {return _texture;}

size_t Animation::size() const {return _frames.size();}

const sf::IntRect& Animation::getRect(size_t index) const {return
    _frames[index];}

Animation& Animation::addFrame(const sf::IntRect& rect)
{
    _frames.emplace_back(rect);
    return *this;
}

Animation& Animation::addFramesLine(int number_x,int number_y,int
    line)
{
    const sf::Vector2u size = _texture->getSize();
    const float delta_x = size.x / float(number_x);
    const float delta_y = size.y / float(number_y);

    for(int i = 0;i<number_x;++i)
        addFrame(sf::IntRect(i*delta_x,line*delta_y,delta_x,delta_y));
    return *this;
}
Animation& Animation::addFramesColumn(int number_x,int
    number_y,int column)
{
    const sf::Vector2u size = _texture->getSize();
    const float delta_x = size.x / float(number_x);
    const float delta_y = size.y / float(number_y);
    for(int i = 0;i<number_y;++i)
        addFrame(sf::IntRect(column*delta_x,i*delta_y,delta_x,delta_y));
    return *this;
}
```

The three `addFrameXXX()` functions allow us to add frames to our animation. The last two ones are some shortcuts to add an entire line or column. The rest of the methods allow us to access to the internal data.

Nothing more is required by our frame container. It's now time to build the `AnimatedSprite` class.

# The AnimatedSprite class

The `AnimatedSprite` class is in charge of the animation displayed on the screen. Due to this, it will keep a reference to an `Animation` class and will change the sub-rectangle of the texture periodically, just like `sf::Sprite`. We will also copy the `sf::Music`/`sf::Sound` API concerning the play/pause/stop ability. An `AnimatedSprite` instance should also be able to display on the screen and be transformable, due to which the class will inherit from `sf::Drawable` and `sf::Transformable`. We will also add a callback that will be triggered when the animation is complete. It could be interesting for the future.

The header looks as follows:

```
class AnimatedSprite : public sf::Drawable, public sf::Transformable
{
  public:
  AnimatedSprite(const AnimatedSprite&) = default;
  AnimatedSprite& operator=(const AnimatedSprite&) = default;
  AnimatedSprite(AnimatedSprite&&) = default;
  AnimatedSprite& operator=(AnimatedSprite&&) = default;

  using FuncType = std::function<void()>;
  static FuncType defaultFunc;
  FuncType onFinished;
  enum Status {Stopped,Paused,Playing};

  AnimatedSprite(Animation* animation = nullptr,Status status=
    Playing,const sf::Time& deltaTime = sf::seconds(0.15),bool
      loop = true,int repeat=0);

  void setAnimation(Animation* animation);
  Animation* getAnimation()const;

  void setFrameTime(sf::Time deltaTime);
  sf::Time getFrameTime()const;

  void setLoop(bool loop);
```

```
    bool getLoop()const;
    void setRepeat(int nb);
    int getRepeat()const;

    void play();
    void pause();
    void stop();
    Status getStatus()const;

    void setFrame(size_t index);
    void setColor(const sf::Color& color);
    void update(const sf::Time& deltaTime);

    private:
    Animation* _animation;
    sf::Time _delta;
    sf::Time _elapsed;
    bool _loop;
    int _repeat;
    Status _status;
    size_t _currentFrame;
    sf::Vertex _vertices[4];

    void setFrame(size_t index,bool resetTime);
    virtual void draw(sf::RenderTarget& target,sf::RenderStates
      states) const override;
};
```

As you can see, this class is bigger than the previous one. Its main functionality is to store an array of four vertices that will represent a frame taken from the associated animation. We also need some other information, such as the time between two frames, if the animation is a loop. This is why we need so many little functions. Now, let's see how all these are implemented:

```
AnimatedSprite::AnimatedSprite(Animation* animation,Status
    status,const sf::Time& deltaTime,bool loop,int repeat) :
      onFinished(defaultFunc),_delta(deltaTime),_loop(loop),
        _repeat(repeat),_status(status)
{
    setAnimation(animation);
}
```

The constructor only initializes all the different attributes to their correct values:

```
void AnimatedSprite::setAnimation(Animation* animation)
{
  if(_animation != animation){
    _animation = animation;
    _elapsed = sf::Time::Zero;
    _currentFrame = 0;
    setFrame(0,true);
  }
}
```

This function changes the current texture for a new one only if they are different, and resets the frame to the first one of the new animation. Note that at least one frame has to be stored in the new animation received as a parameter.

```
Animation* AnimatedSprite::getAnimation()const {return
  _animation;}

void AnimatedSprite::setFrameTime(sf::Time deltaTime){_delta =
  deltaTime;}

sf::Time AnimatedSprite::getFrameTime()const {return _delta;}

void AnimatedSprite::setLoop(bool loop){_loop = loop;}

bool AnimatedSprite::getLoop()const {   return _loop;}

void AnimatedSprite::setRepeate(int nb) {_repeat = nb;}

int AnimatedSprite::getRepeate()const{   return _repeat;}

void AnimatedSprite::play() {_status = Playing;}

void AnimatedSprite::pause() {_status = Paused;}

void AnimatedSprite::stop()
{
  _status = Stopped;
  _currentFrame = 0;
  setFrame(0,true);
}

AnimatedSprite::Status AnimatedSprite::getStatus()const {return
  _status;}
```

All these functions are simple getters and setters. They allow us to manage basic elements of the `AnimatedSprite` class, as depicted in the previous code snippet.

```
void AnimatedSprite::setFrame(size_t index)
{
  assert(_animation);
  _currentFrame = index % _animation->size();
  setFrame(_currentFrame,true);
}
```

This function changes the current frame to a new one taken from the internal `Animation` class.

```
void AnimatedSprite::setColor(const sf::Color& color)
{
  _vertices[0].color = color;
  _vertices[1].color = color;
  _vertices[2].color = color;
  _vertices[3].color = color;
}
```

This function changes the color mask of the displayed image. To do this, we set the color of each internal vertex to the new color received as a parameter:

```
void AnimatedSprite::update(const sf::Time& deltaTime)
{
  if(_status == Playing and _animation)
  {
    _elapsed += deltaTime;

    if(_elapsed > _delta)
    {//need to change frame
      _elapsed -= _delta;
      if(_currentFrame + 1 < _animation->size())
          ++_currentFrame;
      else
      {//end of frame list
        _currentFrame = 0;

          if(not _loop)
          {//can we make another loop an the frames?
            --_repeat;
            if(_repeat<=0)
            { //no, so we stop
                  _status = Stopped;
                  onFinished();
```

```
            }
          }
        }
      }
      //update the frame
      setFrame(_currentFrame,false);
    }
}
```

This function is the main one. Its job is to change from the current frame to the next one when the time limit is reached. Once we reach the last frame of the animation, you can do the following:

- Reset the animation from the first one, depending of the `_loop` value

- Reset the animation from the first one if the `_repeat` value authorizes us to do it

- In all other cases, we trigger the event "on finish" by calling the internal callback

Now, take a look at the function that updates the frame's skin:

```
void AnimatedSprite::setFrame(size_t index,bool resetTime)
{
  if(_animation)
  {
    sf::IntRect rect = _animation->getRect(index);
    //update vertice position
    _vertices[0].position = sf::Vector2f(0.f, 0.f);
    _vertices[1].position = sf::Vector2f(0.f,
      static_cast<float>(rect.height));
    _vertices[2].position =
      sf::Vector2f(static_cast<float>(rect.width),
        static_cast<float>(rect.height));
    _vertices[3].position =
      sf::Vector2f(static_cast<float>(rect.width), 0.f);

    //compute the texture coords
    float left = static_cast<float>(rect.left);
    float right = left + static_cast<float>(rect.width);
    float top = static_cast<float>(rect.top);
    float bottom = top + static_cast<float>(rect.height);

    //set the texture coords
    _vertices[0].texCoords = sf::Vector2f(left, top);
    _vertices[1].texCoords = sf::Vector2f(left, bottom);
    _vertices[2].texCoords = sf::Vector2f(right, bottom);
    _vertices[3].texCoords = sf::Vector2f(right, top);
```

```
    }
    if (resetTime)
    _elapsed = sf::Time::Zero;
}
```

This function is also an important one. Its aims is to update the attributes of the different vertices to those taken from the internal `Animation` class, namely the position and texture coordinates:

```
void AnimatedSprite::draw(sf::RenderTarget&
  target,sf::RenderStates states) const
{
  if (_animation and _animation->_texture)è
  {
    states.transform *= getTransform();
    states.texture = _animation->_texture;
    target.draw(_vertices, 4, sf::Quads, states);
  }
}
```

The final function of this class manages the display. Because we inherit from `sf::Transformable`, we need to take into account the possible transformation. Then, we set the texture we used and finally draw the internal vertices array.

# A usage example

Now that we have the requisite classes to display an animation, let's build a little usage example.

Now, here's the implementation:

```
int main(int argc,char* argv[])
{
  //Creation of the window
  sf::RenderWindow window(sf::VideoMode(600,800),"Example
    animation");

  //load of the texture image
  ResourceManager<sf::Texture,int> textures;
  textures.load(0,"media/img/eye.png");

  //Creation of the different animations
  Animation walkLeft(&textures.get(0));
  walkLeft.addFramesLine(4,2,0);
  Animation walkRight(&textures.get(0));
```

```
    walkRight.addFramesLine(4,2,1);

    //Creation of the animates sprite
    AnimatedSprite sprite(&walkLeft,AnimatedSprite::Playing,sf::secon
ds(0.1));
    //game loop
    sf::Clock clock;
    while (window.isOpen())
    {
      sf::Time delta = clock.restart();
      sf::Event event;
      while (window.pollEvent(event))
      {
        if (event.type == sf::Event::Closed) //close event
        window.close();
      }
      float speed = 50; // the movement speed of the entity
      if(sf::Keyboard::isKeyPressed(sf::Keyboard::Left)) //move left
      {
        sprite.setAnimation(&walkLeft);
        sprite.play();
        sprite.move(-speed*delta.asSeconds(),0);
      }
      else if(sf::Keyboard::isKeyPressed(sf::Keyboard::Right))
        //move right    {
        sprite.setAnimation(&walkRight);
        sprite.play();
        sprite.move(speed*delta.asSeconds(),0);
      }
      window.clear();
      sprite.update(delta); //update the animate sprite for possible
        frame change
      window.draw(sprite); //display the animation
      window.display();
    }
    return 0;
}
```

For a better understanding of this code snippet, I've written some comments in the code.

This short program displays an animation on the screen. You can also change its position by moving it using the arrows on your keyboard. The animation will also change depending on the direction of movement.

Now that the first point of this chapter has been explained, let's continue to the second one, building a map.

# Building a generic Tile Map

For our project, we need something that will manage the map. In fact, the map is nothing but a big grid. The cells can be of any shape (square, hexagonal, and so on). The only restriction is that all the cells of a single map should have the same geometry.

Moreover, each cell can contain several objects, possibly of different types. For example, a cell can contain some background texture for the ground, a tree, and a bird. Because SFML doesn't use a z buffer with sprites (also called a depth buffer), we need to simulate it by hand. This is called the Painter's Algorithm. Its principle is very simple; draw everything but by depth order, starting with the most distant. It's how a tradition art painter would paint.

All this information brings us to the following structure:

- A Map class must be of a specific geometry and must contain any number of layers sorted by their z buffer.
- A Layer contains only a specific type. It also has a z buffer and stores a list of content sorted by their positions.
- The CONTENT and GEOMETRY classes are template parameters but they need to have a specific API.

Here is the flowchart representing the class hierarchy of the previously explained structure:

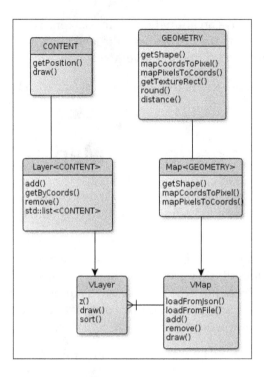

Following is the explanation of the flowchart:

- The CONTENT template class can be any class that inherits from sf::Drawable and sf::Transformable.
- The GEOMETRY class is a new one that we will learn about shortly. It only defines the geometric shape and some helper functions to manipulate coordinates.
- The VLayer class defines a common class for all the different types of layers.
- The Layer class is just a container of a specific type with a depth variable that defines its draw order for the painter algorithm.
- The VMap class defines a common API for the entire Map. It also contains a list of VLayer that is displayed using the painter algorithm.
- The Map class inherits from VMap and is of a specific geometry.

# The Geometry class as an isometric hexagon

For our project, I made the choice of an isometric view with the tile as a hexagon. An isometric view is really simple to obtain but needs to be understood well. Following are the steps we need to follow:

1. First, view your tile from the top view:

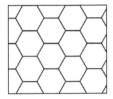

2. Then, rotate it 45 degrees clockwise:

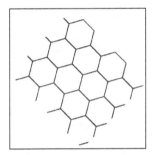

3. Finally, divide its height by 2:

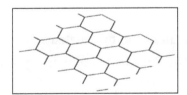

4.  You now have a nice isometric view. Now, let's take a look at the hexagon:

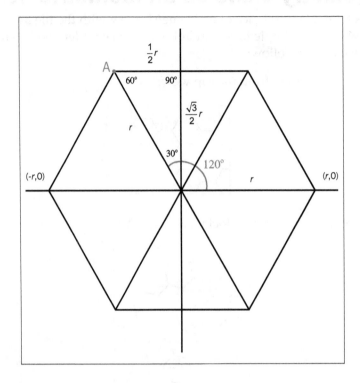

As you know, we need to calculate the coordinates of each of the edges using trigonometry, especially the Pythagoras theorem. This is without taking into account the rotation and the height resize. We need to follow two steps to find the right coordinates:

1.  Calculate the coordinates from the rotated shape (adding 45 degrees).

2.  Divide the total height value by two. By doing this, you will finally be able to build `sf::Shape`:

```
shape.setPointCount(6);
shape.setPoint(0,sf::Vector2f(0,(sin_15+sin_75)/2));
shape.setPoint(1,sf::Vector2f(sin_15,sin_15/2));
shape.setPoint(2,sf::Vector2f(sin_15+sin_75,0));
shape.setPoint(3,sf::Vector2f(sin_15+sin_75+sin_45,sin_45/2
    ));
shape.setPoint(4,sf::Vector2f(sin_75+sin_45,(sin_75+sin_45)
    /2));
shape.setPoint(5,sf::Vector2f(sin_45,(sin_15+sin_75+sin_45)
    /2));
shape.setOrigin(height/2,height/4);
```

3.  The major part of the GEOMETRY class has been made. What remains is only a conversion from world to pixel coordinates, and the reverse. If you are interested in doing this, take a look at the class implementation in the `SFML-utils/src/SFML-utils/map/HexaIso.cpp` file.

Now that the main geometry has been defined, let's construct a `Tile<GEOMETRY>` class on it. This class will simply encapsulate `sf::Shape` , which is initialized by the geometry, and with the different requirements to be able to be use a COMPONENT parameter for the map. As this class is not very important, I will not explain it through this book, but you can take a look at its implementation in the `SFML-utils/include/SFML-utils/map/Tile.tpl` file.

# VLayer and Layer classes

The aim of a layer is to manage any number of components at the same depth. To do this, each layer contains its depth and a container of components. It also has the ability to resort the container to respect the painter algorithm. The `VLayer` class is an interface that only defines the API of the layer, allowing the map to store any kind of layer, thanks to polymorphism.

Here is the header of the `Layer` class:

```cpp
template<typename CONTENT>
class Layer : public VLayer
{
  public:
  Layer(const Layer&) = delete;
  Layer& operator=(const Layer&) = delete;
  Layer(const std::string& type,int z=0,bool isStatic=false);
  virtual ~Layer(){};

  CONTENT* add(const CONTENT& content,bool resort=true);
  std::list<CONTENT*> getByCoords(const sf::Vector2i& coords,const
    VMap& map);
  bool remove(const CONTENT* content_ptr,bool resort=true);
  virtual void sort() override;

  private:
  virtual void draw(sf::RenderTarget& target, sf::RenderStates
    states,const sf::FloatRect& viewport) override;
  std::list<CONTENT> _content;
};
```

As mentioned previously, this class will not only store a container of its `template` class argument, but also its depth (z) and an is static Boolean member contained in the `Vlayer` class to optimize the display. The idea under this argument is that if the content within the layer doesn't move at all, it doesn't need to repaint the scene each time. The result is stored in an internal `sf::RenderTexture` parameter and will be refreshed only when the scene moves. For example, the ground never moves nor is it animated. So we can display it on a big texture and display this texture on the screen. This texture will be refreshed when the view is moved/resized.

To take this idea further, we only need to display content that appears on the screen. We don't need do draw something out of the screen. That's why we have the `viewport` attribute of the `draw()` method.

All other functions manage the  content of the layer. Now, take a look at its implementation:

```
template<typename CONTENT>
Layer<CONTENT>::Layer(const std::string& type,int z,bool isStatic)
  : Vlayer(type,z,isStatic) {}

template<typename CONTENT>
CONTENT* Layer<CONTENT>::add(const CONTENT& content,bool resort)
{
  _content.emplace_back(content);
  CONTENT* res = &_content.back();
  if(resort)
      sort();
  return res;
}
```

This function adds new content to the layer, sort it if requested, and finally, return a reference to the new object:

```
template<typename CONTENT>
std::list<CONTENT*> Layer<CONTENT>::getByCoords(const sf::Vector2i&
coords,const VMap& map)
{
  std::list<CONTENT*> res;
  const auto end = _content.end();
  for(auto it = _content.begin();it != end;++it)
  {
    auto pos = it->getPosition();
    sf::Vector2i c = map.mapPixelToCoords(pos.x,pos.y);
    if(c == coords)
        res.emplace_back(&(*it));
```

```
      }
      return res;
}
```

This function returns all the different objects to the same place. This is useful to pick up objects, for example, to pick objects under the cursor:

```
template<typename CONTENT>
bool Layer<CONTENT>::remove(const CONTENT* content_ptr,bool resort)
{
  auto it =
    std::find_if(_content.begin(),_content.end(),
      [content_ptr](const CONTENT& content)->bool
  {
    return &content == content_ptr;
  });
  if(it != _content.end()) {
    _content.erase(it);
    if(resort)
    sort();
    return true;
  }
  return false;
}
```

This is the reverse function of `add()`. Using its address, it removes a component from the container:

```
template<typename CONTENT>
void Layer<CONTENT>::sort()
{
  _content.sort([](const CONTENT& a,const CONTENT& b)->bool{
    auto pos_a = a.getPosition();
    auto pos_b = b.getPosition();
    return (pos_a.y < pos_b.y) or (pos_a.y == pos_b.y and pos_a.x
      < pos_b.x);
    });
  }
}
```

This function sorts all the content with respect to the painter algorithm order:

```
template<typename CONTENT>
void Layer<CONTENT>::draw(sf::RenderTarget& target, sf::RenderStates
states,const sf::FloatRect& viewport)
```

```
{
  if(_isStatic)
  {//a static layer
    if(_lastViewport != viewport)
    { //the view has change
      sf::Vector2u size(viewport.width+0.5,viewport.height+0.5);
      if(_renderTexture.getSize() != size)
      {//the zoom has change
        _renderTexture.create(size.x,size.y);
        _sprite.setTexture(_renderTexture.getTexture(),true);
      }
      _renderTexture.setView(sf::View(viewport));
      _renderTexture.clear();

      auto end = _content.end();
      for(auto it = _content.begin();it != end;++it)
      {//loop on content
      CONTENT& content = *it;
      auto pos = content.getPosition();
      if(viewport.contains(pos.x,pos.y))
      {//content is visible on screen, so draw it
        _renderTexture.draw(content);
      }
      }
    }
    _renderTexture.display();
    _lastViewport = viewport;
    _sprite.setPosition(viewport.left,viewport.top);
  }
  target.draw(_sprite,states);
}
else
{ //dynamic layer
  auto end = _content.end();
  for(auto it = _content.begin();it != end;++it)
  {//loop on content
    const CONTENT& content = *it;
    auto pos = content.getPosition();
    if(viewport.contains(pos.x,pos.y))
    {//content is visible on screen, so draw it
      target.draw(content,states);
    }
  }
}
```

This function is much more complicated than what we expect because of some optimizations. Let's explain it step by step:

- First, we separate two cases. In the case of a static map we do as follows:
    - Check if the view port has changed
    - Resize the internal texture if needed
    - Reset the textures
- Draw each object with a position inside the view port into the `textureDisplay` the texture for the `RenderTarget` argument.
- Draw each object with a position inside the view port into the `RenderTarget` argument if the layer contains dynamic objects (not static).

As you can see, the `draw()` function uses a naive algorithm in the case of dynamic content and optimizes the statics. To give you an idea of the benefits, with a layer of 10000 objects, the FPS was approximately 20. With position optimization, it reaches 400, and with static optimization, 2,000. So, I think the complexity of this function is justified by the enormous performance benefits.

Now that the `layer` class has been exposed to you, let's continue with the `map` class.

# VMap and Map classes

A map is a container of `VLayer`. It will implement the usual `add()`/`remove()` functions. This class can also be constructed from a file (described in the *Dynamic board loading* section) and handle unit conversion (coordinate to pixel and vice versa).

Internally, a `VMap` class store has the following layers:

```
std::vector<VLayer*> _layers;
```

There are only two interesting functions in this class. The others are simply shortcuts, so I will not explain the entire class. Let us see the concerned functions:

```
void VMap::sortLayers()
{
  std::sort(_layers.begin(),_layers.end(),[](const VLayer* a,
    const VLayer* b)->bool{
    return a->z() < b->z();
  });
  const size_t size = _layers.size();
  for(size_t i=0;i<size;++i)
    _layers[i]->sort();
}
```

This function sorts the different layers by their z buffer with respect to the Painter's Algorithm. In fact, this function is simple but very important. We need to call it each time a layer is added to the map.

```
void VMap::draw(sf::RenderTarget& target, sf::RenderStates
states,const sf::FloatRect& viewport) const
{
  sf::FloatRect delta_viewport(viewport.left - _tile_size,
  viewport.top - _tile_size,
  viewport.width + _tile_size*2,
  viewport.height + _tile_size*2);
  const size_t size = _layers.size();
  for(size_t i=0;i<size;++i)
    _layers[i]->draw(target,states,delta_viewport);
}
```

The function draws each layer by calling its draw method; but first, we adjust the screen view port by adding a little delta on each of its borders. This is done to display all the tiles that appear on the screen, even partially (when its position is out on the screen).

# Dynamic board loading

Now that the map structure is done, we need a way to load it. For this, I've chosen the JSON format. There are two reasons for this choice:

- It can be read by humans
- The format is not verbose, so the final file is quite small even for big map

We will need some information to construct a map. This includes the following:

- The map's geometry
- The size of each tile (cell)
- Define the layers as per the following:
    - The z buffer
    - If it is static or dynamic
    - The content type

Depending on the content type of the layer, some other information to build this content could be specified. Most often, this extra information could be as follows:

- Texture
- Coordinates
- Size

So, the JSON file will look as follows:

```
{
  "geometry" : {
    "name" :"HexaIso", "size" : 50.0
  },
  "layers" : [{
    "content" : "tile", "z" : 1, "static" : true,
    "data" : [{"img" :"media/img/ground.png", "x" : 0, "y" : 0,
      "width" : 100, "height" : 100}]
  },{
    "content" : "sprite", "z" : 3,
    "data" : [
    {"x" : 44, "y" : 49, "img" : "media/img/tree/bush4.png"},
    {"x" : 7, "y" : 91, "img" : "media/img/tree/tree3.png"},
    {"x" : 65, "y" : 58, "img" : "media/img/tree/tree1.png"}
    ]
  }]
}
```

As you can see, the different datasets are present to create a map with the isometric hexagon geometry with two layers. The first layer contains the grid with the ground texture and the second one contains some sprite for decoration.

To use this file, we need a JSON parser. You can use any existing one, build yours, or take the one built with this project. Next, we need a way to create an entire map from a file or update its content from a file. In the second case, the geometry will be ignored because we can't change the value of a template at runtime.

So, we will add a static method to the VMap class to create a new Map, and add another method to update its content. The signature will be as follows:

```
static VMap* createMapFromFile(const std::string& filename);
virtual void loadFromJson(const utils::json::Object& root) = 0;
```

The `loadFromJson()` function has to be virtual and implemented in the `Map` class because of the `GEOMETRY` parameter required by the `Tile` class. The `createMapFromFile()` function will be used internationally. Let's see its implementation:

```
VMap* VMap::createMapFromFile(const std::string& filename)
{
  VMap* res = nullptr;
  utils::json::Value* value =
    utils::json::Driver::parse_file(filename);
  if(value)
  {
    utils::json::Object& root = *value;
    utils::json::Object& geometry = root["geometry"];
    std::string geometry_name = geometry["name"].as_string();
    float size = geometry["size"].as_float();
    if(geometry_name == "HexaIso")
    {
      res = new Map<geometry::HexaIso>(size);
      res->loadFromJson(root);
    }
    delete value;
  }
  return res;
}
```

The goal of this function is pretty simple; construct the appropriate map depending on the geometry parameter and forward it the rest of the job.

```
void Map<GEOMETRY>::loadFromJson(const utils::json::Object& root)
{
    const utils::json::Array& layers = root["layers"];
    for(const utils::json::Value& value : layers) //loop through the
rs
    {
        const utils::json::Object& layer = value;
        std::string content = layer["content"].as_string(); //get the
content type

        int z = 0; //default value
        try{
            z = layer["z"].as_int(); //load value
        } catch(...){}

        bool isStatic = false; //default value
```

```
        try {
            isStatic = layer["static"].as_bool(); //load value
        }catch(...){}

        if(content == "tile") //is a layer or tile?
        {
            auto current_layer = new Layer<Tile<GEOMETRY>>(content,z,i
sStatic); //create the layer
            const utils::json::Array& textures = layer["data"];
            for(const utils::json::Object& texture : textures) //loop
through the textures
            {
                int tex_x = texture["x"]; //get the tile position
                int tex_y = texture["y"];
                int height = std::max<int>(0,texture["height"].as_
int()); //get the square size
                int width = std::max<int>(0,texture["width"].as_
int());

                std::string img = texture["img"]; //get texture path

                sf::Texture& tex = _textures.getOrLoad(img,img); //
load the texture
                tex.setRepeated(true);

                for(int y=tex_y;y< tex_y + height;++y)//create the
tiles
                {
                    for(int x=tex_x;x<tex_x + width;++x)
                    {
                        Tile<GEOMETRY> tile(x,y,_tileSize);
                        tile.setTexture(&tex);
                        tile.setTextureRect(GEOMETRY::getTextureRect(x
,y,_tileSize));

                        current_layer->add(std::move(tile),false);//
add the new tile to the layer
                    }
                }
            }
            add(current_layer,false);//if it's a layer of images
        }
        else if(content == "sprite")
        {
            auto current_layer = new Layer<sf::Sprite>(content,z,isSta
tic);//create the layer
```

```
                    const utils::json::Array& data = layer["data"].as_
array();//loop on data

                for(const utils::json::Value& value : data)
                {
                    const utils::json::Object& obj = value;
                    int x = obj["x"];//get the position
                    int y = obj["y"];
                    float ox = 0.5;//default center value (bottom center)
                    float oy = 1;

                    try{//get value
                        ox = obj["ox"].as_float();
                    }catch(...){}

                    try{
                        oy = obj["oy"].as_float();
                    }catch(...){}

                    std::string img = obj["img"];//get texture path

                    sf::Sprite spr(_textures.getOrLoad(img,img));//load
texture
                    spr.setPosition(GEOMETRY::mapCoordsToPixel(x,y,_
tileSize));

                    sf::FloatRect rec = spr.getLocalBounds();
                    spr.setOrigin(rec.width*ox,rec.height*oy);

                    current_layer->add(std::move(spr),false);//add the
sprite

                }
                add(current_layer,false); //add the new layer to the map
            }
        }
    sortLayers(); //finally sort the layers (recuively)
}
```

For a better understanding, the previous function was explained with raw comments. It's aimed at building layers and filling them with the data picked from the JSON file.

Now that we are able to build a map and fill it from a file, the last thing we need to do is display it on the screen. This will be done with the MapViewer class.

# The MapViewer class

This class encapsulates a `Map` class and manages some events such as mouse movement, moving the view, zoom, and so on. This is a really simple class with nothing new. This is why I will not go into details about anything but the `draw()` method (because of the view port). If you are interested in the full implementation, take a look at the `SFML-utils/src/SFML-utils/map/MapViewer.cpp` file.

So here is the draw method:

```
void MapViewer::draw(sf::RenderTarget& target, sf::RenderStates
states) const
{
  sf::View view = target.getView();
  target.setView(_view);
  _map.draw(target,states,sf::FloatRect
  (target.mapPixelToCoords(sf::
    Vector2i(0,0),_view),_view.getSize()));
  target.setView(view);
}
```

As usual, we receive `sf::RenderTarget` and `sf::RenderStates` as parameters. However, here we don't want to interact with the current view of the target, so we make a backup of it and attach our local view to the rendered target. Then, we call the draw method of the internal map, forwarding the target, and states but adding the view port. This parameter is very important because it's used by our layers for optimization. So, we need to build a view port with the size of the rendered target, and thanks to SFML, it's very simple. We convert the top-left coordinate to the world coordinate, relative to our view. The result is in the top-left coordinate of the displayed area. Now, we only need the size. Here again, SFML provides use all the need: `sf::View::getSize()`. With this information, we are now able to build the correct view port and pass it to the map `draw()` function.

Once the rendering is complete, we restore the initial view back to the rendered target.

# A usage example

We now have all the requirements to load and display a map to the screen. The following code snippet shows you the minimal steps:

```
int main(int argc,char* argv[])
{
  sf::RenderWindow window(sf::VideoMode(1600,900),"Example Tile");
  sfutils::VMap* map =
    sfutils::VMap::createMapFromFile("./map.json");
  sfutils::MapViewer viewer(window, *map);
```

```
sf::Clock clock;
while (window.isOpen())
{
    sf::Event event;
    while (window.pollEvent(event))
    {
        if (event.type == sf::Event::Closed)    // Close window :
            exit
        window.close();
    }
    window.clear();
    viewer.processEvents();
    viewer.update(clock.restart().asSeconds());
    viewer.draw();
    window.display();
}
return 0;
}
```

The different steps of this function are as follows:

1. Creating a window
2. Creating a map from a file
3. Process the events and quit if requests
4. Update the viewer
5. Display the viewer on the screen

The result will be as follows:

Now that the map is done, we need to fill it with some entities.

# Building an entity system

First of all, what is an entity system?

An **entity system** is a design pattern that focuses on data. Instead of creating a complex hierarchical tree of all possible entities, the idea is to build a system that allows us to add components to an entity at runtime. These components could be anything such as health points, artificial intelligence, skin, weapon, and everything but data.

However, if none of the entities and components hold functionalities, where are they stored? The answer is in the systems. Each system manages at least one component, and all the logic is inside these systems. Moreover, it is not possible to build an entity directly. You have to create or update it using an entity manager. It will be in charge of a set of entities, managing their components, creation, and destruction.

The structure is represented by the following chart:

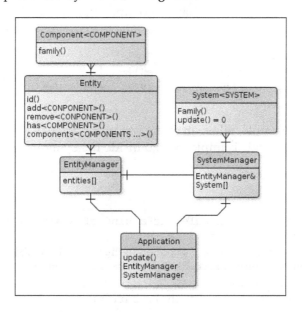

There are many ways to implement such a structure. My choice was to use template and polymorphism.

# Use of the entity system

Without going much into the internal structure, we create a new component with this system as a structure, with no method except a constructor/destructor, and inherit from Component as follows:

```
struct CompHp : Component<CompHp>
{
  explicit Hp(int hp) : _hp(hp){};
  int _hp;
};
```

The inheritance is important to have a common base class between all the components. The same idea is used to create System:

```
struct SysHp : sfutils::System<SysHp>
{
  virtual void update(sfutils::EntityManager& manager, const
    sf::Time& dt) override;
};
```

The reason for the inheritance is to have a common parent and API (the update function). Finally, to create an entity, you will have to do the following:

```
EntityManager entities;
std::uint32_t id = entities.create();
entities.addComponent<CompHp>(id,42); //the first argument is
  always the entity id
```

If we continue this example, when an entity has no hp, we have to remove it from the board. This part of the logic is implemented inside the SysHp::update() function:

```
void SysHp::update(sfutils::EntityManager& manager, const sf::Time&
  dt)
{
  CompHp::Handle hp; //Handler is a kind of smart pointer which
    ensure access to valid data
  auto view = manager.getByComponents(hp); //this object is a
    filter on all our entities by there components
  auto end = view.end();
  for(auto current = view.begin(); current != end;++current)
  {
    if(hp->_hp <= 0)
    manager.remove(current->id());
  }
}
```

This SysHp::update() function is used to create a specific functionality. Its aim is to remove all the entities with hp under or equal to zero. To do this, we initialize ComponentHandler<CompHp> using the CompHp::Handle shortcut (defined in the Component class). Then we create our query on the world. In our case, we need to get all the entities with CompHp attached to them. The multiple criteria query is also possible for more complex systems.

Once we have our view, we iterate on it. Each iteration gives us access to Entity and updates the handler values to the entity components. So, creating access to the hp handler is equivalent to the following:

```
manager.getComponent<CompHp>(current->id())
```

Then, we check the _hp value and remove the entity if needed.

It's important to note that the entity will actually be removed only when the EntityManager::update() function is called to keep data consistent inside the system loops.

Now that the SysHp parameter has been completed, we need to register it to SystemManager that is linked to EntityManager:

```
EntityManager entities;
SystemManager systems(entities);
systems.add<SysHp>();
```

We have now built an entity manager, a component, a system, and an entity. Putting them all together will result in the following code:

```
int main()
{
  EntityManager entities;
  SystemManager systems(entities);
  systems.add<SysHp>();

  for(int i =0; i<10; ++i)
  {//create entities
    std::uint32_t id = entities.create();
    entities.addComponent<CompHp>(id,i*10);
  }
  sf::Clock clock;
  while(/* some criterion*/)
  {//game loop
    systems.updateAll(clock.restart());
    entities.update();
  }
  return 0;
}
```

This little code will create an entity and system manager. Then, we create 10 entities and add them to the `CompHp` component. Finally, we enter the game loop.

As mentioned previously, don't detail the implementation of the entity system; focus on its usage. If you are interested in the implementation, which is a bit complex, take a look at the files in the `SFML-utils/include/SFML-utils/es` directory. This is header only library.

# Advantages of the entity system approach

With a component system, each entity is represented as a single unique integer (its ID). These components are nothing but data. So, this is really simple to create a serialization function that saves the entire world. Database saving is made very simple with this approach but it's not the only point.

To create a flying car with a classic hierarchical tree, you have to inherit it from two different classes, namely car and flying vehicle. Each of these classes could inherit from the other. In fact, when the number of entities become large, the hierarchical tree is too much. For the same example, create an entity with the entity system, attach it to some wheels and wings. That's it! I agree that creating an entity system can be difficult, but its usage simplifies a lot the game's complexity.

# Building the game logic

We now have all the requirements to start our game: resource management, events management, GUI, animations, map, and the entity system. It's time for us to group them into a single project.

First, we need to create our entities. Thanks to the entity system previously described, we only need to build some components and their systems. We can build many of them, but the main components for the project are as follows:

| Components | Entities |
| --- | --- |
| Skin | Animation |
| Health points | Current health |
| | Maximum health |
| Team | Identifier for the team |
| Build area | The authorized range around the entity |
| Movement | Speed |
| | Destination |

| Components | Entities |
|---|---|
| Artificial intelligence for warriors | Delta time |
| | Damage |
| | Length of hit |

The interesting ones are artificial intelligence (to damage) and movement. The others are pretty naive. Of course, you can create your own component in addition/replacement of those proposed.

# Building our components

We know all the data needed by our components, so let's build the two interesting components, namely the `walker` AI and the `warrior` AI:

```
struct CompAIWalker : Component<CompAIWalker>
{
  explicit CompAIWalker(float speed);
  const float _speed;
  sf::Vector2i _pathToTake;
};
```

This component handles the speed and destination. The destination can be updated by anything (for example, when an enemy is detected at proximity):

```
struct CompAIWarrior : Component<CompAIWarrior>
{
  explicit CompAIWarrior(int hitPoint,const sf::Time&
    timeDelta,int range);
  const int _hitPoint;
  const sf::Time _delta;
  sf::Time _elapsed;
  const int _range;
};
```

This component stores the aggressiveness of an entity, with its damaged, attack speed and area of aggressively.

As we will use this component in the system section, I will also explain the `CompSkin` component. This component stores an `AnimatedSkin` and different possible `Animation` that could be applied to it:

```
struct CompSkin : sfutils::Component<CompSkin,Entity>
{
  enum AnimationId : int{ Stand,Spawn, MoveLeft, MoveRight,
    HitLeft, HitRight};
```

```
sfutils::AnimatedSprite _sprite;
std::unordered_map<int,sfutils::Animation*> _animations;
};
```

Now that the components have been built, take a look at the systems.

# Creating the different systems

We need as many systems as the number of components. The skin system simply calls the update function on the animation. We have already built the related system for the health. For the team component, we don't need any system because this component is used only by artificial intelligence. The two systems left are more complex.

Let's start with the movement:

```
struct SysAIWalker : sfutils::System<SysAIWalker,Entity>
{
  explicit SysAIWalker(Level& level);
  virtual void update(sfutils::EntityManager<Entity>&
    manager,const sf::Time& dt) override;
  Level& _level;
};
```

Notice that the `Level` class has not yet been introduced. This class regroups an `EntityManager` and a `SystemManager` classes and gives us access to some functions concerning the map geometry, without having to know it. I will explain it later. In our case, we will need some information about the distance between the actual position of the component and its destination. This is why we need to keep a reference to the level.

Here's the implementation of the walker system:

```
SysAIWalker::SysAIWalker(Level& level) :_level(level) {}
void SysAIWalker::update(EntityManager& manager,const sf::Time&
  dt)
{
  CompAIWalker::Handle AI;
  CompSkin::Handle skin;
  auto view = manager.getByComponents(AI,skin);
  auto end = view.end();
  const float seconds = dt.asSeconds();

  for(auto begin = view.begin();begin != end;++begin)
  {
    sf::Vector2f PosCurrent = skin->_sprite.getPosition();
    sf::Vector2i CoordCurrent =
      _level.mapPixelToCoords(PosCurrent);
```

```
          sf::Vector2i CoordDest = AI->_pathToTake;
          if(CoordDest != CoordCurrent) //need to move
          {
            sf::Vector2f PosDest = _level.mapCoordsToPixel(CoordDest);
            //calculation of the direction to take
            sf::Vector2f directon = PosDest - PosCurrent;
            //calculation of the distance
            const float distance =
              std::sqrt((directon.x*directon.x)+(directon.y*directon.y));
            const float frameDistance = AI->_speed * seconds;
            if(distance > frameDistance)
                skin->_sprite.setPosition(PosCurrent +
              directon*(frameDistance/distance));
            else
            {
              skin->_sprite.setPosition(PosDest);
              AI->_pathToTake = CoordCurrent;
            }

            if(directon.x >0) //update skin direction
                skin->_sprite.setAnimation(skin-
              >_animations.at(CompSkin::MoveRight));
            else
                skin->_sprite.setAnimation(skin-
              >_animations.at(CompSkin::MoveLeft));
          }
        }
      }
```

This system doesn't just move the entity but also makes different things. The position is stored inside the CompSkin component, so we need to iterate on the entities by getting the CompAIWalker and CompSkin components attached to them. Then, we calculate the position of the entity in the world coordinate and check if a move is needed. If we need to move, we calculate the vector corresponding to the total displacement (direction). This vector gives us the direction that the entity needs to follow. Then, we calculate the distance between the end point and the current position. Depending on the speed, we change the current position to the new one.

Once the movement is complete, we also change the current animation to the one matching the movement direction taken by the entity.

Now, let's take an interest in the Warrior AI:

```
SysAIWarrior::SysAIWarrior(Level& level) : _level(level){}
void SysAIWarrior::update(sfutils::EntityManager<Entity>&
  manager,const sf::Time& dt)
```

```cpp
{
    CompAIWarrior::Handle AI;
    CompTeam::Handle team;
    CompSkin::Handle skin;
    auto view = manager.getByComponents(AI,team,skin);
    auto end = view.end();
    for(auto begin = view.begin();begin != end;++begin)
    {
        AI->_elapsed += dt;
        std::vector<Team*> teamEnemies = team->_team->getEnemies();

        //if no enemies
        if(teamEnemies.size() <=0)
            continue;
        std::uint32_t id = std::uint32_t(-1);

        /* ….set id to the nearest enemy ... */

        if(not manager.isValid(id))
            continue;

        //update path
        Entity& enemy = manager.get(id);
        const sf::Vector2f pos = enemy.component<CompSkin>()-
            >_sprite.getPosition();
        const sf::Vector2i coord = _level.mapPixelToCoords(pos);
        const int distance = _level.getDistance(myPosition,coord);
        if(distance <= range) //next me
        {
            //shoot it
            if(AI->_elapsed >= AI->_delta)
            {
                AI->_elapsed = sf::Time::Zero;
                CompHp::Handle hp = enemy.component<CompHp>();
                hp->_hp -= AI->_hitPoint;
                Entity& me = **begin;
                if(enemy.onHitted != nullptr)
                enemy.onHitted(enemy,coord,me,myPosition,_level);
                if(me.onHit != nullptr)
                me.onHit(me,myPosition,enemy,coord,_level);
                //win some gold
                if(hp->_hp <=0){
                    team->_team->addGold(hp->_maxHp/50);
                }
            }

            //no need to move more
            if(begin->has<CompAIWalker>())
            begin->component<CompAIWalker>()->_pathToTake = myPosition;
```

```
        }
        else
        {//too far
            sf::Vector2i path = _level.getPath1(myPosition,coord);
            //move closer
            if(begin->has<CompAIWalker>())
                begin->component<CompAIWalker>()->_pathToTake = path;
        }
    }
}
```

This system requires three components, namely `CompSkin` (for position), `CompTeam` (for detect enemy), and `CompAIWarrior`. The first thing to do is update the delta time. Then, we check if we have some enemies to defeat. Next, we search for an enemy who is closer (I won't detail this part because you can put your own algorithm). If an enemy is found, we check the distance between us and the enemy. If we can shoot the enemy, we do so and reset the delta time to avoid hitting each frame. We also trigger some events (for example, to create sound) and add gold to the team if we just kill the enemy. We also set the destination of the `CompAIWarrior` to the current position (to stay fighting) if we can, or move closer to the next enemy.

We now have all the components and systems to manage them. So, we will continue with the game architecture.

# The level class

As usual, we split the game into several parts. The `level` class represents a map. This class stores all the entities, systems, viewers, maps, sounds, and so on. As previously explained, it also implements an abstraction layer above the map geometry.

In fact, a level is a very simple object; it is just the glue between others. It registers all the systems, constructs the map, initializes a `MapViewer`, events, and regroups all the different update calls into one method. This class also offers users the ability to create new entities, by creating them through the internal `EntityManager`, and adding them to a map layer. The map is always synchronized with the `EntityManager` while doing this.

If you are interested in this implementation, take a look at the `SFML-book/07_2D_iso_game//src/SFML-Book/Level.cpp` file.

# The game class

Now, the `game` class! You should be familiar with this class by now. Its global behavior hasn't changed and still contains the same functionalities (`update()`, `processEvents()`, and `render()`).

The big change here is that the game class will initialize a `Level` and `Team`. One of these will be the one controlled by the player, and the GUI depends on it. This is the reason that the GUI for this project was attached to a team instead of the entire game. I won't say that it's the best way, but it's the simplest and allows us to jump from one team to another.

If you are interested in this implementation, take a look at the `SFML-book/07_2D_iso_game/src/SFML-Book/Game.cpp` file.

## The Team GUI class

This class handles different information and is the interface between the game and the player. It should allow the player to build some entities and interact with them.

The following screen shows you the **Build** menu. This menu shows the player the different entities that can be created and the current gold amount:

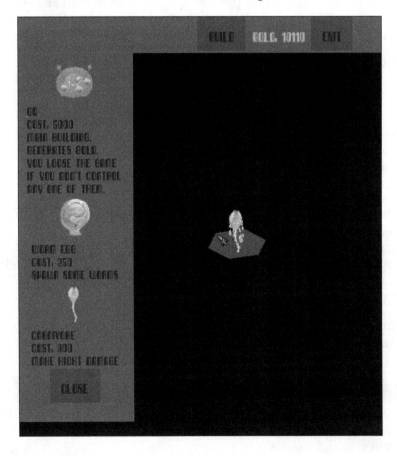

Of course, we can complete this menu a lot, but this is the minimum information required by our game. Using our previously made GUI will facilitate this task a lot.

Once an entity is selected, we just have to place it into the game keeping in mind the following criteria:

- The amount of gold
- The build area

After this, everything will run easily. Don't hesitate to make some helper functions that create different entities by adding some components with specific values.

# Summary

In this chapter, we covered different things, such as creating animations. This class allowed us to display animated characters on screen. Then, we built a `Map` class that was filled with some entities. We also learned how to use an entity system by creating some components and systems to build our game logic. Finally, we put all the accumulated knowledge together to build a complete game with some artificial intelligence, a user interface, sounds, and animations.

With all this knowledge, you are now able to build any kind of game based on a tile system without too much effort.

In the next chapter, we will turn this game in a multiplayer one by using networking.

# 8
# Build a Real-time Tower Defense Game from Scratch – Part 2, Networking

In the previous chapter, we built a complete game from scratch. The only limitation we encountered was that we didn't have real enemies to defeat. We will solve this limitation in the present chapter by adding networking to our game to allow it to interact with players other than you. At the end of this chapter, you will be able to play this game with some friends. This chapter will cover the following topics:

- Network architectures
- Network communication using sockets
- Creating a communication protocol
- Modifying our game by applying the client-server concept
- Saving and loading our game

Now let's dive into this pretty complicated chapter.

## Network architectures

Before constructing our architecture, we need some information about what kind of network architectures are commonly used in a game, and their specificities. There are different types of architectures used in game programming. They greatly depend on the game and the needs of the developer. We will see two common architectures: peer-to-peer (P2P) and client-server. Both of them have their strengths and weaknesses. Let's analyze them individually.

# Peer-to-peer architecture

This architecture was widely used in the past, and is still used today. In this architecture, players know the addresses of each other and directly communicate with each other without any intermediary. For example, for a game with four different players, the network can be represented as the following chart:

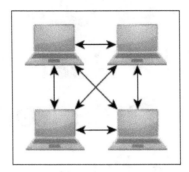

This organization allows a player to directly interact with any or all of the other players. When a client does something, it notifies the others of this action, and they update the simulation (game) consequently.

This approach is efficient for communications, but comes with some limitations that can't be ignored. The main one is that there is no way to avoid cheating. A client can do whatever it wants by notifying the other of that action, even if it's impossible, such as teleporting itself by sending an arbitrary position. A possible result is that the fun of the game is completely destroyed for the other players.

To avoid this kind of cheating, we have to change the architecture to be able to have a kind of referee that can decide if an action is legal.

# Client-server architecture

In game programming, avoiding cheating is very important, because it can completely destroy the experience of the game for the player. To be able to reduce the possibility of cheating, the architecture used can help. With client-server architecture, a game can detect the major part of these exploits. This is one reason that justifies the importance of this part. One other point is that this is the architecture that will be used for our game. Instead of having the players communicating between each other, they will only communicate with a single host called the server. Because all other players will also do the same, we will be able to communicate with them, but with an intermediary.

Moreover, this intermediary will act as a judge that will decide if an action is legal. Instead of having a full simulation on all the different players' computers, the real simulation is made by the server. It holds the real game states that have to be taken into account; the client is just a kind of display that we can interact with. The following chart represents the architecture:

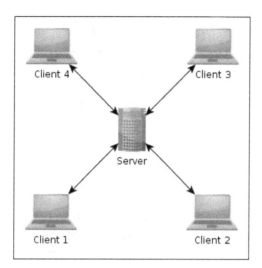

As you can see, we now need to pass through the server to propagate any kind of actions to the other players.

Its main drawback is that the server has to be reactive for all the players (clients), and if your game has a great number of players, this can become hard. Splitting the tasks on different threads is very important to ensure the reactivity of the server.

Some games require so many resources that it can't handle only a limited amount of players, the result is that you have to manage multiple server for one game; for instance, one for logging, another for chatting, another one for a specific area of the map, and so on. We will now see how to use this architecture for our game.

When creating a multiplayer architecture, the first thing to have in mind is that we will have to split our game in two distinct programs: a client and a server. We will have one server hosting several game instances and any number of clients, possibly on different matches.

To be able to have this kind of result, let's first think about what is needed by each part.

# Client

Each player must start a client program to be able to start a match. This program will have to do the following:

- Display the game state
- Handle the different user inputs
- Play effects (sounds, bloodshed, and so on)
- Update its game status according to the information received from the server
- Send requests to the server (build, destroy)

These different features are already present in our actual game, so we will need to adapt them; but there are also some new features:

- Request the creation of a new match
- Request to join a match

Here I use the word *request* because that's what it really is. As a player will not handle the game in totality, it can only send requests to the server to take action. The server will then judge them and react as a consequence. Now let's take a look at the server.

# Server

On the other hand, the server will need to be launched only once, and will have to manage the following functionalities:

- Store all the different matches
- Process each game's steps
- Send updates of the game to players
- Handle player requests

But a server also has to take care of the following:

- Managing connection/disconnection
- Game creation
- Adding a player as a controller for a team

As you can see, there is no need for any kind of display, so the server output will be in console only. It will also have to judge all the different requests coming from the client. In a distributed environment, also true for web development, remember this rule: *don't trust user inputs.*

If you keep this in mind, it will save you a lot of trouble and a lot of time in debugging. Some users, even if it's a very small number of users, can send you random data such as cheats or anything else that you're not supposed to receive. So don't take the inputs at face value.

Now that the functionalities have been exposed, we need a way to communicate between a client and the server. This is the topic that we will now speak about.

# Network communication using sockets

To be able to interact with other players, we will need a way to communicate with them, regardless of the architecture used. To be able to communicate with any computer, we have to use sockets. In short, a socket enables communication with other processes/computers through the network as long as there is an existing way between both sides (LAN or Internet). There are two main kinds of sockets: non-connected (UDP) or connected (TCP). Both these need an IP address and a port number to communicate with their destination.

Notice that the number of available ports on a computer is contained between 0 and 65535. A piece of advice is to avoid the use of ports with a number lesser than 1024. The reason is that most of them are reserved by the system or used by common applications, such as 80 for a web browser, 21 for FTP, and so on. You also have to ensure that both sides of the communication use the same port number to be able to exchange data. Let's now see in detail the two kinds of socket previously introduced.

# UDP

As already said, **User Datagram Protocol (UDP)** is a way of sending data through the network without connections. We can visualize the communication achieved by this protocol, such as sending letters. Each time you want to send a message to someone, you have to specify the destination address (IP and port). The message can then be sent, but you don't know if it really arrives at its destination. This kind of communication is really quick, but comes with some limitations:

- You don't even know if the message has arrived at its destination
- A message can be lost
- A big message will be split in smaller messages
- Messages can be received in a different order than the original order
- A message can be duplicated

Because of these limitations, the messages can't be exploited as soon as they are received. There is a need for verification. A simple way to resolve a majority of these troubles is to add to your data a small header containing a unique message identifier. This identifier will allow us to identify precisely a message, remove possible duplication, and treat each in the correct order. You can also ensure that your message is not too big to avoid splitting and losing a part of the data.

SFML provides us the `sf::UdpSocket` class to communicate using the UDP protocol. This chapter will not cover this kind of socket, but if you are interested in it, take a look at the SFML tutorial on the official website (`www.sfml-dev.org`).

# TCP

**Transmission Control Protocol** (TCP) is a connected protocol. This can be compared to a phone conversation. There are some steps to follow to understand this protocol:

- Ask for a connection to an address (phone is ringing)
- Accept the connection (pick up the phone)
- Exchange data (talk)
- Stop the conversation (hang up)

As the protocol is connected, it ensures that the data arrived at the destination is in the same ordering, structure, and consistency as at its source. By the way, we need to specify the destination address only once during the connection. Moreover, if the connection breaks (the problem is on the other side, for example), we can detect it as soon as it happens. The downside of this protocol is that the communication speed is reduced.

SFML provides us the `sf::TcpSocket` class to deal with the TCP protocol easily. This is the one that we will use in our project. I will discuss its usage in the next section.

# Selector

SFML provides us with another utility class: `sf::SocketSelector`. This class works like an observer on any kind of socket and holds a pointer to managed sockets, as explained in the following steps:

1. Use the `sf::SocketSelector::add(sf::Socket)` method to add a socket to observe.

2. Then, when one or more of the observed sockets receive data, the `sf::SocketSelector::wait()` function return. Finally, using `sf::Socket Selector::isReady(sf::Socket)`, we can identify which one of the sockets received data. This allows us to avoid pooling and use real-time reaction.

We will use this class in this chapter paired with `sf::TcpSocket`.

# The Connection class

Now that all the basic network bricks have been introduced, it's time for us to think about our game. We need to decide the way in which our game will exchange data with another player. We will need to send and receive data. To achieve this, we will use the `sf::TcpSocket` class. As each action on the socket will block the execution of our game, we will need to create a system to disable the blocking. SFML provides a `sf::Socket::setBlocking()` function, but our solution will use a different method.

# The goal of the Connection class

If you remember, in *Chapter 6, Boost Your Code Using Multithreading*, I told you that networking is mostly managed in a dedicated thread. Our solution will follow this path; the idea is to have an object that internally manages a thread as transparently as possible to the user. Moreover, we will design the API to be similar to SFML event management from the `sf::Window` class. The result of these constraints is the construction of a `Connection` class. This class will then be specialized by the architecture that we will choose (described in the next section).

Let's now take a look at the header of this new class:

```
class Connection
{
  public:
  Connection();
  virtual ~Connection();

  void run();
  void stop();
  void wait();

  bool pollEvent(sf::Packet& event);
  bool pollEvent(packet::NetworkEvent*& event);

  void send(sf::Packet& packet);
  void disconnect();
  int id()const;
```

```
    virtual sf::IpAddress getRemoteAddress()const = 0;

    protected:
    sf::TcpSocket _sockIn;
    sf::TcpSocket _sockOut;

    private:
    bool _isRunning;

    void _receive();
    sf::Thread _receiveThread;
    sf::Mutex _receiveMutex;
    std::queue<sf::Packet> _incoming;

    void _send();
    sf::Thread _sendThread;
    sf::Mutex _sendMutex;
    std::queue<sf::Packet> _outgoing;

    static int _numberOfCreations;
    const int _id;
};
```

Let's explain this class step by step:

1.  We start by defining a constructor and a destructor. Notice that the destructor is set to virtual because the class will be specialized.

2.  Then we define some common functions to deal with the internal thread for synchronization issues.

3.  Some methods to deal with events are then defined. We build two methods to deal with incoming events and one to deal with outgoing messages. The overload on the `pollEvent()` function allows us to use raw or parsed data. The `packet::NetworkEvent` class will be described later in this chapter. For now, take it as a message similar to `sf::Event` with type and data, but coming from the network.

4.  We define a function to close the communication properly.

5.  Finally, we define some functions to get information on the connection.

To be able to work, all these functions require some objects. Moreover, to be as responsive as possible, we will use two sockets: one for incoming messages and the other for outgoing messages. This will allow us to send and receive data at the same time and accelerate the responsiveness of the game. Because of this choice, we will need to duplicate all the other requirements (thread, mutex, queue, and so on). Let's discuss the goal of each one:

- `sf::TcpSocket`: It handles the communication between the two sides.

- `sf::Thread`: It allows us to be non-blocking as previously exposed. It will remain alive as long as the connection instance.

- `sf::Mutex`: It protects the queue of data to avoid data race or use them afterwards for free.

- `std::queue<sf::Packet>`: This is the queue of events to processes. Each time it is accessed, the associated mutex is locked.

Now that the different objects have been explained, we can continue with the implementation of the class, as follows:

```
Connection::Connection() :_isRunning(false),
  _receiveThread(&Connection::_receive,this),
  _sendThread(&Connection::_send,this),_id(++_numberOfCreations)
      {}
Connection::~Connection() {}
```

The constructor doesn't have any function in particular. It simply initializes with the correct value without launching a different thread. We have a function for that, which is as follows:

```
void Connection::run()
{
  _isRunning = true;
  _receiveThread.launch();
  _sendThread.launch();
}

void Connection::stop() {_isRunning  = false;}

void Connection::wait()
{
  _receiveThread.wait();
  _sendThread.wait();
}
```

These three functions manage the lifetime of the different threads by launching, stopping, or keeping them waiting. Notice that a mutex to protect _isRunning is not necessary because we don't write in it outside of those functions.

```
int Connection::id()const {return _id;}

bool Connection::pollEvent(sf::Packet& event)
{
  bool res = false;
```

```
    sf::Lock guard(_receiveMutex);
    if(_incoming.size() > 0)
    {
      std::swap(event,_incoming.front());
      _incoming.pop();
      res = true;
    }
    return res;
}

bool Connection::pollEvent(packet::NetworkEvent*& event)
{
  bool res = false;
  sf::Packet msg;
  if(Connection::pollEvent(msg))
  {
    event = packet::NetworkEvent::makeFromPacket(msg);
    if(event != nullptr)
      res = true;
  }
  return res;
}
```

These two functions are important and copy the behavior of the
`sf::Window::pollEvent()` function, so their usage will not surprise you. What we
do here is that we pick up an event from the incoming queue if there is one enabled.
The second function also parses the receiving message to a `NetworkEvent` function.
Most often, we will prefer to use the second method in our code, because all the
verifications are already made to be able to exploit the event. This function just adds
a packet to the outgoing queue. The job is then done by the `_sendThread` object, as
shown in the following code snippet:

```
void Connection::send(sf::Packet& packet)
{
  sf::Lock guard(_sendMutex);
  _outgoing.emplace(packet);
}
```

This function closes the different sockets used. Because we used a connected
protocol, the other side of the communication will be able to detect it and manage
this at its convenience.

```
void Connection::disconnect()
{
  _sockIn.disconnect();
  _sockOut.disconnect();
}
```

This function is one of the two most important ones. It is run into its own thread — this is the reason for the loop. Moreover, we use the `sf::SocketSelector` function to observe our socket. Using this, we avoid useless operations that consume CPU power. Instead, we lock the thread until a message is received on the incoming socket. We also add a timeout of one second to avoid a deadlock, as seen in the following code snippet:

```cpp
void Connection::_receive()
{
  sf::SocketSelector selector;
  selector.add(_sockIn);
  while(_isRunning)
  {
if(not selector.wait(sf::seconds(1)))
  continue;
if(not selector.isReady(_sockIn))
  continue;
    sf::Packet packet;
    sf::Socket::Status status = _sockIn.receive(packet);
    if(status == sf::Socket::Done)
    {
      sf::Lock guard(_receiveMutex);
      _incoming.emplace(std::move(packet));
    }
    else if (status == sf::Socket::Disconnected)
    {
      packet.clear();
      packet<<packet::Disconnected();
      sf::Lock guard(_receiveMutex);
      _incoming.emplace(std::move(packet));
      stop();
    }
  }
}
```

A deadlock is a situation encountered in multithreaded programs where two threads wait indefinitely because they are both waiting for a resource that only the other thread can free up. The most common is a double lock on the same mutex in the same thread, with a recursive call, for example. In the present case, imagine that you use the `stop()` function. The thread is not aware of this change, and will still be waiting for data, maybe forever, because no new data will be received on the socket. An easy solution is to add a timeout to not wait forever, but only a small amount of time that allows us to recheck the loop condition and get out if necessary.

Once a packet is received, or a disconnection is detected, we add the corresponding packet to the queue. The user will then be able to pool in from its own thread and treat it as he wants. The disconnection shows you a specific `NetworkEvent : Disconnected` function. Later in the chapter, I will explain in detail the logic behind this.

```
void Connection::_send()
{
  while(_isRunning)
  {
    _sendMutex.lock();
    if(_outgoing.size() > 0)
    {
      sf::Packet packet = _outgoing.front();
      _outgoing.pop();
      _sendMutex.unlock();
      _sockOut.send(packet);
    }
    else
    {
      _sendMutex.unlock();
    }
  }
}
```

This function complements the previous one. It picks up events from the outgoing queue and sends it through the network using its socket.

As you can see, with the use of classes, we can send and receive data very easily in a multi-threaded environment. Moreover, the disconnection is managed like any other event and doesn't require any special case for the user. Another strength of this class is that it's very generic and can be used in a lot of cases, including on client and server sides.

To sum it up, we can visualize the usage of this class as shown in the following chart:

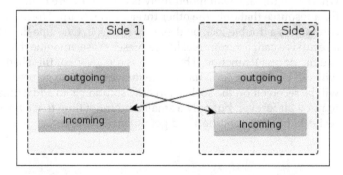

Now that we have designed a class to manage the different messages, let's build our custom protocol.

# Creating a communication protocol

It's now time for us to create our own custom protocol. We will use an SFML class `sf::Packet` to transport our data, but we have to define their shapes. Let's first focus on the `sf::Packet` class and then on the shapes.

## Using the sf::Packet class

The `sf::Packet` class is like a buffer that contains our data. It comes with already-made functions that allow us to serialize primitive types. I don't know if you are familiar with the internal memory storage of computers, but keep in mind that the arrangement is not the same everywhere. This is called endianness. You can see it like reading from the right or from the left. When you send data over the network, you don't know the endianness of the destination. Because of this, the convention is to send data as a big-endian arrangement over the network. I suggest you to take a look at the Wikipedia page (`https://en.wikipedia.org/wiki/Endianness`) for more details.

Thanks to SFML, there are some pre-existing functions that make the job easy for us. The only inconvenience is that we have to use SFML types instead of the primitive types. Following is a table that shows you the primitive types, and the corresponding type to use with `sf::Packet`:

| Primitive | SFML overload |
|---|---|
| char | sf::Int8 |
| unsigned char | sf::Uint8 |
| short int | sf::Int16 |
| unsigned short int | sf::Uint16 |
| Int | sf::int32 |
| unsigned int | sf::Uint32 |
| float | float |
| double | double |
| char* | char* |
| std::string | std:string |
| bool | bool |

The `sf::Packet` class is used like the standard c++ I/O streams using the `>>` and `<<` operators to extract and insert data. Following is an example taken directly from the SFML documentation of the `sf::Packet` class that shows you how simple it is in terms of usage:

```cpp
void sendDatas(sf::Socket& socket)
{
    sf::Uint32 x = 24;
    std::string s = "hello";
    double d = 5.89;
    // Group the variables to send into a packet
    sf::Packet packet;
    packet << x << s << d;
    // Send it over the network (socket is a valid sf::TcpSocket)
    socket.send(packet);
}

void receiveDatas(sf::Socket& socket)
{
    sf::Packet packet;
    socket.receive(packet);
    // Extract the variables contained in the packet
    sf::Uint32 x;
    std::string s;
    double d;
    if (packet >> x >> s >> d)
    {
        // Data extracted successfully...
    }
}
```

Even if this use is pretty simple, there is another way to send data like structure/class more easily, using the operator overload. This is the technique that we will use to send/receive data, an example of which is as follows:

```cpp
struct MyStruct
{
    float number;
    sf::Int8 integer;
    std::string str;
};

sf::Packet& operator <<(sf::Packet& packet, const MyStruct& m){
    return packet << m.number << m.integer << m.str;
}
```

```cpp
sf::Packet& operator >>(sf::Packet& packet, MyStruct& m){
  return packet >> m.number >> m.integer >> m.str;
}

int main()
{
  MyStruct toSend;
  toSend.number = 18.45f;
  toSend.integer = 42;
  toSend.str = "Hello world!";

  sf::Packet packet;
  packet << toSend;

  // create a socket

  socket.send(packet);
  //...
}
```

With this technique, there are two operators to overload, and the serialization/ unserialization is then transparent for the user. Moreover, if the structure changes, there is only one place to update: the operators.

Now that we have seen the system to transport our data, let's think about a way to construct it so that it is as generic as possible.

# RPC-like protocol

We now need to think exactly about our needs concerning the data to send. We have already pretty much completed the job in the first part of this chapter by separating the tasks of the client and the server, but it's not sufficient. We now need a list of all the different possibilities, which have been enlisted here.

Both sides:

- Connection
- Disconnection
- Client event

Log out

- Get game list
- Request for the creation of a game (match)
- Request to join the game
- Request to create an entity
- Request to destroy an entity

Server events

- Entity update
- Entity's events (onHit, onHitted, onSpawn)
- Update team (gold, game over)
- Respond to client events

The good news is that there aren't too many kinds of events; the bad news is that these events don't require the same information, so we can't build only one event, but instead, as many events as the number of possible actions, with their own data.

But there is now another trouble. How do we recognize which one to use? Well, we need an identifier that allows this. An enum function will do the job perfectly, as follows:

```
namespace FuncIds{
  enum FUNCIDS {
    //both side
    IdHandler = 0, IdDisconnected, IdLogOut,
    //client
    IdGetListGame, IdCreateGame, IdJoinGame,IdRequestCreateEntity,
      IdRequestDestroyEntity,
    //server events
    IdSetListGame, IdJoinGameConfirmation, IdJoinGameReject,
    IdDestroyEntity, IdCreateEntity,  IdUpdateEntity,
    IdOnHittedEntity, IdOnHitEntity,  IdOnSpawnEntity,
    IdUpdateTeam
  };
}
```

Now that we have a way to differ the actions, we have to send a packet with a common part for all these actions. This part (header) will contain the identifier of the action. Then all actions will add their own data. This is exactly the way that sf::Event works with the sf::Event::type attribute.

We will copy this mechanism to our own system, by building a new class called `NetworkEvent`. This class works as `sf::Event` does, except that it also adds serialization/unserialization with the `sf::Packet` class, allowing us to send that data across the network easily. Let's now take a look at this new class.

# The NetworkEvent class

The `NetworkEvent` class is built inside the `book::packet` namespace. Now that we have an idea of the global shape of our data to send, it's time for us to build some classes that will help us to deal with them.

We will build one class for each event, with a common parent, the `NetworkEvent` class. This class will allow us to use polymorphism. Following is its header:

```
class NetworkEvent
{
  public:
  NetworkEvent(FuncIds::FUNCIDS type);
  virtual ~NetworkEvent();

  FuncIds::FUNCIDS type()const;
  static NetworkEvent* makeFromPacket(sf::Packet& packet);

  friend sf::Packet& operator>>(sf::Packet&, NetworkEvent& self);
  friend sf::Packet& operator<<(sf::Packet&, const NetworkEvent&
    self);

  protected:
  const FuncIds::FUNCIDS _type;
};
```

As you can see, this class is very short and only contains its type. The reason is that it's the only common point with all the different events. It also contains some default operator and an important function: `makeFromPacket()`. This function, as you will see, constructs the correct events depending on the data stored inside the `sf::Packet` received as parameter. Now take a look at the implementation:

```
NetworkEvent::NetworkEvent(FuncIds::FUNCIDS type) : _type(type){}
NetworkEvent::~NetworkEvent(){}
```

As usual, the constructor and the destructor are very simple and should be familiar:

```
NetworkEvent* NetworkEvent::makeFromPacket(sf::Packet& packet)
{
  sf::Uint8 type;
  NetworkEvent* res = nullptr;
  packet>>type;
  switch(type)
```

```
        {
          case FuncIds::IdDisconnected :
            {
              res = new Disconnected();
              packet>>(*static_cast<Disconnected*>(res));
            }break;

          //... test all the different  FuncIds

          case FuncIds::IdUpdateTeam :
            {
              res = new UpdateTeam();
              packet>>(*static_cast<UpdateTeam*>(res));
            }break;
        }
      return res;
    }
```

The preceding function is very important. This is the one that will parse data received from the network to an instance of `NetworkEvent` with respect to the type received. The programmer will then use this instance instead of `sf::Packet`. Notice that an allocation is made inside this function, so a delete has to be made on the returned object after use:

```
FuncIds::FUNCIDS NetworkEvent::type()const {return _type;}
```

The previous function return the type associated to the `NetworkEvent`. It allows the programmer to cast the instance into the correct class.

```
sf::Packet& operator>>(sf::Packet& packet, NetworkEvent& self)
{
    return packet;
}

sf::Packet& operator<<(sf::Packet& packet, const NetworkEvent&
  self)
{
  packet<<sf::Uint8(self._type);
  return packet;
}
```

These two functions are in charge of the serialization/unserialization functionality. Because the unserialization function (>> operator) is only called inside the `makeFromPacket()` function and the type has already been extracted, this one does nothing. On the other hand, the serialization function (<< operator) adds the type of the event to the packet, as there is no other data.

I will now show you one of the event classes. All the others are built on the same logic, and I'm sure that you already understand how it is done.

Let's take the `RequestCreateEntity` class. This class contains the different data to request the creation of an entity on the battlefield:

```
namespace EntityType {
    enum TYPES {IdMain = 0,IdEye,IdWormEgg,IdWorm,IdCarnivor,};
}

class RequestCreateEntity : public NetworkEvent
{
  public :
  RequestCreateEntity();
  RequestCreateEntity(short int type,const sf::Vector2i& coord);

  short int getType()const;
  const sf::Vector2i& getCoord()const;

  friend sf::Packet& operator>>(sf::Packet&, RequestCreateEntity&
    self);
  friend sf::Packet& operator<<(sf::Packet&, const
    RequestCreateEntity& self);

  private:
  short int _entitytype;
  sf::Vector2i _coord;
};
```

First of all, we define an `enum` function that will contain all the identifiers for the entities, and then the class that requests their construction. The `RequestCreateEntity` class inherits from the previous `NetworkEvent` class and defines the same functions, plus those specific to the event. Notice that there are two constructors. The default is used in the `makeFromPacket()` function, and the other by the programmer to send an event. Take a look now at the following implementation:

```
RequestCreateEntity::RequestCreateEntity() :
  NetworkEvent(FuncIds::IdRequestCreateEntity){}

RequestCreateEntity::RequestCreateEntity(short int type,const
  sf::Vector2i& coord) : NetworkEvent(FuncIds::IdRequestCreateEntity),
_entitytype(type),
  _coord(coord) {}

short int RequestCreateEntity::getType()const
```

```
{
    return _entitytype;
}

const sf::Vector2i& RequestCreateEntity::getCoord()const {return
  _coord;}

sf::Packet& operator>>(sf::Packet& packet, RequestCreateEntity&
  self)
{
  sf::Int8 type;
  sf::Int32 x,y;
  packet>>type>>x>>y;

  self._entitytype = type;
  self._coord.x = x;
  self._coord.y = y;
  return packet;
}
```

This function unpacks the different data specific to the event and stores them internally. That's all:

```
sf::Packet& operator<<(sf::Packet& packet, const
  RequestCreateEntity& self)
{
  packet<<sf::Uint8(self._type)
  <<sf::Int8(self._entitytype)
  <<sf::Int32(self._coord.x)
  <<sf::Int32(self._coord.y);
  return packet;
}
```

This function serializes the different data using the SFML object corresponding to the primitive types used.

As you can see, creating an event is really simple with this system. It only requires an identifier for its class along with some parsing functions. All the other events are built on the same model as this one, so I will not explain them. To see the complete code, you can take a look at the include/SFML-Book/common/Packet.hpp file if you want.

Now that we have all the keys in hand to build the multiplayer part, it's time for us to modify our game.

# Modifying our game

To add this functionality to our game, we will need to rethink the internal structure a bit. First of all, we need to split our code to build two different programs. All the common classes (such as those used for communication) will be put into a common directory. All the other functionalities will be put into the server or client folder with respect to their usage. Let's start with the most complicated part: the server.

# Server

The server will be in charge of all the simulation. In fact, all our game will reside in the server. Moreover, it will have to ensure the possibility of having multiple matches running at the same time. It will also have to deal with connections/ disconnections and player events.

Because the server will not render anything, we don't need any graphic class anymore on this side. So the `AnimatedSprite` function in the `CompSkin` component will have to be removed, as will the `sf::RectangleShape` component in the `CompHp` function.

Because the positions of the entities were stored by the `CompSkin` component (more precisely `_sprite`), we have to add an `sf::Vector2f` function in each entity that will store its position.

The main loop will also be changed a lot. Remember that we need to manage multiple clients and matches and listen for a new connection on a specific port. So to be able to do this, we will build a `Server` class, and each match will have its own game instance running in its own thread. So let's do this:

# Building the Server entry point

The server class will be in charge to manage new clients, to create new matches and to add clients to existing matches. This class can be seen like the main menu of the game. By the way the corresponding display on the player screen will be as follows:

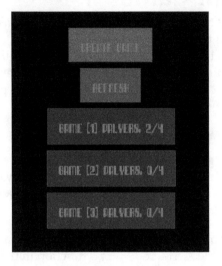

So, we will need to:

- Store the running match (games)
- Store the new clients
- Listen for new clients
- Respond to some request (create a new match, joint a match, get the list of running match)

Let's now build the server class.

```
class Server
{
    public:
        Server(int port);
        ~Server();
        void run();

    private:
        const unsigned int _port;
        void runGame();
        void listen();
```

```
    sf::Thread _gameThread;
    sf::Mutex _gameMutex;
    std::vector<std::shared_ptr<Game>> _games;

    sf::Mutex _clientMutex;
    std::vector<std::shared_ptr<Client>> _clients;

    sf::Thread _listenThread;
    sf::TcpListener _socketListener;
    std::shared_ptr<Client> _currentClient;
};
```

This class handle all the information describe above, and some threads to run separated functionalities independently (logging and request). Now take a look to its implementation:

First of all we need to declare some global variable and function as followed:

```
sig_atomic_t stop = false;
void signalHandler(int sig) {stop = true;}
```

The previous function will be call when the user will ask to stop the server by pressing the *Ctrl* + *C* key. This mechanism is initialized in the `Server::run()` function as you will see in a moment..

```
Server::Server(int port) :
    _port(port),_gameThread(&Server::runGame,this),_listenThread(&Server
::listen,this)
{
  rand_init();
  _currentClient = nullptr;
}
```

The previous function initialize the different threads, and the random function.

```
Server::~Server()
{
  _gameMutex.lock();
  for(Game* game : _games)
  game->stop()
  _gameMutex.unlock();
  _clientMutex.lock();
  for(Client* client : _clients)
  client->stop();
  _clientMutex.unlock();
}
```

Here, we destroy all the running matches and clients to stop the server properly.

```
void Server::run()
{
  std::signal(SIGINT,signalHandler);
  _gameThread.launch();
  _listenThread.launch();
  _gameThread.wait();
  _listenThread.terminate();
}
```

This function start the server that is blocked until the SIGINT (*Ctrl + c*) signal is sent to it:

```
void Server::runGame()
{
  while(!stop)
  {
    sf::Lock guard(_clientMutex);
    for(auto it = _clients.begin(); it !=
      _clients.end();++it)//loop on clients
    {
      std::shared_ptr<Client> client = *it; //get iteration
        current client
      packet::NetworkEvent* msg;
      while(client and client->pollEvent(msg)) //some events
        incomings
      {
        switch(msg->type()) //check the type
        {
          case FuncIds::IdGetListGame :
          {
            sf::Packet response;
            packet::SetListGame list;
            sf::Lock guard(_gameMutex);
            for(Game* game : _games) { //send match informations
            list.add(game->id(),game->getPlayersCount(),game-
              >getTeamCount());
            }
            response<<list;
            client->send(response);
          }break;
          case FuncIds::IdCreateGame :
          {
            sf::Packet response;
            packet::SetListGame list;
```

```
            sf::Lock guard(_gameMutex);
            _games.emplace_back(new Game("./media/map.json"));
              //create a new match
            for(Game* game : _games){ //send match informations
            list.add(game->id(),game->getPlayersCount(),game-
              >getTeamCount());
          }
          //callback when a client exit a match
          _games.back()->onLogOut = [this](std::shared_ptr<Client>
            client){
            _clients.emplace_back(client);
          };
          _games.back()->run(); //start the match
          response<<list;
          for(auto it2 = _clients.begin(); it2 !=
            _clients.end();++it2){ //send to all client
          (*it2)->send(response);
        }
      }break;
    case FuncIds::IdJoinGame :
    {
      int gameId = static_cast<packet::JoinGame*>(msg)->gameId()
      sf::Lock guard(_gameMutex);
      //check if the player can really join the match
      for(auto game : _games) {
        if(game->id() == gameId) {
          if(game->addClient(client)){ //yes he can
          client = nullptr;
          it = _clients.erase(it); //stop to manage the client
            here. Now the game do it
          --it;
        }
        break;
      }
    }
  }break;
  case FuncIds::IdDisconnected : //Oups, the client leave the game
  {
    it = _clients.erase(it);
    --it;
    client = nullptr;
  }break;
  default : break;
}
delete msg;
}
```

This function is the server's most important function. This is the one that handles all the events coming from players. For each client, we check if there is an event waiting to be processed, and then, depending on its type, we take different actions. Thanks to our `NetworkEvent` class, the parsing on the event is easy, and we can reduce the code to the functionalities only:

```
void Server::listen()
{
  if(_socketListener.listen(_port) != sf::Socket::Done) {
    stop = true;
    return;
  }
  _currentClient =   new Client;
  while(!stop)
  {
    if (_socketListener.accept(_currentClient->getSockIn()) ==
      sf::Socket::Done) {
      if(_currentClient->connect()) {
        sf::Lock guard(_clientMutex);
        _clients.emplace_back(_currentClient);
        _currentClient->run();
        _currentClient = new Client;
      }
      else {
        _currentClient->disconnect();
      }
    }
  }
}
```

This function is the final function of the server. Its job is to wait for a new connection, initialize the client, and add it to the list managed by the previous function.

Nothing else has to be done in this class since as soon as the client joins a match, it's the match and no more the `Server` class that will have to deal with it. Each match is managed by a `Game` instance. Let's now take a look at it.

# Reacting to players' actions during a match

The Game class hasn't changed a lot. The event processing has changed, but is still very similar to the original system. Instead of using sf::Event, we now use NetworkEvent. And because the API is very close, it should not disturb you too much.

The first function that interacts with a player is the one that receives the match information. For example, we need to send it to the map file and all the different entities. This task is created by the Game::addClient() function, as follows:

```cpp
bool Game::addClient(Client* client)
{
    sf::Lock guard(_teamMutex);
    Team* clientTeam = nullptr;
    for(Team* team : _teams)
    {
        // is there any team for the player
        if(team->getClients().size() == 0 and team->isGameOver())
        { //find it
            clientTeam = team;
            break;
        }
    }

    sf::Packet response;
    if(clientTeam != nullptr)
    {
        //send map informations
        std::ifstream file(_mapFileName);
        //get file content to as std::string
        std::string content((std::istreambuf_iterator<char>(file)),(st
d::istreambuf_iterator<char>()));

        packet::JoinGameConfirmation conf(content,clientTeam->id());//
send confirmation

        for(Team* team : _teams)
        { //send team datas
            packet::JoinGameConfirmation::Data data;
            data.team = team->id();
            data.gold = team->getGold();
            data.color = team->getColor();
            conf.addTeam(std::move(data));
        }
```

```
            response<<conf;
            client->send(response);
            {
                //send initial content
                response.clear();
                sf::Lock gameGuard(_gameMutex);
                packet::CreateEntity datas; //entites informations
                for(auto id : entities)
                    addCreate(datas,id);
                response<<datas;
                client->send(response);
            }

            client->setTeam(clientTeam);
            sf::Lock guardClients(_clientsMutex);
            _clients.emplace_back(client);
        }
        else
        { //Oups, someone the match is already full
            response<<packet::JoinGameReject(_id);
            client->send(response);
        }
        return clientTeam != nullptr;
    }
```

This function is separated into four parts:

1. Checking if we can add a new player to the match.
2. Sending map data.
3. Sending entity informations.
4. Adding the client to the team.
5. Once a client has been added to the game, we have to manage its incoming events. This task is made by the new function processNetworkEvents(). It works exactly as the old processEvents() function, but with NetworkEvent instead of sf::Events:

```
void Game::processNetworkEvents()
{
    sf::Lock guard(_clientsMutex);
    for(auto it = _clients.begin(); it != _clients.end();++it)
    {
        auto client = *it;
        packet::NetworkEvent* msg;
```

```
      while(client and client->pollEvent(msg))
  {
      switch(msg->type())
      {
          case FuncIds::IdDisconnected :
          {
              it = _clients.erase(it);
              --it;
              delete client;
              client = nullptr;
          }break;

          case FuncIds::IdLogOut :
          {
              it = _clients.erase(it);
              --it;
              client->getTeam()->remove(client);
              onLogOut(client); //callback to the server
               client = nullptr;
          }break;

          case FuncIds::IdRequestCreateEntity :
          {
              packet::RequestCreateEntity* event =
static_cast<packet::RequestCreateEntity*>(msg);
              sf::Lock gameGuard(_teamMutex);
               // create the entity is the team as enough
money
          }break;

          case FuncIds::IdRequestDestroyEntity :
          {
              packet::RequestDestroyEntity* event =
static_cast<packet::RequestDestroyEntity*>(msg);
               // destroy the entity if it shares the same
team as the client
          }break;
           default : break;
      } //end switch          } //end while      } //
end for
  }
```

There's no surprise here. We have to deal with the possible client disconnection/logout, and then with all the different events. I don't have to put the entire code of the different events, as there is nothing complicated there. But if you are interested, take a look at the `src/SFML-Book/server/Game.cpp` file.

Notice that we never send any confirmation to the client for any request. The synchronization of the game will ensure this.

# Synchronization between clients and the server

A big change in the `Game` class is the way to manage the synchronization between the clients and the server. In the previous chapter, only one client received data. Now we have some of the clients, and the logic changes. To ensure synchronization, we have to send updates to clients.

To be able to send the updates, we have to keep in memory each change during the game loop, and then send them to all the players. Because a request will change the game, it will be included in the updates. This is why in the previous points we don't send any response to the player for the requests. In the game, we will need to keep track of the following:

- Entity creation
- Entity destruction
- Entity updates
- Entity events (onHitted, onHit, onSpawn)
- Update of team status, gold amount, and so on

Most of these events only require the entity ID without any other information (destruction entity events). For other events, some extra data is required, but the logic is still the same: add the information to a container.

Then, in the `Game::update()` function, we have to send the updates to all the players. To do this, we add to a queue the outgoing events (exactly as in the `Connection` class). Another thread will be in charge of their propagation.

Here is a code snippet that makes the destruction event:

```
if(_destroyEntityId.size() > 0)
{
  packet::DestroyEntity update;
  for(auto id : _destroyEntityId)
  update.add(id);
  sf::Packet packet;
```

```
    packet<<update;
    sendToAll(packet);
    _destroyEntityId.clear();
}
```

As you can see, there is no complexity here, and all the magic is done by the
`sendToAll()` function. As you can suppose, its aim is to broadcast the message to
all the different players by adding the packet to the outgoing queue. Another thread
will then enter that queue to broadcast the message.

In terms of the game's logic, nothing else has changed. We still use the entity system
and the map to manage the level. Only the graphical elements have been deleted. It
is the client's job to display on the screen the game state to the player, speaking of
which, let's now look into this part in detail.

# The Client class

This is the final part of this chapter. The client is even simpler than the server, since
it only has one player to manage but is still a bit complex. The client will have a
graphical rendering but no more game logic. The only job made by the client is
handling player inputs and updating the game states with the incoming network
events.

Because starting a client is now not sufficient to start a match, we have to
communicate with the server to initialize a game, or even create a new match. In fact,
a client is composed of two main components: the connection menu and the game.
The client game class has changed a lot to handle the new functionalities, which is
why I will now show you the new Game header before continuing the explanation:

```
class Game
{
  public:
  Game(int x=1600, int y=900);
  ~Game();
  bool connect(const sf::IpAddress& ip, unsigned short
    port,sf::Time timeout=sf::Time::Zero);
  void run(int frame_per_seconds=60);
  private:
  void processEvents();
  void processNetworkEvents();
  void update(sf::Time deltaTime);
  void render();
  bool _asFocus;
  sf::RenderWindow _window;
```

```
      sf::Sprite _cursor;
      Client _client;
      bool _isConnected;
      enum Status {StatusMainMenu,StatusInGame, StatusDisconnected}
        _status;
      MainMenu _mainMenu;
      GameMenu _gameMenu;
      Level* _level;
      Level::FuncType _onPickup;
      int _team;
    };
```

As you can see, there are some new functions to manage the network, and the GUI has been separated in other classes (`MainMenu`, `GameMenu`). On the other hand, some classes such as `Level` haven't changed.

Now let's take a look at the main menu.

# Connection with the server

Before starting a match, a connection to the server is required, following which we have to choose which match we want to play. The connection is achieved exactly as in the server, but in the reverse order (changing received to send, and vice versa).

The choice of the match is then made by the player. He has to be able to create a new match and join it as well. To simplify this, we will use our GUI by creating a `MainMenu` class:

```
    class MainMenu : public sfutils::Frame
    {
      public:
      MainMenu(sf::RenderWindow& window,Client& client);
      void fill(packet::SetListGame& list);
      private:
      Client& _client;
    };
```

This class is very small. It's a frame with several buttons, as you can see in the following image:

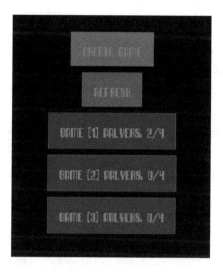

The implementation of this class is not too complicated; rather much more consequential:

```
MainMenu::MainMenu(sf::RenderWindow& window,Client& client) : sfutils:
:Frame(window,Configuration::guiInputs), _client(client)
{
        setLayout(new sfutils::Vlayout);
}

void MainMenu::fill(packet::SetListGame& list)
{
    clear();
    sfutils::VLayout* layout = static_cast<sfutils::VLayout*>(Frame::
getLayout());
    {
        sfutils::TextButton* button = new sfutils::TextButton("Create
game");
        button->setCharacterSize(20);
        button->setOutlineThickness(1);
        button->setFillColor(sf::Color(48,80,197));
        button->on_click = [this](const sf::Event&, sfutils::Button&
button){
            sf::Packet event;
            event<<packet::CreateGame();
            _client.send(event);
        };
        layout->add(button);
```

```
        }

        {
            sfutils::TextButton* button = new
sfutils::TextButton("Refresh");
            button->setCharacterSize(20);
            button->setOutlineThickness(1);
            button->setFillColor(sf::Color(0,88,17));
            button->on_click = [this](const sf::Event&, sfutils::Button&
button){
                sf::Packet event;
                event<<packet::GetListGame();
                _client.send(event);
            };
            layout->add(button);
        }

        for(const autoe& game : list.list())
        {
            std::stringstream ss;
            ss<<"Game ["<<game.id<<"] Players: "<<game.
nbPlayers<<"/"<<game.nbTeams;
            sfutils::TextButton* button = new sfutils::TextButton(ss.
str());
            button->setCharacterSize(20);
            button->setOutlineThickness(1);
            button->on_click = [this,game](const sf::Event&,
sfutils::Button& button){
                sf::Packet event;
                event<<packet::JoinGame(game.id);
                _client.send(event);
            };
            layout->add(button);
        } //end for
    }
```

All the logic of the class is coded within the `fill()` function. This function receives the list of running matches on the server and displays them as buttons to the player. The player can then press one of the buttons to join the match or request the creation of a game.

When the player requests to join the game, if all is good on the server side, the client receives a `JoinGameConfirmation` event with the data to initialize its level (remember the `addClient()` function in the server):

```
void Game::processNetworkEvents()
{
    packet::NetworkEvent* msg;
```

```
while(_client.pollEvent(msg))
{
  if(msg->type() == FuncIds::IdDisconnected) {
    _isConnected = false;
    _status = StatusDisconnected;
  }
  else
  {
    switch(_status)
    {
      case StatusMainMenu:
      {
        switch(msg->type())
        {
          case FuncIds::IdSetListGame :
          {
            packet::SetListGame* event =
              static_cast<packet::SetListGame*>(msg);
            _mainMenu.fill(*event);
          }break;
          case FuncIds::IdJoinGameConfirmation :
          {
            packet::JoinGameConfirmation* event =
              static_cast<packet::JoinGameConfirmation*>(msg);
            // create the level from event
            if(_level != nullptr) {
              _team = event->getTeamId();
              // initialize the team menu
              _status = StatusInGame;
            }
          }break;
          case FuncIds::IdJoinGameReject :
          {
            //...
          }break;
          default : break;
        }
      }break;
      case StatusInGame :
      {
        _gameMenu.processNetworkEvent(msg);
        _level->processNetworkEvent(msg);
      }break;
```

```
          case StatusDisconnected :
          {
            // ...
                }break;
              } //end switch
          } //end else
          delete msg;
      } //end while
    }
```

This function handles the events coming from the server and dispatches them depending on the internal states. As you can see, a `JoinGameConfirmation` event launches the creation of the level, and a change of the internal state, which shows by displaying the game to the player.

# The Level class

Some additions have been made to the `Level` class to handle network events. We still have to deal with construction/destruction requests, but now we also have to manage events coming from the server, such as position update, entity creation/ destruction, and entity events.

This management is very important because this is the place that adds dynamism to our game to synchronize it with the server. Take a look at the following function:

```
void Level::processNetworkEvent(packet::NetworkEvent* msg)
{
  switch(msg->type())
  {
    case FuncIds::IdDestroyEntity :
    {//need to destroy an entity
      packet::DestroyEntity* event =
        static_cast<packet::DestroyEntity*>(msg);
        for(auto id : event->getDestroy())
          {
              destroyEntity(id);
          }
    }break;
    case FuncIds::IdCreateEntity :
    {//need to create an entity
      packet::CreateEntity* event =
      static_cast<packet::CreateEntity*>(msg);
      for(const autoa& data : event->getCreates())
      {
        Entity& e = createEntity(data.entityId,data.coord);
          //create the entity
```

```
    makeAs(data.entityType,e,&_teamInfo.at(data.entityTeam),
      *this,data); //add the components
  }
}break;
case FuncIds::IdUpdateEntity :
{//an entity has changed
  packet::UpdateEntity* event =
    static_cast<packet::UpdateEntity*>(msg);
  for(const auto& data : event->getUpdates())
  {
    if(entities.isValid(data.entityId)) //the entity is still
      here, so we have to update it
    {
      CompSkin::Handle skin =
        entities.getComponent<CompSkin>(data.entityId);
      CompHp::Handle hp =
        entities.getComponent<CompHp>(data.entityId);
      //... and other updates
      hp->_hp = data.hp;
    }
  }
}break;
case FuncIds::IdOnHittedEntity :
{//entity event to launch
  packet::OnHittedEntity* event =
  static_cast<packet::OnHittedEntity*>(msg);
  for(const auto& data : event->getHitted())
  {
    if(entities.isValid(data.entityId))
    {
      Entity& e = entities.get(data.entityId);
      if(e.onHitted and entities.isValid(data.enemyId)) //to
        avoid invalid datas
      {
        Entity& enemy = entities.get(data.enemyId);
        //call the callback
        e.onHitted(e,_map->mapPixelToCoords(e.getPosition()),
          enemy, _map->mapPixelToCoords
            (enemy.getPosition()),*this);
      }
    }
  }
}break;
case FuncIds::IdOnHitEntity :
{//another event
  //same has previous with e.onHit callback
}break;
case FuncIds::IdOnSpawnEntity :
```

```
{ //other event
  packet::OnSpawnEntity* event =
    static_cast<packet::OnSpawnEntity*>(msg);
  for(auto id : event->getSpawn())
  {
    if(entities.isValid(id))
    {
      Entity& e = entities.get(id);
      CompAISpawner::Handle spawn =
        entities.getComponent<CompAISpawner>(id);
      if(spawn.isValid() and spawn->_onSpawn) //check data
        validity
      {//ok, call the call back
        spawn->_onSpawn(*this,_map-
          >mapPixelToCoords(e.getPosition()));
      }
    }
  }
}break;
default : break;
  }
}
```

As you can see, this function is a bit long. This is because we have to manage six different types of events. The destruction and the creation of entities are easy to make because the major part of the job is done by the `EntityManager` function. The updates are another piece of cake. We have to change each value to the new one, one by one, or activate the callbacks for the entity events with all the necessary verifications; remember *don't trust user inputs*, even if they come from the server.

Now that the major part of the game has been made, we just have to clean all the unnecessary components from the client to only have `CompTeam`, `CompHp`, and `CompSkin`. All the others are only used by the server for the entities' behavior.

The final result of this chapter will not change a lot from the previous one, but you will now be able to play with friends, and the game will become interesting to play because the difficulties are now real:

# Adding data persistence to the game

If, like me, you can't imagine a game without a save option, this part couldn't interest you more. In this final part of the book, I will introduce you to the persistence of data. Data persistence is the ability of a program to save its internal state for future restoration. This is exactly what a save option does in a game. In our particular case, because the client received data directly from the server, all the jobs have to be done on the server part. First of all, let's think a bit about what we need to save:

- The entities and their components
- The teams
- The games

We then need a way to store that data to be able to restore it later. The solution is to use files or something else that can grow with time, as easy to copy. For this functionality, I've made the choice of using Sqlite. This is a database engine available as library. More information can be found on the website at https://sqlite.org/.

The usage of a database engine is a bit of overkill for our project, but the goal here is to show you its usage in our actual game. Then you will be able to use it for more complex projects of your creation. The persistence data will be stored in a database that is a single file, which can easily be copied or modified using some GUI for Sqlite.

The only drawback of this solution is that some knowledge on the SQL language is required. Because this book doesn't aim to cover that topic, I propose to you an alternative usage: **Object-relational Mapping (ORM)**.

# What is ORM?

To say as simply as possible, an ORM is between the database engine and the API of the program and automatically makes the SQL query when it's needed without the need to write it by hand. Moreover, most of them support multiple database engines, allowing you to change the engine with only one or two lines of code.

Following is an example that will help illustrate my words (in pseudo code). First, using a standard library:

```
String sql = "SELECT * from Entity WHERE id = 10"
SqlQuery query(sql);
SqlResults res = query.execute();
Entity e;
e.color = res["color"];
//.. other initializations
```

And now using an ORM:

```
Entity e = Entity::get(10);
// color is already load and set
```

As you can see, all is made by the ORM without the need to write anything. This remains exactly the same when it comes to saving data. Just use the save() method, and that's it.

# Using cpp-ORM

We will use the cpp-ORM library which was written by me, so there is no trouble to use it in our project. It can be found at https://github.com/Krozark/cpp-ORM.

To be able to work, the library needs some information on your class; this is why some custom types have to be used for the data that you want to save.

| ORM types | C++ types |
|---|---|
| orm::BooleanField | bool |
| orm::CharField<N> | std::string (of length N) |
| orm::DateTimeField | struct tm |
| orm::AutoDateTimeField | |
| orm::AutoNowDateTimeField | |
| orm::IntegerField | int |
| orm::FloatField | float |
| orm::DoubleField | double |
| orm::TextField | std::string |
| orm::UnsignedIntegerField | unsigned int |
| orm::FK<T,NULLABLE=true> | std::shared_ptr<T> NULLABLE specify if T can be null |
| orm::ManyToMany<T,U> | std::vector<std::shared_ptr<U>> Use it when T need to keep an unknown number of reference of U class |

Moreover, your class will need to have a default constructor with no parameters, and extends from `orm::SqlObject<T>` where `T` is your class name. To understand well, let's build a component as persistent, such as `CompHp`:

```
class CompHp : public sfutils::Component<CompHp,Entity>, public
orm::SqlObject<CompHp>
{
  public:
  CompHp(); //default constructor
  explicit CompHp(int hp);
  orm::IntegerField _hp; //change the type to be persistent
  orm::IntegerField _maxHp; //here again
  //create column for the query ability (same name as your
    attributes)
  MAKE_STATIC_COLUMN(_hp,_maxHp);
};
```

There is not much to explain. We just add `orm::SqlObject<CompHp>` as the parent class and change `int` to `orm::IntegerField`. The `MAKE_STATIC_COLUMN` is used to create some additional fields that will contain the column name of each field in the database. With regards to the implementation, there is another macro to avoid repetitive work: `REGISTER_AND_CONSTRUCT`. Its usage is as follows:

```
REGISTER_AND_CONSTRUCT(CompHp,"CompHp",\
_hp,"hp",\
_maxHp,"maxHp")
```

This macro will construct the entire default constructor implementation. Then, in your code, use the field as usual. There is no need to change anything concerning your class.

The last requirement is to reference the default database to use. In our case, we will use the `Sqlite3` engine, so we need to create it somewhere, for example, in the `main.cpp` file:

```
#include <ORM/backends/Sqlite3.hpp>
orm::Sqlite3DB def("./08_dataPersistence.sqlite"); //create the
   database (need to be include before file that use SqlObject)
orm::DB& orm::DB::Default = def;//set the default connection
   (multi connection is possible)
#include <ORM/core/Tables.hpp>
#include <SFML-Book/server/Server.hpp>
int main(int argc, char* argv[])
{
  // get port parameter
  orm::DB::Default.connect(); //connect to the database
  orm::Tables::create(); //create all the tables if needed
  book::Server server(port);
  server.run();
  orm::DB::Default.disconnect(); //disconnect the database
  return 0;
}
```

In this short example, the database is created and the connection connected to it. It's important to keep in mind that all the access to the database will use the default connection by default.

# Turning our object persistent

Now that the database is created, we don't need to touch it anymore. Now let's interest ourselves with how to save our objects in the database or restore them.

## Saving an object in a database

This functionality is very simple thanks to the entity system. Let's take our previous `CompHp` class. Create an instance of it and call the `.save()` method on it. If you want to update an object already stored in the database, use `save()` as well. Only the field that changes will be updated:

```
CompHp chp;
chp._hp = 42;
chp.save();
//oups I've forgotten the other field
chp._maxHp = 42;
chp.save();
std::cout<<"My id is now "<<chp.getPk()<<std::endl;
```

Now let's move on to the object loading.

## Loading an object from the database

There are basically two ways to load an object. The first one is when you know its primary key (identifier), and the second one is to search all the objects corresponding to a specific criterion:

```
CompHp::type_ptr chp = CompHp::get(10); //load from database
//chp.getPk() = -1 on error, but chp is a valid object so you can use
  it
std::cout<<"My id is "<<chp->getPk()<<" And my content is
  "<<*chp<<std::endl;
```

These two lines of code load an object from the database and then display its content to the console output. On the other hand, if you don't know the identifier value but you have a specific criterion, you can also load objects in the following manner:

```
CompHp::result_type res;
CompHp::query()
.filter(
  orm::Q<CompHp>(25,orm::op::gt,CompHp::$_hp)
  and orm::Q<CompHp>(228,orm::op::lte,CompHp::$_maxHp)
  or (orm::Q<CompHp>(12,orm::op::gt,CompHp::$_hp) and
    orm::Q<CompHp>(25,orm::op::exact,CompHp::$_maxHp))
```

```
)// (_hp > 25) and (_maxHp <= 228) or (_hp > 12 and _maxHp ==25 )
. orderBy(CompHp::$_hp,'+')// could be +,-,?
.limit(12) //only the first 12 objects
.get(res);
for(auto chp : res)
std::cout<<"My id is "<<chp->getPk()<<" And my content is
  "<<*chp<<std::endl;
```

In this example, we get the entire CompHp component through a complex query and then display the content to the console output.

Now you have all the keys in hand to add loading/saving into our actual game without too much pain, so I will not enter further into the implementation details.

# Summary

In this final chapter, you have learned how to add basic networking using sockets, selectors, and even creating a custom protocol. You have integrated this new knowledge to the previous game and turned it into a multiplayer game in real time.

You have also learned how to add persistence to your data using an ORM, and how to add a save/load option to the game. By now you have seen many aspects of game programming, and you now have all the keys in hand to build every kind of game you want in 2D.

I hope that this book gives you useful tools. If you want to reuse some part of the framework made across this book, the code is available on GitHub at https://github.com/Krozark/SFML-utils.

I hope you have enjoyed reading this book, and developed the games well. I wish you good luck for your future games!

# Index

## Symbols

2D physics engines  110
3D physics engines  110

## A

**Action class**
  using  35-38
**AnimatedSprite class  192-197**
**Animation class  190-192**
**animations, Real-time Tower Defense game**
  AnimatedSprite class  192-197
  Animation class  190-192
  building  189, 190
  A usage example  197, 199
**application**
  converting, to Asteroid clone game  61-63
  entity component system  70
  hierarchical entity system  70
  modifying  63, 64
  World class  65-69
**assert() function  95**
**Asteroid clone game**
  application, converting to  61
  building  61-63
  designing  71, 72
  Enemy class  78, 79
  Entity class  73, 74
  levels  62
  Meteor class  83, 84
  Player class  62-78
  Saucer class  79-82
  Shoot class  85-87

## B

**Board class  101**
**Box2D**
  about  111
  build process  112
  collision functionality  111
  installation  112
  pairing, with SFML  112, 113
  physics functionality  111
  preparing  111
  URL  111
  working  113-118
**Button class  146-148**

## C

**C++11**
  about  1
  features  2, 3
**C++11 compiler**
  installing  4
  installing, for all users  4
  installing, for Linux users  4
  installing, for Mac users  4
  installing, for Windows users  4
**class hierarchy, GUI**
  about  140-142
  Button class  146-148
  Container class  151-153
  Frame class  141-155
  Label class  140-145
  Layout class  156
  TextButton class  140-151

VLayout class  157-159
Widget class  142, 143
**Client class**
about  257, 258
connecting, with server  258-262
Level class  262-265
**client-server architecture**
about  228, 229
client  230
server  230, 231
**CMake**
installing  5
installing, for Linux users  5
URL  5
**Code::Blocks**
configuring  11-14
URL  5
**communication protocol**
creating  239
NetworkEvent class  243-246
RPC-like protocol  241-243
sf::Packet class, using  239-241
**configuration menu**
building  166, 167
**Connection class, sockets**
about  233
goal  233-238
sf::Mutex  235
sf::TcpSocket  235
sf::Thread  235
std::queue<sf::Packet>  235
**Container class  151, 152**
**cpp-ORM library**
URL  266
using  267, 268

**D**

**data persistence**
adding  265, 266
cpp-ORM, using  266, 267
object, loading from database  269
object, saving in database  269
ORM  266

**E**

**endianness**
URL  239
**enemies, Asteroid clone game**
about  62
flying saucers  63
meteors  62, 63
**Entity  70**
**entity system, Real-time Tower Defense game**
about  215
advantages  218
using  216, 217
**Euclidean torus**
URL  62
**exec() family functions  176**

**F**

**Font class  52**
**fork() function  175, 176**
**Frame class  153-155**
**frame rate**
about  22
fixed time steps approach  23
minimum time steps  25-27
variable time steps approach  25
**frames per second (FPS)  21**

**G**

**game**
general structure  17
physics, adding  119, 120
**game engine**
versus physics engine  110
**game loops**
about  21, 22
fixed time steps approach  24
frame rate  22
**game structure**
Game class  18-20
game loop  21, 22
Player object, moving  27

generic Tile Map, Real-time Tower
    Defense game
  building 199
  dynamic board loading 208-212
  Geometry class, as isometric
    hexagon 201-203
  Layer class 203-207
  Map class 207, 208
  MapViewer class 213
  usage example 213-215
  VLayer class 203-207
  VMap class 207
GitHub
  URL 187
Graphical User Interface (GUI)
  about 139
  class hierarchy 140-142
  creating, from scratch 140

I

Image class 52
installations
  C++11 compiler 4
  CMake 5
  SFML 2.2 5

L

Label class 144, 145
Layer class 203-207
Layout class 156
Level class 223
Linux
  C++11 compiler, installing 4
  CMake, installing 5
  SFML, compiling 9

M

Mac users
  C++11 compiler, installing for 4
makeFromPacket() function 243
MapViewer class 213

menu
  adding, to game 160
  configuration menu, building 166, 167
  main menu, building 161-164
  pause menu, building 164, 165
multithreading
  about 175
  adding, to games 181-185
  exec() family functions 176, 177
  fork() function 175, 176
Music class 53

N

network architectures, Real-time Tower
    Defense game
  about 227
  client-server architecture 228, 229
  peer-to-peer architecture 228
NetworkEvent class 243, 247

O

Object-relational Mapping (ORM) 266

P

pause menu
  building 164, 165
peer-to-peer architecture 228
physics, adding to game
  Game class, using 132-135
  Piece class, using 121-125
  Stats class, using 136
  World class, using 125-131
physics engine
  2D physics engine 110
  3D physics engine 110
  about 109
  Box2D 111
  versus game engine 110
Player object
  moving 27
  Player class 27-31
processEvent() method 148

# R

**Real Time Strategy (RTS) 187**
**Real-time Tower Defense game**
 about 187
 animations, building 189
 Client class 257
 clients and server synchronization 256, 257
 communication protocol, creating 239
 data persistence, adding 265
 entity system, building 215
 generic Tile Map, building 199
 goal 188
 logic, building 218
 modifying 247
 network architectures 227
 network communication, with sockets 231
 player's action, reacting to 253-256
 server 247-252
**Real-time Tower Defense game logic**
 building 218
 components, building 219
 different systems, creating 220-223
 Game class 223
 Level class 223
 Team GUI class 224, 225
**render() function 19**
**Resource Acquisition Is Initialization**
 **(RAII) idiom 55**
**resources**
 Font class 52
 Image class 52
 in SFML 50, 51
 manager, building 55-58
 Music class 53
 player's skin, modifying 58, 59
 Resource Acquisition Is Initialization
  (RAII) idiom 55
 Shader class 53
 SoundBuffer class 53
 Texture class 51
 tracking 50
 use cases 54

# S

**SFGUI**
 about 167
 features, using 168
 installing 168
 starting level, building 169-172
 URL 168
 using 167
**SFML**
 about 3
 Box2D, pairing with 112, 113
 building 5
 building, on Linux 6
 building, on other operating system 6
 compilation, in Linux 9
 compilation, on Windows 9, 10
 compilation, with CMake 6-8
 dependencies, installing 6
 URL 4, 232
**SFML 2.2**
 Code::Blocks, configuring 11-14
 example 14, 15
 installing 5
 URL 5
**SFML, modules**
 audio 3
 graphics 3
 network 3
 system 3
 window 3
**Shader class 53**
**Simple and Fast Graphical User Interface.**
 *See* **SFGUI**
**Simple and Fast Multimedia**
 **Library.** *See* **SFML**
**sleep() function 27**
**sockets**
 Connection class 233
 sf::SocketSelector 232, 233
 Transmission Control Protocol (TCP) 232
 used, for network communication 231
 User Datagram Protocol (UDP) 231, 232

SoundBuffer class 53
Sqlite
  URL 265
stop() function 237

# T

Team GUI class 224, 225
Tetris clone game
  about 88
  Board class, using 96-103
  building 88
  Game class, using 103-106
  Piece class, using 91-95
  Stats class, using 89-91
TextButton class 148-151
Texture class 51
thread functionality
  about 177
  need for 178
  thread, using 179, 180
  using 178
Transmission Control Protocol (TCP) 232

# U

update() function 19
User Datagram Protocol (UDP)
  about 231
  limitations 231
user inputs
  Action class, using 35-38
  action target 39-49
  event map 44
  events, polling 32
  handling 35
  managing 31, 32
  real-time events 33, 34

# V

VLayer class 203-207
VLayout class 157-159
VMap class 207, 208

# W

Widget class 142, 143
Windows
  SFML, compiling 9, 10
  C++11 compiler, installing for 4

## Thank you for buying
# SFML Blueprints

# About Packt Publishing

Packt, pronounced 'packed', published its first book, *Mastering phpMyAdmin for Effective MySQL Management*, in April 2004, and subsequently continued to specialize in publishing highly focused books on specific technologies and solutions.

Our books and publications share the experiences of your fellow IT professionals in adapting and customizing today's systems, applications, and frameworks. Our solution-based books give you the knowledge and power to customize the software and technologies you're using to get the job done. Packt books are more specific and less general than the IT books you have seen in the past. Our unique business model allows us to bring you more focused information, giving you more of what you need to know, and less of what you don't.

Packt is a modern yet unique publishing company that focuses on producing quality, cutting-edge books for communities of developers, administrators, and newbies alike. For more information, please visit our website at www.packtpub.com.

# About Packt Open Source

In 2010, Packt launched two new brands, Packt Open Source and Packt Enterprise, in order to continue its focus on specialization. This book is part of the Packt Open Source brand, home to books published on software built around open source licenses, and offering information to anybody from advanced developers to budding web designers. The Open Source brand also runs Packt's Open Source Royalty Scheme, by which Packt gives a royalty to each open source project about whose software a book is sold.

# Writing for Packt

We welcome all inquiries from people who are interested in authoring. Book proposals should be sent to author@packtpub.com. If your book idea is still at an early stage and you would like to discuss it first before writing a formal book proposal, then please contact us; one of our commissioning editors will get in touch with you.

We're not just looking for published authors; if you have strong technical skills but no writing experience, our experienced editors can help you develop a writing career, or simply get some additional reward for your expertise.

## SFML Game Development

ISBN: 978-1-84969-684-5       Paperback: 296 pages

Learn how to use SFML 2.0 to develop your own feature-packed game

1. Develop a complete game throughout the book.

2. Learn how to use modern C++11 style to create a full featured game and support for all major operating systems.

3. Fully network your game for awesome multiplayer action.

4. Step-by-step guide to developing your game using C++ and SFML.

## SFML Essentials

ISBN: 978-1-78439-732-6       Paperback: 156 pages

A fast-paced, practical guide to building functionally enriched 2D games using the core concepts of SFML

1. Learn to utilize the features of SFML quickly to create interactive games.

2. Realize your game ideas by following practical tutorials based on the essential features of SFML.

3. Step-by-step guide describing the fundamental concepts of SFML with the help of plenty of examples.

Please check **www.PacktPub.com** for information on our titles

## SDL Game Development

ISBN: 978-1-84969-682-1        Paperback: 256 pages

Discover how to leverage the power of SDL 2.0 to create awesome games in C++

1. Create 2D reusable games using the new SDL 2.0 and C++ frameworks.

2. Become proficient in speeding up development time.

3. Create two fully-featured games with C++ which include a platform game and a 2D side scrolling shooter.

4. An engaging and structured guide to develop your own game.

## HTML5 Game Development HOTSHOT

ISBN: 978-1-84969-546-6        Paperback: 366 pages

Build interactive games with HTML, DOM, and the CreateJS game library

1. Create eight different games using HTML5.

2. Learn essential games development techniques, such as game loop, animations, and browser storage.

3. Follow the project-based approach to build games from start to finish with in-depth explanations on game management.

Please check **www.PacktPub.com** for information on our titles

www.ingramcontent.com/pod-product-compliance
Lightning Source LLC
Chambersburg PA
CBHW060518060326
40690CB00017B/3316